PRAISE FOR *REVOLUTION IN 35MM*

"Andrew Nette, Samm Deighan, and their boisterous band of noteworthy collaborators serve up an impressive, breathlessly globe-trotting tour of Cold War left-wing cinemas of resistance in this beautifully appointed volume. Movie lovers will find a new trove of treasures to screen; film aficionados will dive into the debates stimulated by these provocative contributions."
—Jonathan Kirshner, author of *Hollywood's Last Golden Age*

"Navigating the rivers of blood between exploitation films, revolutionary cinema, and beyond, this is a vital, lively, necessary book for anyone interested in cinema, or politics, or both. Nette and Deighan seem to have seen everything: they make connections that change and deepen our understanding of the moving image, the moving world."
—Howard A. Rodman, former president, Writers Guild of America West

"*Revolution in 35mm* is a fantastic collection of essays, as vital and compelling as the films they analyze. The authors engage in the cinema of the time mindful of the context but also underline the relevance of the work today. Highly recommended."
—John Bleasdale, host of *Writers on Film* podcast

"The writing in *Revolution in 35mm* not only conveys a wholehearted enthusiasm for a diverse cross-section of cinema from around the world, but thoughtfully considers the sociopolitical conditions these films were aiming to challenge. An invaluable blend of cultural history and film critique, the book is a celebration of iconoclasts who channeled righteous anger into all manner of 'political cinema,' whether by attacking issues directly or covertly smuggling topical themes into popular genre fare. Even the most seasoned cinephile will come away with dozens of unfamiliar titles to seek out."
—Bill Ackerman, host of *Supporting Characters* podcast

REVOLUTION IN 35mm

Political Violence and Resistance in Cinema from the Arthouse to the Grindhouse, 1960–1990

Edited by **Andrew Nette** and **Samm Deighan**

Revolution in 35mm: Political Violence and Resistance in Cinema from the Arthouse to the Grindhouse, 1960–1990
Edited by Andrew Nette and Samm Deighan
All text copyright © 2024 the individual authors
This edition © 2024 PM Press

ISBN: 979–8–88744–060–6 (paperback)
ISBN: 979–8–88744–069–9 (ebook)
Library of Congress Control Number: 2024930556
Cover by John Yates / www.stealworks.com
Interior design by briandesign

10 9 8 7 6 5 4 3 2 1

PM Press
PO Box 23912
Oakland, CA 94623
www.pmpress.org

Printed in the USA.

CONTENTS

INTRODUCTION

A CINEMA OF RESISTANCE ON THE MARGINS

Political violence is generally described as violence perpetrated to achieve political goals: war at home or abroad, military coups, genocide, a state's repression of its own people, terrorism, guerrilla warfare, kidnappings and assassinations, violent protests, and organized crime. It also includes violence that occurs because of the ideological oppression associated with racism, sexism, and classism. Although it has always been part of human history and took on particular importance in the modern world with the French Revolution in the 1790s (which birthed the term *terrorism*), political violence was enacted on an unimaginable scale in the twentieth century, with World War I and World War II as defining global events. World War II in particular is often described as the key historical event of the twentieth century, one that irrevocably shaped modern life. On a cultural level, this especially makes sense because narratives about the war often provide a clear hero (the Allied powers, democracy, the ideal of freedom) and an obvious villain (the Axis powers, fascism, the horrors of genocide).

The decade that followed World War II was marked by a series of murkier, more nebulous conflicts: the Cold War, which had been brewing since the surrender of Nazi Germany in 1945 but is viewed as officially starting with the exclusion of pro-Soviet Communist parties from government in Italy and France in 1947; the Korean War (1950–53); the Cuban Revolution (1953–59); and the Algerian War (1954–62), which became symbolic of the struggle for independence many countries faced around the world. In much the same way that Vietnam defined the American left in the second half of the '60s and

A still from *Born in Flames* (1983)

the first half of the '70s, the war for independence in Algeria was a dominant focus for the European left in the 1950s. It also helped to inspire a series of wars fought to achieve freedom from colonialist states like France, England, and Portugal, which would eventually lead to dozens of African countries achieving independence. This must be considered alongside the near-global outrage over the Vietnam War and the West's worldwide campaign to eradicate communism, which helped birth, among other developments, a series of disastrous military dictatorships in Latin America and Africa. These coincided with fascist dictatorships in places like Spain and Greece, Stalinist totalitarianism in the Soviet Union and its satellite states, and so on.

In the West, various social movements arose in response to these struggles, particularly in the '60s and '70s, resulting in wide-scale protests, primarily from students, blue-collar workers, leftist groups, and those linked to the civil rights, Black Power, and feminist movements. In addition to challenging dominant economic and political structures, some of these movements sought to engender broader cultural and social transformation. Dissatisfied with the slow pace of change, others broke away and formed urban guerrilla groups, inspired primarily by national liberation movements in the Global South and also by each other: the Red Army Faction of Germany and Japan; organizations like the Black Liberation Army, Symbionese Liberation Army, and the Weathermen, to name a few in the

Diego Reggente and Mariangela Melato in *Execution Squad* (1972)

US; the Red Brigades in Italy; and the Provisional Irish Republican Army, among others. While these movements developed as a response to specific local and cultural concerns, they were also connected on a global scale. Not only were there parallels between radical groups around the world, they also became intertwined in a more literal way. As Martin Klimke writes in *The Other Alliance: Student Protest in West Germany and the United States in the Global Sixties* (2011), "Whether we describe sixties' protest as a revolution in the world-system, a global revolutionary movement or a conglomerate of national movements with local variants but common characteristics, its transnational dimension was one of its crucial motors."

Many of these protest movements were also connected with and expressed their values through art, literature, popular culture, and, of course, cinema. *Revolution in 35mm: Political Violence and Resistance in Cinema from the Arthouse to the Grindhouse, 1960–1990* is an examination of how filmmakers around the world reacted to the political violence and resistance movements of the period and how this was expressed on-screen, primarily in arthouse and cult films. There is not the space here to engage in a debate about the precise meaning of "arthouse" and "cult" film, except to acknowledge that both terms are contested and slippery. At its most basic, "arthouse cinema" refers to the nebulous body of films—often independent productions for smaller markets—created as art, rather than as commercial

Investigation of a Citizen Above Suspicion (1970)

products; arthouse films are often deliberately made as a counterpoint to Hollywood. "Exploitation films" refer to a body of low-budget films that emerged in the mid-'60s that rely on graphic representations of violence and sex for their audience appeal and were often shown in so-called lower-class inner-city cinemas, sometimes referred to as grindhouses. Our emphasis on these two strands of cinema, rather than the mainstream film market, is because both provided more freedom of expression for filmmakers.

The focus of this book is on films made during the decades between the Algerian War in the late '50s and the fall of the Soviet Union in the early '90s. While there are certainly films made before and after that period that depict political violence and resistance, the films made in this rough thirty-year span have a certain unique cohesion and interconnectedness. Many emerged from and reflected a historical era often referred to as the "long Sixties," a shorthand term for a period of rapid change that began in the late '50s and continued well into the '70s. We have also chosen to include cinema from the '80s, which depicts a continuation of key issues and themes: the transformation of the global order, in particular the gradual dissolution of the Soviet Union and its notion of "actually existing socialism," which birthed and continued to influence much of the politics of the '80s; the decline of a certain type of solidarity politics and anti-imperialist and anticolonial movements in the Global South, a development related to the political

Kapò (1960)

degeneration of many of the liberation movements they were aligned to and, in cases where they came to power, the governments they formed; and the shift from industrial to finance capitalism, which had major impacts worldwide, including on cinema.

Clearly, 1968 is especially significant as a radical watershed of sorts that had been many years in the making and that would continue to reverberate well into the '80s. This is best exemplified by literary critic and philosopher Fredric Jameson's notion of the "long 1968." The political, social, philosophical, and cultural ripples of 1968 were particularly influential for cinema. Christos Tsiolkas's essay in this book on Costa-Gavras's 1969 political thriller *Z* discusses how its reception was framed by the post-'68 call on filmmakers to take a political position, "to commit to the popular (and therefore capitalist) or to the experimental (and therefore radical), [which] had already convulsed much of international cinema." Academic Sarah Hamblin notes in an article in the 2019 issue of *Cultural Politics* how the political maelstrom of 1968 also led many filmmakers to reject the more "authoritarian model in which the film maker is positioned as the master who aims to impart specific wisdom to the unaware audience." This shift, which was obviously influenced by numerous factors, is touched on in several of the pieces in this book, from Latin America's "new cinema" movement of the 1960s and 1970s to the evolution of European directors like Jean-Luc Godard. In *European Cinema: Face*

La Chinoise (The Chinese, 1967)

to *Face with Hollywood* (2004), German film historian Thomas Elsaesser discusses how 1968 "coincides with a period of stagnation and structural changes in Hollywood which led to larger-scale mergers, takeover bids and boardroom struggles for control of the industry's assets." Among many changes, this led to Hollywood's attempt to attract younger audiences with films depicting the campus revolt that was sweeping the US, and much of the West, and the violence associated with it. Some of these efforts are explored by Kimberly Lindbergs in her piece on campus revolt cinema, as well as by Michael A. Gonzales in his essay on the 1973 film *The Spook Who Sat by the Door*, once little known but now considered an important revolutionary film from the period. In reference to the earlier point about the porous nature of film categories, these movies arguably straddle the divide between arthouse, grindhouse, and mainstream cinema.

Revolution in 35mm does not seek to be a conclusive account of the political period concerned. The essays in this book—both full chapters and shorter "outtake" essays—do seek to explore the films of politically active, for the most part overtly left-wing filmmakers from a wide range of countries, including the Global South, who were depicting and/or responding to real-life political violence in their work during these decades. These depictions

Police attack students as the sit-in is busted.

MGM Presents
A Robert Chartoff-Irwin Winkler Production   "THE STRAWBERRY STATEMENT"   Metrocolor

70/141

The Strawberry Statement (1970)

include overt political violence (revolution, assassinations, guerrilla warfare, riots, and state-sanctioned kidnapping, disappearance, and torture) as well as violence that is not overtly political but represents historical political symbolism in its subtext (like the Italian *poliziotteschi* crime films and the "Zapata" spaghetti westerns, bank-heist movies in West Germany, Bollywood gangster cinema, and so on).

Within the scope of one volume, it is of course impossible to cover every film made from 1960 to 1990 that includes depictions of political violence. We have chosen to focus on certain subjects that heavily feature this theme: key filmmaking movements like the French, Japanese, German, and Yugoslavian New Waves; subgenres like spaghetti westerns, Italian crime films, Blaxploitation, and mondo movies; groups of films that reflect beliefs held by specific movements like feminists or Vietnam War protesters; and the work of particularly influential political filmmakers such as Costa-Gavras and Gillo Pontecorvo. Likewise, in the interest of focus, this book does not include popular mainstream films, made-for-TV movies, or more straightforward, conventional documentaries.

That there are large gaps in this book's coverage is due to many issues. A lack of films featuring political violence is evident from certain regions, because of reasons such as censorship or political repression. With that said, filmmakers living under dictatorships often developed their own strategies for making, distributing, and screening their work, sometimes with lethal consequences for those involved. Evidence of this can be found in essays discussing cinema from the '60s and '70s in Argentina, Bolivia, and Yugoslavia, for example. Another obstacle was locating and viewing some films. This is a particular problem in relation to the work of directors from many regions within the Global South, but as many essays in this book address, it is also a much broader problem for directors with radical political views regardless of geographical location: American filmmaker Robert Kramer is a notable example, as his films from the '60s and early '70s are incredibly difficult to track down.

This book aims to be something other than an encyclopedia of non-mainstream films concerned with political violence and resistance. It seeks to show how filmmakers outside the mainstream, from different countries and often different decades, and generally working in different cinematic genres, are in conversation with one another and often share many similarities. Examining these films as a collective body also allows for a broader view of their filmmakers' shared explorations of radical politics, political violence, and modes of resistance. Many of the films discussed in this book raise questions and instigate discussions about the aims of political violence and its effectiveness, still relevant at a time when such violence is on the rise again globally: war in Eastern Europe, protests and executions in Iran, a wave of right-wing violence and an attempted extremist overthrow of the government in the United States, the persecution of Palestinians by the Israeli state—the list goes on. By comparing what is a largely marginal cinema, from the arthouse to the grindhouse, we are hoping to expose a more complex understanding of certain types of cinema, like low-budget genre fare that is often dismissed from more serious conversations of cinema as an art form. Finally, we hope to highlight underseen films and the important work of neglected filmmakers, many of whom made incredible sacrifices—including their lives in some cases—to contribute culturally to the ongoing global fight for radical freedom.

Samm Deighan and Andrew Nette

GILLO PONTECORVO'S BATTLE OF IDEAS

O ne of the most arresting aspects of watching Gillo Pontecorvo's *La battaglia di Algeri* (*The Battle of Algiers*, 1966) over half a century after its release is how contemporary the images of Western soldiers involved in a bloody counterinsurgency campaign in an Arab country feel today. Two imperial wars in the Middle East, along with the circulation of images from Abu Ghraib and Guantánamo Bay and their pop-culture reflections in countless films and television series, make Pontecorvo's iconography of counterinsurgency and political violence look familiar. Using the tools of Italian neorealism, documentary filmmaking, and the political thriller, the director and his scriptwriter, Franco Solinas, document the first stage of Algeria's struggle against French colonial authorities, a campaign of urban warfare from 1954 to 1957. Militants of the pro-independence Front de Libération Nationale (National Liberation Front, or FLN for short) infiltrated the Arab section of the capital, Algiers, known as the casbah, and began to organize the population and launch armed attacks on French colonial authorities and European settlers, known as *pieds-noirs*. The FLN met with resistance from colonial police and armed vigilante settlers. The violence escalated until Paris was forced to deploy French army units, many of whom were veterans of the country's then-recent defeat in Indochina, and Algiers was effectively placed under military rule. Between January and September 1957, French troops commanded by General Jacques Massu undertook a campaign of torture, forced disappearances, and executions.

The Battle of Algiers opens in 1957, at which point Massu has largely succeeded in hunting down and capturing or eliminating the FLN's urban

American poster for *The Battle of Algiers* (1966)

leadership, ending the first phase of their struggle. In a dingy room, white men in military fatigues stand over a broken Arab male. That he has just been tortured and given his captors information against his will is etched on his traumatized features. His captors reinforce their physical domination by dressing him in their uniform and forcing him to accompany them on a raid to capture the individuals he has informed on. In a hidden compartment off a room in an apartment block are two men, a woman, and a child, the last survivors of the FLN's remaining urban-based leadership, including Ali La Ponte (Brahim Hadjadj) and Halima (Fusia El Kader), both based on real-life FLN figures. The French soldiers wire the entrance to the hiding space with explosives and threaten to detonate it unless they surrender. But the French victory is temporary. As a coda at the film's conclusion informs the audience, the insurgents regrouped in the rural areas and succeeded in driving out the colonial authorities, and Algeria gained independence on July 2, 1962.

"Algeria was de Gaulle's linchpin, the link between metropolitan France and the former French colonies in North, West, and Central Africa," writes Elaine Mokhtefi in her 2018 book *Algiers, Third World Capital: Freedom Fighters, Revolutionaries, Black Panthers*. In the same way that Vietnam defined the American left in the late '60s and the first half of the '70s, the war in Algiers was a dominant political issue in '50s Europe. France was forced to deploy twelve of its fourteen active military divisions to fight the insurgency, and its loss was a huge defeat for the country and, by association, colonialism globally. It also came at significant human cost. As many as 1.5 million Algerians, twenty-five thousand French soldiers, and six thousand European settlers died during the conflict, and two million out of a population of nearly nine million were displaced.

The Battle of Algiers was one of several films about the war in Algeria. Appearing the same year as Pontecorvo's effort, the most commercial of these, Mark Robson's *The Lost Command*, stars Anthony Quinn, Alain Delon, Claudia Cardinale, and George Segal (the latter in brownface as a commander in the Algerian resistance). Taking place in the same historical period as *The Battle of Algiers*, the film focuses on Quinn as a veteran French paratrooper leader given one more chance to prove his military worth and salvage his wounded pride after unsuccessfully commanding French forces at Dien Bien Phu. Set in 1957, Laurent Heynemann's *La Question* (*The Question*, 1977) recounts the experience of a newspaper editor in Algiers, sympathetic to the FLN cause, who is detained by the French military. Based on a 1958 autobiography by Henri Alleg, the book and its film adaptation caused a scandal in France for depicting the military's dirty tactics in Algeria, including the widespread use of torture. Algerian-born Mohammed Lakhdar-Hamina's *Ahdat sanawovach el-djamr* (*Chronicle of the Years of Fire*, 1975) is a multigenerational tale of the struggle against French colonialism spanning World War II to independence.

That *The Battle of Algiers* remains by far the best known and most influential of these films is due to the way it became not just a call to arms in a period of accelerating anticolonial struggle, but also a how-to manual for Third World liberation struggles and urban guerrilla movements in the north. It was used as a primer by the Black Panthers, and according to a 2017 *Film Comment* piece by Mark Harris, during its first run on Manhattan's Upper East Side, Black audiences cheered during each anti-French terror attack. It was supposedly a favorite film of Italian Brigate Rosse (Red Brigades) head Mario Moretti and Andreas Baader, one of the initial leaders of the West German Rote Armee Fraktion (Red Army Faction, or as it was better known the Baader-Meinhof Group). The Provisional Irish Republican Army, the Palestine Liberation Army, and the Jammu Kashmir Liberation Front (the separatist organization active in both the Indian- and Pakistani-held areas of Kashmir), all reportedly used it as a training tool. And it was also viewed by those seeking guidance for how to tackle insurgency movements. Showings were held for military cadets in Argentina's infamous Navy Mechanics School, the site of an illegal and secret detention center during the "Dirty War" carried out by that country's military dictatorship from 1976 to 1983. And the Pentagon held a now-infamous screening for officers and civilian military experts following the American invasion of Iraq. A flyer for the event said: "How to win a battle against terrorism and lose the war of ideas. Children shoot soldiers at point-blank range. Women plant bombs in cafes. Soon the entire Arab population builds to a mad fervor. Sound familiar? The French have a plan. It succeeds tactically, but fails strategically. To understand why, come to a rare showing of this film."

Argentinian poster for *The Battle of Algiers* (1966)

Less commented on is that *The Battle of Algiers* is only one of four feature films in Pontecorvo's slim cinematic oeuvre (he directed five feature films in total and numerous documentaries and shorts) that together can be viewed as a sustained interrogation of the practicalities and impacts of the use of political violence. The others are the Italian/French/Yugoslavian coproduction *Kapò* (1960), the Italian/French coproduction *Queimada* (*Burn!*, 1969), and his least-known but I would argue potentially most interesting film from the standpoint of its discussion of political violence, the Italian/Spanish coproduction *Operación Ogro* (*Ogro*, 1979). Pontecorvo collaborated with Solinas, one of postwar Europe's most politically committed screenwriters, on all these films but *Ogro*. And all but *Kapò* were scored by Ennio Morricone.

Born into a wealthy secular Jewish family in the northern Italian city of Pisa in 1919, Pontecorvo grew up during the early period of fascist control. He moved to Paris in 1938 to escape increasing antisemitism, returning in 1941, when he joined the Italian Communist Party (PCI). The dates and exact nature of Pontecorvo's wartime activities vary, but there is no doubt he was deeply enmeshed in dangerous work for the communist-led resistance. After the war, he edited the PCI's journal but broke ties with the party over the Soviet suppression of the Hungarian uprising in 1956. In addition to his wartime experience and Marxism, Pontecorvo was influenced by the writings of Frantz Fanon, particularly *Les damnés de la terre* (*The Wretched*

Gillo Pontecorvo (left) with Enrico Berlinguer, future head of the Italian Communist Party, Milan, November 1945

of the Earth), originally published in France in 1961. Fanon posited the use of political violence not only as a military and political strategy but as a means of rehumanizing the colonized subject. As Alan O'Leary and Neelam Srivastava write in a 2009 article on Pontecorvo in the journal *the italianist*, versions of Fanon's "wretched of the earth" are all represented in the four Pontecorvo films discussed in this piece: "the jew of the concentration camp, the colonized Algerian, the slave on the Caribbean plantation, the oppressed Basque people in Franchist Spain." These films not only debate how revolutionary movements might use political violence but also examine the ethics of doing so over a period in which the context facing Third World national liberation movements and European far-left guerrilla groups shifted considerably.

Kapò is a story of political resistance in one of the most horrific situations imaginable, a Nazi death camp. Without warning, a young French Jewish girl, Edith (American actress Susan Strasberg), finds herself and her family imprisoned by German soldiers. She avoids the fate of her parents, being marched naked to a gas chamber, with the help of a communist doctor (Sima Janićijević), a prisoner working in the camp's medical center. The doctor swaps Edith's identity for Nicole, a recently deceased French girl of approximately the same age, on whose clothes is sewn a black star, the sign she

French poster for *Kapò* (1960)

Laurent Terzieff and Susan Strasberg in a still from *Kapò* (1960)

had been arrested as a criminal. The doctor shaves Edith's head so she will blend in with the other inmates and tells her to focus on one thing: survival. Transferred to a female labor camp in Poland, Edith puts the doctor's advice into practice. She hides her Jewish identity, prostitutes herself to the German officers for food and other comforts, including being allowed to grow back her hair, and becomes a *kapò*, a prisoner assigned to supervise other inmates. *Kapòs*, usually recruited from among the camp's criminal prisoners, were renowned for their brutality toward their fellow inmates. Edith's collaboration is counterposed with the "politicals," prisoners who attempt to maintain anti-Nazi resistance by engaging in political debate and small acts of sabotage in the camp factory, for which, if discovered, they are sentenced to death. Camp life is disrupted by the arrival of a large group of male Russian prisoners, who bring word that Germany is losing the war. Edith starts to question what she has been doing after she falls in love with one of the Russians, Sascha (Laurent Terzieff), and they fantasize about life together after the war. As Russian forces can be heard advancing in the distance, rumors spread that the Nazis intend to liquidate the prisoners and retreat. The Russians hatch a mass escape plan, which Edith volunteers to assist by disabling the electric fence that surrounds the camp, unaware it is a suicide mission.

Appearing just fifteen years after the war's end, *Kapò* generated condemnation for its sometimes melodramatic depiction of Nazi mass industrialized slaughter. Particularly contentious was a scene in which a political prisoner commits suicide by throwing herself on the camp's electrified fence. But the film is the product of thorough historical research, including interviews with survivors of the Treblinka death camp, located northwest of Warsaw. This was the site of a major revolt in August 1943, when prisoners seized arms, set camp buildings on fire, and rushed the main gate. Several hundred prisoners escaped, more than half of whom were then traced and killed by the Nazis. The film depicts the horror of concentration camp life and the decision of some inmates to collaborate. But it also shows the reassertion of Edith's humanity through her decision to participate in an act of collective political resist-ance. This forms part of a much larger narrative about the need to maintain faith in some sort of radical project, even in the most politically hopeless of circumstances. Discussion about the ethics of political struggle and violence percolates throughout the film. Sascha questions the morality of sending Edith on a suicide mission to his superior officer, because he loves her and because the deception and decision to sacrifice her feels, to him, morally wrong. The commander responds that "in this case, it becomes necessary and even right to kill someone in order to save many others." Edith succeeds in disabling the electric fence but is mortally wounded, living long enough to reaffirm her Jewish identity to Sascha and rip the swastika emblem off her uniform.

A similar commitment to historical authenticity informs *The Battle of Algiers*. Pontecorvo and Solinas initially had the idea for a film about a former French paratrooper, a veteran of the Indochina war, who travels to Algeria as a reporter. This approach was jettisoned when the director was approached by Saadi Yacef, a former FLN leader and the head of Casbah Films, an Algerian government-backed production house with funds at its disposal. Yacef, who had already approached and been rebuffed by Francesco Rosi and Luchino Visconti, was looking for a director to help him film his screenplay, based on his 1962 memoir, *Souvenirs de la bataille d'Alger* (*Memories of the Battle of Algiers*). Pontecorvo accepted the project on the condition that he and Solinas could rewrite Yacef's script to inject it with more objectivity. Director and screenwriter spent considerable time in Algiers researching the story, mostly in the casbah, where they interviewed the inhabitants and developed a sense of the city's spatial dimensions and political history. Yacef said in a 2008 interview with *Framework: The Journal of Cinema and Media* that filming took five months, much of which took place in the same locations where the events portrayed occurred. This often included streets too narrow to use a dolly, necessitating the use of a single handheld camera. The cast were mostly nonprofessional actors, including Yacef as the FLN commander El-hadi Djafar. The only exception was French actor Jean Martin as Colonel

A still from *The Battle of Algiers* (1966); former National Liberation Front commander Yacef Saadi as Djafar can be seen second from the left

Mathieu, the leader of the French forces. Mainly known for his stage work, Martin had been dismissed several years earlier from his job in Théâtre National Populaire for signing a petition against France's military intervention in Algeria. Mathieu's character was based on several of the French commanders involved in counterinsurgency operations in Algeria, especially Massu. In addition to on-the-ground research, *The Battle of Algiers* pulsates with a sense of the revolutionary possibility that existed in post-independence Algiers, a city on the cusp of becoming a center for exiled national liberation movements. Amílcar Cabral, the Pan-African poet, intellectual, and revolutionary who led the movement against the colonial administration in Portuguese Guinea, called Algiers the "capital of revolutions." "Muslims go on pilgrimage to Mecca," he said in the late 1960s, "Christians to the Vatican, and national liberation movements to Algiers."

The Battle of Algiers moves between the end of the first phase of the FLN's struggle and the beginnings of the insurgency in 1954. In this earlier period, La Pointe is an unemployed laborer and petty criminal arrested for hustling cards in the European quarter of Algiers. Arrested and jailed, Le Pointe becomes politicized while imprisoned and on his release is recruited by Djafar. Mathieu, the main representation of the colonialist forces, is a kind of

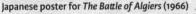

Japanese poster for *The Battle of Algiers* (1966)   Italian poster for *The Battle of Algiers* (1966)

warrior-intellectual whose orders are to do whatever is necessary to maintain French rule and who understands that the ideological aspects of occupation are as important as brute force. That Mathieu's character is neither one-dimensional nor entirely unsympathetic is an aspect of the film criticized by some. But it is characteristic of the political nuance that Pontecorvo and Solinas breathe into their work. While unambiguously pro-FLN, the film does not romanticize its characters or the political violence they commit. Whether it is the shooting of a lone policeman, or the bombing of crowded cafés by the FLN, or reprisal attacks by plainclothes colonial police and the torture and brutality committed by the French military, violence is never fetishized, and the consequences are shown in full: the horrific impact on fragile bodies, white and brown; the anguish of widowed women and orphaned children; and the profound trauma of those who have been tortured.

Three other aspects of the film's treatment of political violence are worth mentioning, as they were no doubt central to its popularity as a guide for aspiring revolutionaries. First, it shows the participation of the Arab population in the uprising. Children act as FLN scouts and, in one of the film's most tense sequences, women drop their veils and assume a modern Western look to infiltrate the capital's heavily guarded European quarter and plant bombs—a re-creation of an actual FLN operation in September 1956. Second, screen time is devoted to examining how the struggle over Algeria takes place on different levels simultaneously: tactics and overall strategy are debated between different FLN factions; there is the fight for French public opinion; and on an international level, there is the battle for global public opinion in the United Nations. Last, the story explores the psychological aspects of the liberation struggle. Early in his time with the FLN, La Pointe is ordered to kill a colonial policeman. A woman carrying a basket gives him the gun, but he discovers after confronting the policeman that it has no bullets, forcing him to beat up his target and flee with the woman. She then introduces him to Djafar, who informs him the mission was a test of his loyalty to make sure he was not a police spy. At another point, the FLN bans the sale of alcohol and drugs in the casbah and prohibits prostitution and procuring. Djafar explains that this is necessary to cleanse the organization's ranks of unreliable elements and prepare the populace psychologically for the upcoming conflict. La Pointe is shown enforcing this policy by executing a former criminal associate who has continued his activities in the face of the FLN's dictate.

The psychology of insurgency is explored further in *Burn!* The story takes place on an imaginary Caribbean island called Queimada in the 1880s. Marlon Brando is William Walker, an English mercenary and spy who arrives with orders to rid the island of its Portuguese rulers and bring the territory and its lucrative sugar industry under British control. He does this by skillfully fomenting a revolt among the Black slave population and convincing the island's wealthy plantation-owning Creole class to support it. Walker manipulates a rebellious slave, José (Evaristo Márquez, an illiterate herdsman that Pontecorvo encountered in the Columbian jungle, where the film was made, and who would go on to make another four films before returning to his previous profession), to lead the rebellion. But no sooner have the Portuguese been overthrown and slavery theoretically abolished than José faces the more difficult task of administrating the island's sugar-dependent economy with no knowledge of economics or government. With the sugar crop rotting in the fields, Walker again manipulates José into the outcome desired by the British, getting him and his ex-slave army to agree to lay down their arms, return to work on the plantations, and pass power to the Creoles, led by the weak puppet ruler Teddy Sanchez (Renato Salvatori). "Civilization is not a simple matter," Walker tells José. "You cannot learn its secrets overnight. Today civilization belongs to the white man, and you must learn to use white civilization. Without it you cannot go forward." Fast-forward ten years and Walker is lured back to Queimada to put down another revolt led by José. Walker again tries to manipulate José. But the former slave has learned his lesson and become much more militant. His advances rebutted, Walker resorts to the other strategy at his disposal: violence.

The product of European auteurism and Hollywood's industrial model of film production and star system, the tone of *Burn!* veers between arthouse film and exploitation cinema. This is possibly one reason why it flopped on release. The screenplay has parallels with the revolutionary history of the Caribbean archipelago of Guadeloupe and Haiti. Brando's character also shares a name with

Italian lobby card for *Burn!* (1969); left to right: Renato Salvatori, Marlon Brando, and Evaristo Márquez (far right)

the historical American doctor, lawyer, and mercenary William Walker, a believer in the doctrine of "manifest destiny," the idea that white America was destined to take control of the entire American continent. Played by Ed Harris in the 1987 Alex Cox film *Walker*, the real Walker was involved in blood-soaked military adventures in Mexico, Nicaragua (where he briefly set himself up as its president, before being deposed), and Honduras (where he was executed). Despite these historical antecedents, it is hard to view *Burn!* as anything other than Pontecorvo's take on the Vietnam War. *Burn!* depicts an oppressed colonial people fighting a seemingly one-sided struggle against a local ruling class backed by a larger international power. Despite this, the revolt proves difficult to suppress, forcing Sanchez to call on British soldiers, or in his words "technical support and instructors," for assistance. With British help, Walker oversees a similar strategy to that pursued by the Americans in South Vietnam, the forced relocation of villagers into what are effectively open-air prisons, to deprive the insurgents of food and logistical support. He then orders the burning of the forests and sugarcane fields in which the insurgents are hiding, to flush them out into the open where his troops can kill them. Burning Queimada to the ground to defeat the revolt is not only reminiscent of the widespread use of napalm in Vietnam. It also recalls the famous quote from an American officer to an Associated Press reporter in 1968, in reference to the obliteration of a South Vietnamese town thought to be harboring Viet Cong guerrillas, that "it became necessary to destroy the town to save it." *Burn!* shows the logic of colonial domination taken to its extreme, that it will literally destroy everything to maintain control. The systematic nature of the slaughter is so brazen that even Sanchez tires of it, at which point Walker has him replaced by a more pliant member of the island's plantation-owning class and executed for treason.

US poster for *Burn!* (1969)

The psychology of colonialism—the mental dependency it engenders in the oppressed, and what must be done to reverse this—is the film's key theme. To paraphrase Fanon, violence must be used to reconstitute the slave as human. Or as the captured José states to a Black soldier who is guarding him near the end of the film, "If someone gives you freedom, it is not freedom. Freedom is something that nobody can give you. You alone must take it." But *Burn!* takes its exploration of political violence one step further by depicting the dilemma that while an oppressed people can use violence to overthrow the old order, how does a revolution sustain itself in the face of hostile powers who control its economy and trade?

A decade passed before Pontecorvo's last and least-examined feature. *Ogro* was based on a real event, the 1973 assassination of Admiral Carrero Blanco by members of Euskadi Ta Askatasuna (Basque Homeland and Freedom), better known as ETA. Nicknamed "the Ogre," Blanco was right-hand man and successor to then-ailing Spanish dictator Francisco Franco and a leading member of the hard-line faction opposed to any loosening of fascist control. ETA had initially planned to kidnap Blanco from the church where he attended mass each morning and hold him hostage in return for the release of 150 Basque political prisoners. But the plan changed when Blanco suddenly became prime minister and security around him was heightened, making assassination the only viable option. A squad of ETA operatives dug a tunnel under the road on which Blanco's car passed each morning on the way to mass, and planted and successfully detonated explosives, killing him.

Cowritten with Giorgio Arlorio and prominent Italian screenwriter and PCI member Ugo Pirro, *Ogro* utilizes a similar dual-narrative structure to *The Battle of Algiers.* It opens in Spain's Basque region in 1978, after the downfall of the Franco regime. Txabi (Eusebio Poncela), part of a militant underground Basque nationalist group that still believes in armed struggle, is reunited with Amaiur (Ángela Molina), a member of the now-legal Basque independence movement. Txabi argues that little has changed for the Basque population postfascism and that independence can only be won through violence. Amaiur counters that while imperfect, Spain's fragile democracy offers a chance to pursue a more moderate path, based on nonviolent activism. The film then jumps back to 1973, when Txabi and Amaiur, along with Izarra (Gian Maria Volonté), Iker (José Sacristán), Luque (Saverio Marconi), and Karmele (Nicole Garcia), were assigned by ETA to travel to Madrid to kidnap Blanco. In addition to having to avoid detection by Franco's security apparatus, the group must navigate political differences between Txabi and the group's leader, Izarra. Txabi argues it would be preferable to assassinate

GIAN MARIA VOLONTE
JOSE SACRISTAN
ANGELA MOLINA
EUSEBIO PONCELA
SAVERIO MARCONI

PRODUCIDA POR
José Sámano

Un film de
GILLO PONTECORVO

OPERACIÓN OGRO

Una coproducción SABRE(Madrid)VIDES(Roma)ACTION(Paris)

DIRIGIDA POR
Gillo Pontecorvo

French lobby card for *Ogro* (1979)

Blanco, while Izarra maintains they follow orders and proceed with the kidnapping, a divide that foreshadows the men's political trajectory in post-Franco Spain. Txabi, impatient and his politics more extreme, suspects that even after the end of dictatorship, the Spanish mindset toward Basque independence will not shift. Izarra is just as committed to the Basque cause but more measured and cautious. He also allows himself a degree of optimism as to what might transpire after fascism. Their debates take place in parallel with the painstaking details of scouting Blanco's movements and developing a plan to snatch him while he attends daily mass. When the situation changes and ETA orders the group to assassinate Blanco, Pontecorvo takes the viewer through the difficult task of digging a tunnel so the group can lay explosives under the road along which Blanco travels daily.

Ogro feels more like a political thriller than Pontecorvo's previous films. It is also more subdued and lacks the visual and narrative power of works such as *The Battle of Algiers* and *Burn!* Most of the story takes place in cramped rooms, dingy bedsits, and, toward the end, in the claustrophobic confines of the tunnel the men are digging, which evokes the feel of a prison break story. So too does belief in the possibility of radical change seem contracted. Gone is the optimism in large-scale social transformation that characterized the left in the '60s, replaced by paranoia, internal conflict, and a sense of mounting political desperation. The shift in sensibility is reflected in the film's much more didactic dissection of the use of political violence: overtly supportive of a violent act against a hard-line Francoist politician by ETA under a fascist dictatorship, but far less so when carried out by Basque militants after Franco's death and the slow emergence of a nascent Spanish democracy. Toward the end of the narrative strand set in 1978, Txabi accuses Amaiur and Izarra of surrendering the goal of Basque independence, insisting on the need for a "revolution, not only in the streets but in people's minds, in their souls." "Even at the cost of a coup?" Amaiur asks. "Of fascism coming back?" Txabi breaks off their

French poster for *Ogro* (1979)

argument to go on a mission, the assassination of two Spanish police. Unlike the similar scene in *The Battle of Algiers*, the act is coldly rendered without any political context, making it feel almost like a common street crime. The encounter leaves Txabi badly wounded. Izarra, now a senior leader in the mainstream Basque independence movement, arrives at the hospital his former comrade has been taken to. Reporters quiz Izarra about his previous involvement in armed resistance. That was under fascism, he says. "Now it's different. Democracy, though fragile and incomplete, allows us to use other weapons. We can circulate our ideas, and it's only with those we want to fight." In a far cry from the mass uprising at the end of *The Battle of Algiers*, *Ogro*'s politically subdued ending sees Txabi die in his hospital bed, unrepentant and surrounded by his wife and the former comrades from whom he has disassociated himself.

While Blanco's assassination has been viewed as a key factor in accelerating the downfall of the Franco dictatorship, some claim the attack was part of ETA's own strategy of tension to heighten repression against Spain's Basque minority and thus generate greater support for ETA. Whatever the case, Txabi's position is not without some political justification. While Basque areas of Spain were granted autonomy, there is still no independent Basque state, and police repression against Basques continues. Pedro Costa's *El caso Almería* (*The Almería Case*, 1984) is a dramatization of a Spanish judge's investigation into one of the most infamous examples of this, the torture and murder of three young Basque men by the Spanish police in 1981, because they were wrongly suspected of being responsible for an attack on a police general in Madrid the previous day.

Ogro's political ambivalence has been seen as Pontecorvo's comment on growing violence by both the far right and far left that occurred during the *Anni di piombo* (Years of Lead) in the director's home country. He could also have been dismayed by the political violence wracking Western Europe more generally in the 1970s, including France and West Germany, and the fragile status of Spain's own democracy following the Franco regime. As will be discussed elsewhere in this book, hard-line Francoist elements of Spain's military, political, and business elite, unhappy with the transition, developed a strategy to destabilize democracy. This included a planned coup by elements of Spain's military in late 1978, discovered and thwarted before it could take place, and another failed attempt to seize state power in February 1981.

Pontecorvo's reappraisal of political violence is also emblematic of changing global conditions more generally. Margaret Thatcher had just taken power in Great Britain, and America was about to elect Ronald Reagan. And many among the wave of postcolonial independence movements were settling into what would often prove to be corrupt, authoritarian governments. Volonté's character, still dedicated to Basque independence but, as he puts it, through "the courage of patience," can also be seen as a cipher for the less pro-Soviet and more overtly reformist Eurocommunist path embraced by Western European communist parties in the 1970s and 1980s, an ideological shift spearheaded by Spain's party.

Political violence may have been an acceptable strategy—or indeed the sole one—available to the inmates in a Nazi concentration camp, Algeria's FLN in the 1950s, the impoverished slaves of the fictitious Queimada, or left groups under Franco's dictatorship. But the question posed in *Ogro* is whether it can be justified in a democracy, even a very imperfect one, and particularly a democracy already under threat by hard-right groups seeking to destabilize its foundations.

Andrew Nette

OUTTAKE: YOUSSEF CHAHINE AND EGYPTIAN NEOREALISM

Depictions of political violence in Middle Eastern cinema are somewhat complicated to explore, because of the very nature of how cinema has developed in the region. Many countries in the area either have not produced a large body of films or only got into cinema production in more recent years. There are several reasons for this, including colonialism, war, and extremist Islamic governments restricting art and culture in specific countries, like Saudi Arabia. Exceptions include Iran, Lebanon, and Egypt, the latter of which has produced not only the greatest number of films in the total history of Middle Eastern cinema, but also the most with complex depictions of political violence. Egypt, which is situated in North Africa but is also considered part of the Middle East, is one of the only countries in either region to develop its own film industry under colonial rule, beginning in the 1890s. Initially, documentaries, newsreels, and nonfiction films were most common, but soon melodramas, musicals, and romantic comedies came to dominate, thanks to leading companies like Misr Studios in Cairo.

Egyptian cinema reached a golden age in the '50s and '60s, and though more upbeat mainstream films were the most common, certain directors took advantage of periods of creative freedom. The first of such periods occurred in the late '50s between the Egyptian Revolution of 1952—when King Farouk was overthrown in a coup d'état, kicking off a wave of anticolonial revolutionary fervor that spread through the Middle East—and the nationalization of the film industry in 1966 under President Nassar, when censorship became more restrictive.

One young director to take advantage of this relative freedom was Youssef Chahine. After his family helped nurture a passion for cinema throughout his childhood, Chahine studied theater and television in California as a young man and went on to work in the publicity department at 20th Century Fox before returning to Egypt and launching his career as a director in 1950. He would go on to become one of Egypt's most important filmmakers and often found ways to incorporate transgressive political material within popular genres like melodrama, romance, and historical drama. Chahine's early crime drama *Bāb al-Ḥadīd* (*Cairo Station*, aka *The*

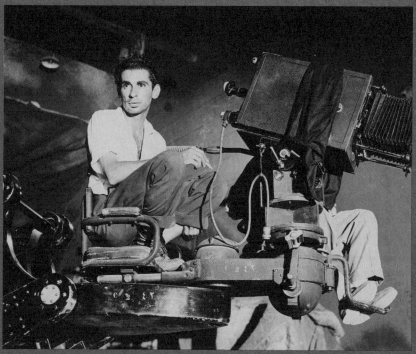

Egyptian director Youssef Chahine

Iron Gate, 1958) is a key example. Set in the bustling, often violent central train station in Cairo, the film focuses on a love triangle unfolding amid labor strife and a wave of serial murders. The beautiful, brash Hannuma (Hind Rostom) sells cold drinks as a sort of black market business, and the police are always one step behind her and her friends. She is engaged to be married to Abu Siri (Farid Shawqi), who is trying to organize the exploited train station porters into a labor union. But a disturbed, disabled newspaper seller, Qinawi (Youssef Chahine himself), is also in love with Hannuma, though he is ostracized or at least mocked by much of the community because he walks with a limp. As he becomes more delusional, he is determined to go to any lengths to have her and is inspired by news of a local serial killer murdering young women and hiding their bodies in luggage.

   Cairo Station was particularly radical at the time because of the three themes it centers on, which would recur in many of Chahine's later films: a transgressive approach to sexuality and representation of women, a somewhat ribald portrayal of poor and working-class Egyptians, and the struggle of average citizens against corrupt businessmen or government officials. Within *Cairo Station*, this plays out through the many bold, playful expressions of Hannuma's beauty and sexuality, including an implied (though not directly depicted) premarital sex scene between Hannuma and Abu Siri. Chahine suggests that Hannuma's extravagance—her awareness of her own beauty, the hint of cleavage she shows, her loud singing and dancing—are what really draws both the police and perverse male attention (from Qinawi and others) to her, more than just her black market business. But Chahine also undoubtedly celebrates Hannuma,

Cairo Station (1958)

which apparently garnered the film some criticism.

Like many of Chahine's later films, *Cairo Station* embraces nuance; even the tormented Qinawai is depicted with sympathy and humor, while showing how a predatory, often cruel world has twisted him into a murderous predator. In several scenes, the film embraces a lurid crime-thriller aesthetic, calling to mind Chahine's contemporaries like Alfred Hitchcock and Henri-Georges Clouzot, and even Herschell Gordon Lewis with seedy shots of Qinawi's hovel, decorated obsessively with cut-out pictures of partially nude women. But *Cairo Station* also evokes film noir, with its gorgeous chiaroscuro cinematography and suspense sequences, as well as elements of Italian neorealism, with its focus on the plight of working-class Egyptians. This includes the lengthy subplot in which Abu Siri tries to organize his fellow workers into forming a union to get out from under the oppression and corruption they face, and even shots of a women's rights parade toward the end of the film, with a marching band of women protesting against marriage.

Many of these themes would recur in Chahine's more overtly revolutionary drama *Jamila al-Jaza'iriyya* (*Jamila, the Algerian*, 1958), about real-life Algerian Front de Libération Nationale (National Liberation Front, or FLN) freedom fighter Djamila (or Jamila) Bouhired. Set during Algeria's war for independence against France, the film follows a young

Djamila Bouhired, the inspiration for Youssef Chahine's 1958 film *Jamila, the Algerian*

Jamila, the Algerian (1958)

but determined heroine (Magda Sabbahi) who becomes an underground commando (or freedom fighter) during the conflict. After several acts of bravery, she is arrested and severely tortured, but the occupied government is convinced to give her a public trial. Though it is meant to be a show trial leading to her swift sentencing and execution, the trial inadvertently brings international awareness of her plight and of the secret French torture campaign, turning the tide of the war.

Though there are elements of *Jamila, the Algerian* that could be seen as nationalistic or propagandistic in a modern light, it is a surprisingly subversive film, partly because of its focus on a female freedom fighter. The film doesn't shy away from presenting Jamila as beautiful and feminine, though it also doesn't suggest that these qualities interfere with her work as a budding revolutionary in any way; among the side characters are other impassioned young female commandos who are her schoolmates and friends. Many of them are tortured, beaten, and murdered, often quite graphically on-screen, and she ultimately joins the FLN because she's horrified by the violence used against them. When Jamila herself is tortured later in the film, it is even implied that some of this is sexual in nature. And as in some of Chahine's later films, her love for her country is presented in an almost romantic light; though she shares a mutual attraction with the leader of the independence movement (Ahmed Mazhar), she declares that she can't consider any feelings beyond her love for Algeria.

المؤسسة المصرية العامة للسينما
تقدم

الاختيار
بالألوان

سعاد حسني
عزت العلايلي
سيف الدين
يوسف وهبي

اخراج، يوسف شاهين

بطولة،
هدى سلطان
محمود المليجي

قصة، نجيب محفوظ   يوسف شاهين   موسيقى، على اسماعيل   مديرالتصوير، احمد خورشيد

توزيع، المؤسسة المصرية العامة للسينما

The Sparrow (1972)

Both the Jamila of Chahine's film and her real-life counterpart, who survived her ordeal and is still a renowned militant into her eighties, remain a symbol of a free Middle East. And while *Jamila, the Algerian* is a powerful film that brought Chahine some international acclaim, it horrified the French government and was banned or withheld from distribution in Egypt and Algeria off and on for decades. It is less clear why the film was banned in Algeria after independence, though the depiction of women as figures capable of independence, intelligence, and even incredible violence is likely one reason for the film's controversy, which Chahine was forced to tone down in some of his later films. He was not entirely alone among Middle Eastern or African directors depicting strong female characters, but Jamila is relatively unique in the way she is shown to be self-sufficient and capable of enduring and inflicting great violence. For example, filmmaker Henry Barakat has several dramas centered on poor and working-class village women overcoming harrowing ordeals, like *Doaa al-Karawan* (*The Nightingale's Prayer*, 1959) or *El Haram* (*The Sin*, 1965), but they are much more tragic in tone and the female protagonists become heroic through death or self-sacrifice.

Jamila's passionate nationalism—which is mostly depicted as a yearning for independence from colonialism at any cost—connects it to a series of films made later in the '60s by Chahine and other directors that reflect the aims of the anticolonial Non-Aligned Movement. His later films were forced to be somewhat more restrained, and many are either period-set historical films exploring revolutionary themes through the lens of the past, such as *El Nasser Salah Ed-Din* (*Saladin, the Victorious*, 1963); more conventional crime thrillers like *Al-Ikhtiyar* (*The Choice*, 1970); or more restrained dramas about class conflict like *Al-Ard* (*The Land*, 1969). But nearly all of these continue his focus on the plight of exploited working-class Egyptians, often at odds with the wishes of the Egyptian government.

An important example of this is *Al-Asfour* (*The Sparrow*, 1972), about a firebrand journalist and young police officer who attempt to expose local and national government corruption leading up to the Six-Day War against Israel in 1967. Ultimately, Chahine seems to blame Egypt's defeat on corruption in the government. The film ends with an incredibly emotional sequence that parallels *Jamila, the Algerian*, where a chorus of poor and working-class voices rise up in song to affirm that the people love their country and their communities above all else and will always go on to fight regardless of the government's position. Such depictions of love of one's country and the need to fight for it—but disdain for the country's governing body—is all but unheard of in Western mainstream cinema.

And while political cinema with revolutionary themes became relatively popular again in the '70s, many of these films were either period pieces or focused more heavily on romantic melodrama or comedic plots. Though there are some exceptions, such as *Al-Rasasa La Tazal Fi Gaiby* (*The Bullet Is Still in My Pocket*, 1974), *Ala Mn Notlik Al-Rosas* (*Whom Should We Shoot?*, 1975), *Al Mothneboon* (*The Guilty*, 1975), and especially Ali Badrakhan's *Al-Karnak* (*Karnak*, 1975), which all deal explicitly with corruption and the political causes of poverty and social misery, there are few directors in Middle Eastern cinema who continually explored radical political and transgressive themes like sexuality, gender roles, and even queer relationships within their films as frequently or as boldly as Youssef Chahine.

Samm Deighan

OUTTAKE: OUSMANE SEMBÈNE AND THE BIRTH OF AFRICAN CINEMA

Cinema is like an ongoing political rally with the audience.
—Ousmane Sembène, 1994

From 1957 to roughly 1977, Africa experienced a determined and often violent period of self-liberation, when as many as thirty African nations attempted to throw off colonial rule. This ongoing revolt—and the hope it symbolized—are central to the films of Senegalese director Ousmane Sembène, considered the father of African cinema. Many of Sembène's films are a response to the process of achieving

Ousmane Sembène

independence in Africa. They offer a harsh polemic against colonialism, but also explore its lasting impact in postcolonial Africa. Alongside his revolutionary colleagues who became political leaders—like Patrice Lumumba of the Democratic Republic of the Congo and Amílcar Cabral of Guinea-Bissau and Cape Verde—Sembène was fighting a war, but on a more cultural front. His demand for representation helped birth a long-overdue wave of films made in and about Africa, by Black Africans, for an African audience, in African languages. Because of the repressive conditions of colonialism, this did not exist before Sembène's first film in 1963.

Sembène turned to filmmaking relatively late in his life. As a young man, he worked manual labor jobs in Senegal's capital, Dakar, in the late '30s, until he was drafted into an African branch of the French army and later the Free French Forces to fight in World War II. In the late '40s, he lived in France, working in factories in Paris and on the docks in Marseille, and it was there that he became interested in radical politics. He took an active role in labor unions, participated in strikes, and joined the Communist Party.

He also explored French writing, which widened his access to the robust world of francophone Pan-African fiction, poetry, philosophy, and political writing.

Sembène himself soon found success as a novelist, which brought him international acclaim, particularly among socialist states. Many of his novels—as well as his later films—have autobiographical elements: his first book, *Le docker noir* (*The Black Docker*, 1956), is about an African's experience with racism working on the docks in Marseille; a later novel, *Les bouts de bois de Dieu* (*God's Bits of Wood*, 1960), is a fictionalized account of the 1947 railroad strike

British poster for *Black Girl* (1971)

he participated in on the Dakar-Niger border. But he came to believe that literature was not the best medium to reach his intended audience: Africans. He realized that high rates of illiteracy in Africa and issues like the lack of access to books would limit his audience to a relatively privileged few. So he turned to cinema.

Like his fellow revolutionary director Sarah Maldoror, Sembène was invited to study filmmaking in Moscow in the early '60s and used a Soviet camera to make his first short film, *Borom sarret* (*The Wagoner*, 1963). This follows a wagon driver (Ly Abdoulay) struggling to survive in Dakar. His clients either intentionally rip him off or are too destitute to pay; when he is tricked into driving into the forbidden, wealthy area of the city, he is fined and his cart is confiscated. The implication is that his wife will have to resort to sex work to feed their family. In many ways, *Borom sarret* anticipates his first and most celebrated feature, *La noire de . . .* (*Black Girl*, 1966), and is a harrowing psychological portrait of the toll colonialism and economic exploitation take on an individual, with the protagonist representing the misery of an entire continent.

Sembène's searing sixty-minute feature debut, *Black Girl*, is based on a short story he wrote and follows Diouana (Mbissine Thérèse Diop), a young woman in Dakar hired as a nanny by a French couple (Anne-Marie Jelinek and Robert Fontaine). Initially, her work for them is easy and they treat her with kindness. But when she agrees to accompany them to France, they begin to treat her as a slave. "Madame" forces her to do all the cooking and cleaning and becomes increasingly oppressive: Diouana is not paid, is not allowed to leave the house, and is even told to dress more like a servant. Limitations are put on how much she is allowed to eat or sleep. After a fight, Diouana responds with an unmistakably political act of violence: suicide. Generally considered the first sub-Saharan African film, *Black Girl* helped bring Sembène—and early African cinema—to a more global stage. Notably, it deals with the legacy of oppression, racism, and slavery that still haunts Africans, even in a seemingly postcolonial period. The way the French couple treats Diouana suggests that colonialism cannot be abolished with war or declarations of independence alone.

Diouana is a key example of the prominence of women in Sembène's films, who often respond to oppression and colonial violence with silent defiance and acts of coordinated resistance. Women's suicide is not often interpreted as a political act, but rather one associated with more personal, psychological motivations: mental illness, or as a response to suffering caused by trauma or abuse. But Diouana's suicide is an act of resistance, a way to reclaim agency over her labor and her own body, which also links her to the history of the transatlantic slave trade and the thousands of Africans who attempted or committed suicide to escape slavery. In a 2019 essay for *Voyages: Africana Journal*, Zoë Hopkins writes, "Diouana's life is one of various violences, constant rupture. Rupture from her homeland, from her free personhood, and finally from her own body and the physical world. While Sembène's Afro-pessimism is unsettling, it is also part of diasporic consciousness. We must contend with death as rebellion and rebellion as necessity and thus—what it means when liberating the self means leaving the self."

Like Maldoror, Sembène's films often explore how colonialism negatively impacts women in specific, gendered ways, and how they are important partners in the fight for liberation. Sembène was not afraid to depict how African society repressed women, during and after colonial rule, though following *Black Girl*, he typically centered his films on communities rather than individual protagonists, showcasing different regions of Africa and even exploited workers from other continents. Broadly, his output as a writer and filmmaker explores the complex, sometimes fraught process of Africans liberating themselves from European colonialism. In this way, his work can be seen as a cultural extension of influential movements

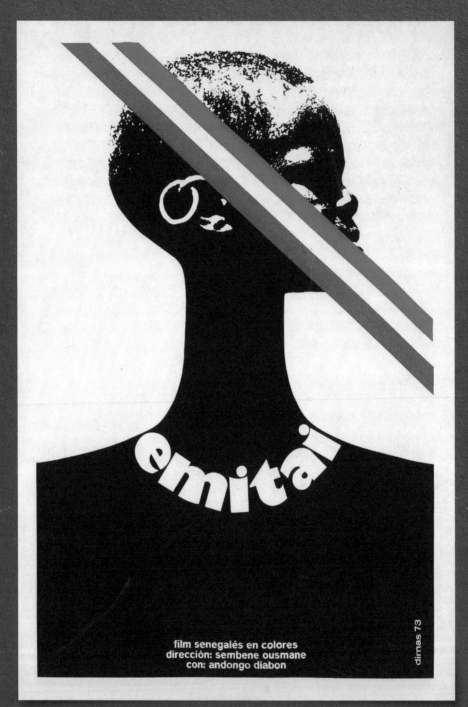

Cuban poster for *Emitaï* (1971)

like the African National Congress and the Organization of African Unity. These were connected to the broader Non-Aligned Movement, which included many countries in the so-called Third World who sought to free themselves from colonial oppression and forge new societies that followed a different model than the predatory capitalism of the West. Many of these, particularly in Africa, were Marxist and socialist. Sembène furthered this movement by creating not only some of the first African films, but the first film in an African language: his second feature, *Mandabi* (*The Money Order*, 1968), another tale of economic exploitation, which he produced in Wolof, a majority language in Senegal. He would follow this with later films in Diola (another Senegalese language) and Bambara (the national language of Mali).

Many of his films after *Black Girl* center African greed and corruption in their narratives, which are explicitly depicted as caused by colonialism. These films feature Black characters—namely soldiers, businessmen, and government officials—who subjugate other Africans. This is particularly true of his loose '70s trilogy comprising *Emitaï* (1971), *Xala* (1975), and *Ceddo* (1977), which includes Africans serving white colonialist leaders to increase their own power (as in *Emitai*), wealthy Africans in local government exploiting poor workers (as in *Xala*), and foreign leaders imposing their own religious or cultural values on African communities and enslaving those who resist (as in *Ceddo*). *Emitaï* and *Ceddo* follow similar narrative arcs: a village is subjugated by external colonizers, who demand much of them, and ultimately the villagers revolt under the direction of local women. Notably, both films are period pieces. *Emitaï* is set during World War II and focuses on the roundup of young men in a village, who are then sent to join the French forces, much like in Sembène's own experience. But taking most of the village's men is not enough, and soon there is a demand for their rice as well. The women hide their supply of rice—which they believe has a sacred link to the gods—refusing to turn it over even when they are taken hostage and threatened with death. Ultimately, the women of the village orchestrate a rebellion, which is successful, at least in the short term. Similarly, *Ceddo* (meaning "outsider") is set in nineteenth-century Senegal, before French colonizers took over the country. The villagers are essentially turned into slaves or serfs by their king (Makhouredia Gueye), who has given in to the demands of both Christian missionaries and particularly domineering imams. A number of villagers kidnap his daughter, the princess (Tabata Ndiaye), demanding the king reject slavery, forced Christianity, and forced Islam. When the king is in turn murdered, the outraged princess leads the villagers in revolt.

Both *Emitaï* and *Ceddo* were censored or banned outright in Senegal and other parts of Africa. Sembène got around this by organizing his own screenings in villages around the country and widely promoting the material that was censored. In the 2023 essay "One Hundred Years of Ousmane Sembène" for *Jacobin*, Tsogo Kupa writes, "He would tour projector screens around remote villages, setting up chairs and hosting discussions until late into the night. These 'night schools' aimed to encourage conversations among the Senegalese poor and working class. They challenged patriarchy, critiqued Senegal's political elite, sought to raise class consciousness, and unashamedly defended the notion that there was a cosmopolitan and pluralist culture indigenous to Africa."

Sembène's work as a writer, filmmaker, and intellectual confronted the intertwined legacy of colonialism, racism, capitalism, and patriarchal oppression within Africa and around the globe. In the '70s and '80s, he inspired other African directors, kick-started a Senegalese film industry, and opened the door to a more international audience for radical African films like Med Hondo's *Soleil Ô* (Oh, Sun, 1970) and *West Indies ou les nègres marrons de la liberté* (*West Indies: The Fugitive Slaves of Liberty*, 1979); the Soviet-African collaboration *Chyornoye solntse* (*Black Sun*, 1971), a fictionalized account of Patrice Lumumba's life, costarring Sembène regular Mbissine Thérèse Diop; Safi Faye's *Kaddu beykat* (*Letter from My Village*, 1975); and later films like Flora Gomes's *Mortu nega* (*Death Denied*, aka *Those Whom Death Refused*, 1988), about the war for independence in Guinea-Bissau. Until his death in 2007, Sembène was a champion of Africa, but his often confrontational work also challenged current and future generations of Africans to aspire to a greater, more egalitarian future, a message that lives on in his films.

Samm Deighan

OUTTAKE: SARAH MALDOROR'S PAN-AFRICAN CINEMA OF LIBERATION

Director Sarah Maldoror was born in France as Sarah Ducados, the daughter of a Guadeloupean émigré. Her somewhat defiant assumption of the name "Maldoror" is a reference to the Comte de Lautréamont's transgressive novel *Les chants de Maldoror* (1869), which follows a Byronic, evil protagonist and was influential to both nineteenth-century Gothic writers and the early twentieth-century Surrealists. It also reflects Maldoror's tendency to be a trailblazer from early in her career. In 1956, she helped start the first all-Black French theater group, Les Griots—"griot" meaning a West African storyteller, singer, or poet responsible for passing down

Sarah Maldoror in Guinea-Bissau, while she was shooting her first feature film, *Guns for Banta* (1970)

tradition and history orally. Inspired by her early love for Sergei Eisenstein, she traveled to Moscow in 1961 for a scholarship to study cinema. There she wound up studying alongside another highly influential future African filmmaker, Ousmane Sembène. Maldoror went on to live in Algeria, where she assisted Gillo Pontecorvo on *La battaglia di Algeri* (*The Battle of Algiers*, 1966) and Algerian director Ahmed Lallem.

In Algiers, she met representatives from other African, Latin American, and even East Asian anticolonial liberation movements, and the Algerian Front de Libération Nationale (National Liberation Front, or FLN) notably supported her early career as a filmmaker. From the first, her films were focused on anticolonialism; her initial short film, *Monangambé* (1968), explored the cultural conflicts between Angolans and their Portuguese colonizers and the violence caused by such failures in communication between them. It serves as something of a dry run for her most famous feature, *Sambizanga* (1972). Both films are based on the writings of José Luandino Vieira, set in Angola, concern freedom fighters, and feature a woman in a central role. As Yasmina Price notes in her 2002 essay "Sambizanga: Everyday Revolution," "Maldoror was adept at conveying the brutalities of the colonial regime without reducing suffering to a consumable spectacle."

Like *Monangambé*, her films often centered communities, families, and women in revolutionary struggle, rather than solely focusing on violence or open warfare. This did not always have a positive outcome; Maldoror's first planned feature film project, *Des fusils pour Banta* (*Guns for Banta*, 1970), was intended to follow a woman involved with the African Party for the Independence of Guinea and Cape Verde. The project was financed by the FLN, who allegedly canceled and buried the film because it featured women too much in its resistance narrative. But this didn't slow down Maldoror, who was outspoken about the importance of women in political movements. In a 2020 interview, she asserted that "a war cannot be won if women and children are not involved. . . . A war waged solely by soldiers is a failure."

This sentiment is at the heart of her early films, where Maldoror had two primary aims: to show communities as central to political resistance and to highlight the struggles for independence being waged throughout Africa. In the late '60s and early '70s, much of the international outrage about colonial and interventionist struggles was focused on American imperialism, particularly the American war in Vietnam. Maldoror sought to use her films to raise awareness about the various battles for liberation being waged throughout Africa. As Kate Goh writes for the British Film Institute (2021), she used "the camera as a tool for radical, feminist liberation for a continent bearing the weight of colonial oppression."

Sambizanga, Maldoror's most celebrated film and the first feature in Africa to be directed by a woman, is a particularly moving example of this mission and focuses on the Angolan War of Independence against the Portuguese occupation. The war, which lasted from 1961 to 1974, was one of many that swept Africa after World War II. Particularly following Ghana's independence from the United Kingdom in 1957, dozens of countries liberated themselves from the colonial rule of France, the UK, Belgium, Spain, and Portugal throughout the '60s and '70s. Because *Sambizanga* was made during the war in Angola, it was shot in the neighboring Republic of the Congo and features many people involved in the conflict. The film

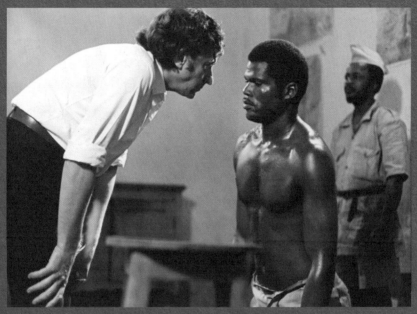

Domingos (Domingos de Oliveira) being interrogated by a Portuguese jailer in Sarah Maldoror's *Sambizanga* (1972)

was cowritten by Maldoror's husband and collaborator, Mário Pinto de Andrade, a poet who helped found the Angolan Communist Party and the Movimento Popular de Libertação de Angola (People's Movement for the Liberation of Angola, or MPLA). French writer Maurice Pons also contributed to the script, based on José Luandino Vieira's 1961 novel *A vida verdadeira de Domingos Xavier* (*The Real Life of Domingos Xavier*).

The book focuses on the titular Domingos Xavier, who is arrested, tortured, and killed, because he is believed to be associated with the MPLA and their fight for liberation. *Sambizanga* broadens the narrative to include not only Domingos (Domingos de Oliveira), who is abruptly arrested in his village and taken to the Angolan capital of Luanda for interrogation, but also his family and community. His wife, Maria (Elisa Andrade), searches for him tirelessly, with the help of people from their village and from Luanda, and with a baby strapped to her back. Local men—including some implied freedom fighters—as well as women and even children are shown to be central to events. Maldoror's decision to change the title of the film to *Sambizanga*, the name of a district in Luanda, moves the novel's focus even further away from the male protagonist.

Shot in Portuguese, as well as the Lingala and Kimbundu languages, the film was cast with amateur actors, many of whom were real Angolan

Maria (Elisa Andrade) in *Sambizanga* (1972)

militants, including the two leads. *Sambizanga* devotes an equal amount of screen time to Domingos's arrest and mistreatment in prison as it does to depictions of communal care. Maldoror does not shy away from the violence; this includes relatively graphic sequences in which Domingos is beaten and tortured, though he refuses to give his captors any information. Ultimately, he is beaten to death, his bloodied and broken body coming to rest on the floor of a shared jail cell. In one of the most affecting death scenes in anticolonial cinema, Domingos's fellow prisoners tenderly touch his dying body and spontaneously break out into a mournful song of remembrance.

Singing is of central importance to *Sambizanga* and marks moments of sorrow, but also solidarity and joy, emphasizing Maldoror's message that hope and celebration is possible even in the midst of tragedy and violence. This is bolstered throughout the film by intimate domestic scenes between Domingos and Maria early on, and later when Maria travels from their village to the city, where she is mostly treated with kindness and experiences acts of care from the community. There are some mild autobiographical elements here: Maldoror was on her own making the film with her young children in tow and her husband hiding in exile.

With *Sambizanga*, and much of her later work, Maldoror seems to suggest that a struggle for liberation is not just about fighting and experiencing violence, it is about living within a vibrant community. A film full of poetry, beauty, and—even in its conclusion—joy, *Sambizanga* is a shining example of work that highlights a more complex, rounded side of the African experience, beyond just suffering and oppression. Maldoror's thesis that community is the only way of winning a war—and that women and families are integral to this—results in a far more hopeful film than much of the political cinema of the early '70s. In a memorial to Maldoror in the December 2020 issue of *Sight and Sound*, Sukhdev Sandhu writes, "Time and again, she explored not only the violated histories of Black peoples—from Africa and the Caribbean to the fringes and suburbs of the modern European metropolis—but the ways in which they reimagined their futures."

Sambizanga—and Maldoror's career in general, from her short films to documentaries like *Aimé Césaire: Un homme une terre* (*Aimé Césaire: One Man One Land*, 1976) and TV movies like *Dessert for Constance* (1981)—remains a celebration of Africa and African history, as told by Africans. Maldoror participated in the influential Pan-African Festival of Algiers in 1969 and would go on to collaborate with Chris Marker on the shoot for *Sans soleil* (1983) in Guinea-Bissau. She went on to make dozens of films and television documentaries throughout her life, covering a wide range of subjects, including portraits of artists and writers like poet Aimé Césaire, who was a frequent focus of Maldoror's later nonfiction films, Jean Miró, Louis Aragon, and Édouard Glissant, as well as other key Pan-African cultural figures, including a never-realized documentary about philosopher Frantz Fanon planned at the end of her life. Like Fanon and Césaire—all francophone and Afro-Caribbean—Maldoror is a powerful symbol of Pan-African art, thought, and resistance. Her films, which deserve to be celebrated and made more widely available, are a continuation of the work that began with the Négritude movement that emerged in the US in the '20s and '30s during the Harlem Renaissance and developed in the work of figures like Césaire. Négritude's focus on anticolonialism, Marxism, and Surrealism, its connection to French literature and the Afro-Caribbean, and its promotion of creating alternative ways of life beyond First World capitalism are all also elements of Maldoror's inspiring life and cinema.

Samm Deighan

OUTTAKE: JEAN-LUC GODARD IN THE 1960S

French New Wave auteur Jean-Luc Godard rose to prominence with a series of films that deconstructed Hollywood cinema and reimagined genre tropes. But alongside New Wave colleagues such as François Truffaut, Éric Rohmer, and Jacques Rivette, Godard's early films are generally considered apolitical, or even somewhat politically conservative, with his radical leftist awakening not unfolding until 1967 and 1968. But even from some of his first films, he was concerned with the issue of political violence, and I would argue that his use of radical violence as a tool of social critique only intensified through his films of the '60s.

Godard's second feature film, *Le petit soldat* (*The Little Soldier*, 1963), is the first important example of this. Though it was shot right after his seminal debut, *À bout de souffle* (*Breathless*, 1960), it wasn't released until a few years later, because of its incendiary political content. The film follows a photojournalist, Bruno (Michel Subor), living in Geneva to escape military enlistment in France during the Algerian War. Though Bruno seems rather apolitical, he is secretly working for La Main Rouge (the Red Hand), a real right-wing paramilitary faction of the French foreign intelligence agency, whose primary purpose was to wage a covert war on the Algerian independence movement and its sympathizers. Bruno falls in love with a young model, Véronica (Anna Karina, in her first collaboration with Godard), who is later revealed to be supporting the Front de Libération Nationale (National Liberation Front, or FLN). When the Red Hand tries to force Bruno into assassinating an FLN leader, Véronica is tragically caught in the middle.

The release of *The Little Soldier* was delayed because it was one of the first French films to depict the torture that occurred during the Algerian War. Bruno is captured by the FLN and tortured, while the Red Hand later kidnaps, tortures, and murders Véronica. Though the film is politically rather ambiguous—like Bruno himself—it undeniably condemns the use of kidnapping, coercion, torture, and murder on both sides. The FLN torturers are implied to be acting out of desperation, while members of the Red Hand seem more sinister. Godard likely knew that the French government would never have approved a film made during the Algerian War about the war itself and specifically about the torture that occurred. And, indeed,

The Little Soldier (1963)

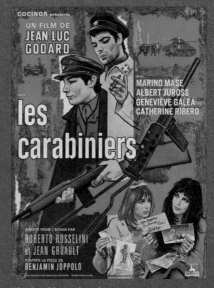

The Carabineers (1963)

despite being a Swiss production, shot in Godard's native Geneva, its release was barred by the French government for several years. As Richard Brody writes in *Everything Is Cinema: The Working Life of Jean-Luc Godard* (2008), "As early as April 3, 1955, the French government had used the pretext of the Algerian uprising to justify wide-ranging censorship in all domains, including newspapers, books, magazines, and films.... The film was nonetheless a provocation aimed principally at the French government: by implicating France in a dirty war to which it had never admitted, *Le petit soldat* was an act of defiance that belonged naturally to the left. It was a singular rejection of the Gaullist regime's censorship, an attempt to break the silence about the war."

In this light, *The Little Soldier* can be seen as the beginning of Godard's growing radicalism throughout the '60s. Though he is best known for experimenting with subgenres like crime and romance during the decade, he also increasingly explored the theme of political violence from various angles. For example, his little-seen, deeply cynical *Les carabiniers* (*The Carabineers*, 1963) presents a scathing critique of war as it follows two soldiers who are convinced to join the army of a fictionalized European country because they are promised economic spoils—which is revealed to be a lie when the soldiers return home to a country erupting into violence, empty-handed. Godard would return to the concept of guerrilla warfare and political terrorism even more overtly in *Pierrot le fou* (*Pierrot the Fool*, 1965).

Pierrot le fou (1965)

Pierrot le fou follows Ferdinand, aka Pierrot (Jean-Paul Belmondo), an unhappily married man who flees his family and repressive bourgeois lifestyle to go on the run with his ex-girlfriend Marianne (Karina). He soon learns that Marianne is a leftist operative being pursued by the right-wing counterterrorist group Organisation de l'Armée Secrète (Secret Armed Organization, or OAS), another real group dedicated to continuing French colonial rule in Algeria. The real assassinations, kidnappings, torture, and bombings they carried out are reflected in *Pierrot le fou*. Ferdinand and Marianne are caught up in carnage, some of which they flee from, but some of which Marianne herself is responsible for. To his horror, Ferdinand learns that she is using him as a sort of cover until she can return to her real boyfriend and her revolutionary cell. Marianne is alluring and enigmatic, but she ultimately betrays Ferdinand; in return, he murders Marianne and her boyfriend and then blows up their hideout, committing suicide in the process. Anna Karina starred in *Pierrot le fou* as a character that can be seen as a loose continuation of her role in *The Little Soldier*. *Pierrot le fou* is also about the end of their romantic and cinematic relationship; Karina and Godard married just after *The Little Soldier* and made several acclaimed films together, but they were in the process of divorcing in 1965.

Despite its stylish pop-art sensibilities and story of a frustrated love affair, with *Pierrot le fou* Godard began to depict a war being waged against bourgeois France by left-wing radicals, one he would soon take part in more directly. His immediate follow-up films contained similarly shocking, politically motivated acts of violence; these occur casually and rather spontaneously in *Masculin féminin* (1966), while *Made in U.S.A.* (1966) offers a pulpy, convoluted follow-up to *Pierrot le fou*, starring Karina as a leftist journalist caught up in more kidnapping, murder, and terrorism. As in *Pierrot le fou*, she is again presented as a sort of sinister agent pulling strings from the background, committing politically motivated and espionage-related crimes, including several murders, with impunity. But these murkier depictions of political violence would change when Godard met and began a romantic relationship with a young actor and student radical, Anne Wiazemsky. The bitter disappointment, resentment, and betrayal of his later films with Karina was replaced with hope and idealism.

Godard's earlier films often had two main themes: a dissection of romantic relationships and his troubles in love, and his own deeply personal intellectual musings on cinema and culture. These aims continued in his films with Wiazemsky, in which he would explore more emotional issues alongside his own growing political radicalism. *La Chinoise, ou plutôt à*

Italian lobby card for *La Chinoise* (1967)

la Chinoise: un film en train de se faire (The Chinese, or, Rather, in the Chinese Manner: A Film in the Making, 1967) is an important example of this evolution in his career. Based loosely on Fyodor Dostoyevsky's novel *Demons* (1872), about a group of student radicals, *La Chinoise* focuses on a similar group in 1967 Paris, young Maoists living in close quarters and trying to determine how to turn Maoist theory into practice.

Like *Masculin féminin*, *La Chinoise* features a series of cinema verité–like interviews with the young actors, including Wiazemsky and French New Wave icons like Jean-Pierre Léaud and Juliet Berto, who seemingly play versions of their real selves, with Léaud as somewhat of a stand-in for Godard. Wiazemsky's character, Véronique,

Italian poster for *La Chinoise* (1967)

Jean-Luc Godard being arrested in Paris, May 1968

seems obsessed with the idea of violence as the only possible course forward. She declares that "politics are the starting point of a practical revolutionary action" and plans to shut down French universities with bombs—not bomb threats, but actual detonated bombs intended to kill teachers and students. Though this doesn't move beyond conversation, she ultimately assassinates the Soviet minister of culture in town for a state visit, after first accidentally killing another man because she confused their hotel room numbers.

For a film so concerned with violence, none is shown on-screen. Like several of Godard's political films to follow, there is much more of a focus on discussion and references to philosophy, art, and pop culture, with shots of real-world strife intruding via stock footage or documentary sequences. Despite Véronique's words in *La Chinoise*, the veneration of certain cultural objects—like Mao's Little Red Book, which dominates certain scenes— seems to be more important than the actual planning of direct actions. But in this way, Godard highlights a contradictory element of the youth revolt on the rise in the period: genuinely frustrated individuals desperate for social change who are also young and naive, caught up in symbolism and optics.

This formula would be turned on its head with his nihilistic, chaotic, and quite violent follow-up, *Weekend* (1967), which follows a bourgeois couple (Mireille Darc and Jean Yanne) waiting to come into money, each eager to betray the other. But their journey by car through the French countryside erupts in violence: traffic jams, grisly car accidents, gang rape, and murder, culminating with the wife allowing a group of revolutionaries to kill her husband, who is dismembered and eaten with her participation. Certainly, much of the violence in *Weekend* could be described as political, but it is blackly comic in tone, even apocalyptic. Notably, *Weekend* was to be Godard's last "commercial" film—though it is anything but conventional—before forming the leftist Dziga Vertov Group with Jean-Pierre Gorin, where they would make highly political, documentary-like films until 1973, far outside the realm of conventional narrative cinema.

Samm Deighan

GHOSTS AND WEEDS

What Is and Isn't in Costa-Gavras's Z

Costa-Gavras's influential 1969 political thriller, *Z*, begins with a colonel delivering a lecture to a group of military officers and government officials. Using horticultural metaphors, the colonel argues that just as a gardener is ruthless in weeding, "antisocial" and "decadent" elements in society must be eliminated at their roots. His delivery is fiery and emphatic: he is self-righteous and clearly believes in the truth of his authoritarian doctrines.

It's an effective opening scene, powerful yet comic, with the humor in the bombastic overreach of the colonel's language. The scene also slyly echoes the voice-overs that punctuated much of Hollywood film noir, such as Alfred L. Werker's and Anthony Mann's *He Walked by Night* (1948) or John Huston's *The Asphalt Jungle* (1950), where a stern and masculine authoritative voice—usually a police commissioner or a judge—would counsel the audience against taking too much pleasure in the activities of the underworld antiheroes. It's impossible to view this opening without also thinking of the almost documentary-styled scenes in Gillo Pontecorvo's *La battaglia di Algeri* (*The Battle of Algiers*, 1966), in which the frustrated French general outlines what is at stake for the French state to maintain their colonial mandate in Algiers.

Part of what makes *Z* so exuberant—a liveliness that helped it achieve colossal popular and critical approval—is in its daring to pilfer across global cinema. Tropes and narrative strategies associated with classic Hollywood cinema, such as film noir and melodrama, are melded to formal and stylistic techniques that are influenced by Italian neorealism and the French

Nouvelle Vague. Even watching the film now, over a half century later, the present-day viewer is struck by its *committed* playfulness. *Z* deals with highly charged political events, events that had overwhelming import for the filmmakers, but is nevertheless enormously pleasurable to watch. The film is over two hours long, but it never lets up in its breathless pacing. Costa-Gavras gleefully immerses himself in the conventions of the thriller and of the *noir policier*, but he isn't apologizing for the disconcerting edits, the vertiginous zooms, and the abrupt

Director Costa-Gavras on the set of his 1983 film *Hanna K.*

flashbacks that he borrows from his contemporaries in the New Wave. There's not either/or at work in *Z*, no sense that a filmmaker must choose between the popular and the avant-garde, or between pleasure and earnestness. There's no subtlety in its brazenness, and that's part of what makes it feel like a youthful work. Even the musical score by Mikis Theodorakis, written when he was a political prisoner and which had to be smuggled out of Greece, is provocatively lively and nose-thumbing, cheekily utilizing a jaunty martial air.

Z is adapted from a 1967 novel by Vassilis Vassilikos, which is itself based on the real-life murder of Greek politician Grigoris Lambrakis in 1963. Lambrakis had been a member of the Greek resistance during World War II and subsequently, as a leftist politician, had played a key part in opposing the overdetermining role of the US government in Greek politics. His assassination, which was covertly supported by the Greek police and military, intensified the political turmoil in the country. The military coup of 1966, which resulted in a ten-year brutal dictatorship, was led by many of the military personnel who had unofficially sanctioned Lambrakis's murder. The "Regime of the Colonels" was a period of extreme political oppression, including curfews, the suspension of civil liberties, and widespread torture. The makers of *Z* were working in exile while the dictatorship was still taking place. It is absolutely no wonder that we still experience the intensity of the drive of everyone involved in making the film.

Costa-Gavras himself was from a family who understood the ferocity of Greece's modern history only too well. His father had been a member

French poster for *Z* (1969)

of the resistance and a communist intellectual. Once the Axis powers were defeated, Greece became a frontline battle in the emerging Cold War between the superpowers. The communists, who had been the leaders of the resistance, were ready to assume electoral victory, but that eventuality led to the US and Great Britain—utilizing powers acceded to them by the newly conceived Marshall Plan for Europe—intervening to support the royalist opposition. The result was a four-year civil war that saw horrific atrocities committed by both sides. Even with the end of that war, and the defeat of the communists, there

Japanese poster for Z (1969)

was continuing oppression against leftists in Greece. Though born in Greece, as the child of a communist, Costa-Gavras could not continue further education there. His family made the choice to migrate to France.

Z was made deliberately to delegitimize the military dictatorship. It was lauded with critical praise, garnering two Academy Awards in the US, and it did indeed lead to a greater global awareness of the vileness of the junta in Greece. However, by the time of its production, almost concurrent with the events in Paris in May 1968, the call for artists and filmmakers to take a position, to commit to the popular (and therefore capitalist) or to the experimental (and therefore radical), had already convulsed much of international cinema. The popular and critical success enjoyed by Costa-Gavras's film was viewed with suspicion by an increasingly radicalized film culture. As Daniel Fairfax notes in his 2021 book, *The Red Years of Cahiers du cinéma (1968–1973): Volume I, Ideology and Politics*, Z was scornfully censured and "derided as fictions de gauche" precisely for its use of popular cinematic forms. In the cultural and political upheavals of the late 1960s, film theory and criticism were increasingly dominated by a dogmatic poststructuralism, heavily influenced by the avowedly antihumanist Marxism of Louis Althusser, which prioritized the material and the formal over intention and manifest content. From such a perspective, Costa-Gavras's own personal history didn't matter any more than Theodorakis's own suffering under the junta. What mattered was what was on-screen, and what the post-1968 Maoist critics saw was a film that utilized narrative tropes and film-making techniques borrowed from capitalist Hollywood cinema. That sneering word, *fictions,* is meant as an indictment of the straightforward genre elements utilized in *Z.*

Z is a thriller. And it is also a courtroom drama, and it is a highly romanticized lionization of a left-wing political hero. Early in the film, we are introduced to a group of antiwar activists organizing a lecture for a visiting politician (Yves Montand as the Lambrakis figure)

Yves Montand · Irene Papas · Jean-Louis Trintignant
A Film by Costa-Gavras · Music by Mikis Theodorakis   Z   A Cinema V Presentation · Eastmancolor

Irene Papas as Hélène, the wife of the murdered deputy in *Z*

and another group of right-wing extremist thugs doing their best to sabotage the lecture. The activists are being constantly stymied in their attempts to book an auditorium, while we witness the support of the police and military for the fascist thugs. A hall is finally secured and the lecture is delivered, but when the politician goes out to talk to the crowd after his speech, he is run down and murdered. The rest of the film becomes a tense investigation, led by the stern, cool-headed investigator, played by Jean-Louis Trintignant, who is seeking to work out if the killing was an accident or a planned assassination.

The scenes oscillate between the investigation and the attempts by the right-wing paramilitaries to cover up their crimes. The film reaches its conclusion in a triumphant scene in which the military officers responsible for ordering the murder are rounded up and charged. It's a release for the audience. But in a final denouement, a caustic mirror of the lecture of the opening scene, a journalist reveals how many of the accused will go on to become leaders of the junta. This coda is a warning to the audience not to underestimate the hyperbole of the sentiments expressed in the opening lecture. The colonels are deadly serious about weeding out the undesirables. Like the firm avuncular voice in film noir reminding us that crime is serious, that criminals intend harm, the ending of *Z* is a reminder that though we've had fun, the consequences of this "fiction" are deadly serious as well.

Once stripped of its haute academic obtrusiveness, the critique of the film from the Maoist *Cahiers du cinéma* critics isn't a world away from Pauline

Jean-Louis Trintignant as the examining magistrate in *Z* (1969)

Kael's perceptive contemporaneous review of *Z* in the *New Yorker* (December 1973), "Exiles," where she expressed doubts about turning political events into melodrama. Though she found the film "almost intolerably exciting," she observed that similar breathless "techniques of excitation" could be used by fascist filmmakers to galvanize an audience.

I like that doubt. I think I respond to it because I have seen *Z* numerous times now, first when I was a late adolescent and most recently as a man in his mid-fifties, and yet I still am not sure what I think of it. Every time I watch it, I am impressed by its effectiveness. Raoul Coutard's cinematography is remarkable, equally luminous and forbidding in daylight or at night. The cast is superlative, clearly chosen for the iconic strength the actors bring to their roles: Montand as the assassinated hero, his craggy and handsome face recalling both Albert Camus and Humphrey Bogart; Irene Papas's wounded and heroic haughtiness as his widow; the callowness and earnestness of Trintignant as the prosecutor; and the simultaneously repellent and attractive leering visage of Marcel Bozzuffi as the villainous, sadistic killer, Vago, the most ruthless of the thugs who organizes the assassination. There's that propulsive rousing music, of course, and the tautness of that economical and proficient script.

My conflicted relationship to *Z* arises from it being part of my consciousness even as a very small child, a long time before I ever saw the film. I have a memory of being four or five years old, playing with my tiny toy cars under

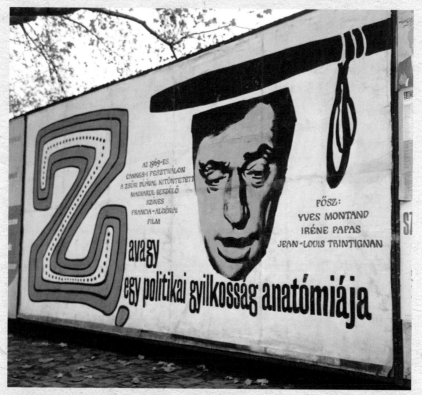

Poster for *Z*, Budapest, Hungary, 1970

the kitchen table while my parents discussed the film. As with all such distant remembrances, I can't vouch for how much of what I remember is factual and how much has been recalibrated and reconstructed by the act of recollection itself. Yet there are elements of the memory that are still so sharply vivid after decades. My sitting cross-legged under the table, of how cool the black-and-white lino felt on my bum, of how my father was complaining that his friend Kostas was late and that they would miss the beginning of the film. Did my mother voice that she wished she too was going to attend the screening? Or was that a moot point, it being understood that it was her role to stay at home and watch over the children? I remember hearing the title of the film, their giving it the Greek inflection: *Zei*, not the Australian English *Zed*, with that sharp consonant at the end.

As a child in the pre-video era, my parents would take my brother and I to the movies most weekends, to the Greek-speaking cinemas in Melbourne. The films were often slapstick comedies or tear-jerking melodramas. But the way the adults talked about *Z* made it seem apart from the usual Greek-language fare. It wasn't playing in the inner-city neighborhoods where most migrants lived. My father and his friends had to get a tram out to the bourgeois eastern suburbs to see it. And something about the film had precipitated an argument, even before my father and his friend had viewed it. Their voices were raised; they were clearly emotional. The argument was about politics. I went back to playing with my toy cars.

Z came back into my life as a teenager, when I began to share my mother's love for film. I started devouring books on cinema history, as well as searching out literature on radical politics and revolutionary aesthetics, and all this reading became entwined with the understanding I had of the Greek political turmoil that was central to my parents' migration to Australia.

Z itself doesn't deal with the Greek Civil War (1946–49), but for anyone of Greek heritage, the shadow of that awful conflict is a persistent ghost within the movie. The war was never successfully resolved, leading inevitably to the wretched failure of a successful democracy to emerge in Greece in the '50s and '60s. The resistance to Axis powers was fought mainly in rural areas, and the countryside of Greece was devastated by that conflict and the ensuing poverty. The migration from the countryside to the cities and then the massive emigration across the globe has its roots in the terror of that period. Even before I watched Z, I knew that the shadow of the Civil War would guide my relationship to the film.

I was also struck by the incongruence of it being my father who so keenly sought out the film. Both my parents were born to peasant rural households and grew up during the Civil War. My father's oldest brother was brutally murdered by the communists while he was undertaking military service for the royalist regime, which initiated my father's lifetime antipathy to communism. My mother's story was a stark contrast: her left-wing family experienced oppression from the rightist forces. Most pertinently, her oldest brother was held prisoner and tortured by the military junta of the colonels, the culmination of the story that Costa-Gavras's film details. It was my mother, not my father, who explained to me the tragic story of Grigoris Lambrakis. He was murdered in the year that she left Athens for Melbourne, and she remembers her brother coming home to the apartment they shared in Kalifea, crying, "The bastards have killed Grigoris." And she added, in a statement that has remained a constant guide for me throughout my life, "That's what fascists do, they destroy the good."

I was eighteen and in my first year at university when I first saw Z, at a repertory arthouse cinema. I do recall the anticipation I felt at finally watching a film that had such importance for political cinema, a film that I knew was going to resonate with my engagement with cinema and politics and—more importantly—with the history of my migrant parents. I was animated by the movie, caught up in the thriller components of the plot. I was at the edge of my seat throughout, and along with the rest of the audience, I cheered the conviction of the murderers. And I felt the punch of that final coda.

Yet leaving the cinema, my mood was conflicted. I had gone into the screening wanting to love *Z* and assuming that I would. But the specters of the Civil War and of the colossal emigration that followed were missing from the film. Unlike most of the Greek communists I knew, factory workers like my parents, none of the left-wingers in the film were peasants or workers. They seemed all to be students and intellectuals. Having grown up in a family where the material and existential costs of the Greek Civil War had a determining effect on how I viewed international relations, I was disappointed by the absence of that historical context within the narrative of the film. I was unconvinced by the buffoonery of the rightist thugs who carry out the assassination at the behest of the military. I didn't question the critique and abhorrence of their violence, but I wanted more nuance around why their anticommunism was expressed so vehemently.

There's a sequence late in the film where a Greek dockworker from Odessa nicknamed "the Russian" (Guy Mairesse) collaborates with the investigation into the assassination. He is promised his long-desired visa and passport to the US in return for his assistance. The "Russian" fingers various men involved in a right-wing Christian paramilitary group: a butcher, a barber, a grocer, a mechanic, and a boxer. The lumpen and petit bourgeois makeup of this group is too neat and smacks of left-wing theorizing. Their adherence to fascism has no context and is simply reduced to an inherent malevolence or ignorance. This reductive portrayal of the thugs is further compounded by the heroic grace given to the liberal and left-wing activists in the film. I wanted to see my mother's oldest brother reflected in the film, a rural youth without any formal education who migrated to Athens in his early teens, a unionist whose activism had led to his imprisonment by the institutional forces condemned in the film. The Civil War and its consequences are erased in *Z*. More profoundly, so are class issues.

At that moment of my first seeing *Z*, in 1983, I was a member of a Greek-speaking political group, Greek Progressive Youth of Australia (EPNA). Many of my fellow cadres in the organization were young people who had recently migrated from Greece. Democracy had been restored in Greece with the fall of the junta in 1975, and in 1981 Andreas Papandreou led PASOK, the major democratic-socialist party, to victory in the Greek elections. Nevertheless,

Still from Theodoros Angelopoulos's *The Travelling Players* (1975)

memories of the Civil War, of the junta, and of the decades-long punishment and harassment of Greek leftists were still fresh, and the tensions and consequences of these conflicts remained unresolved. It was with these Greek friends, many of whom considered themselves exiles, that I first debated the merits and contradictions of *Z*. They explained to me that in Greece, Costa-Gavras had a contentious position within Greek leftist and activist thought. "He's a French filmmaker" is a critique I heard again and again. As a migrants' child, I am sure I was hurt by this peremptory disavowal of the filmmaker as not "Greek." After years of interrogating questions of exile and migration, I am convinced that diasporic experiences can be integrated into notions of statehood and identity. Thus, for me, Costa-Gavras is both a Greek *and* a French filmmaker. There was also an issue with the nature of the film's distribution. "It's not for us, it's a film for the West," one of my friends explained. "If you want to understand Greek cinema and Greek history, then watch Angelopoulos."

It so happened that not long afterward, EPNA screened *O Thiasos* (*The Travelling Players*), the 1975 masterwork from Theodoros Angelopoulos, one of the great cinematic poets of time. The film details the struggles of a group of actors in Greece from 1939 to 1952, who travel the countryside putting on the play *Golfo the Shepherdess*. At the same time, within the dynamics of the troupe, there are reverberations of the ancient Aeschylean tragedies in the *Oresteia*. I knew *Golfo the Shepherdess* already, for this tragic melodrama of a young shepherd girl was one of my mother's favorite stories; I had seen an old black-and-white film version as a child at the Greek cinema. Though I was

Giorgos Arvanitis and Theodoros Angelopoulos (right) on the set of *The Travelling Players* (1975)

baffled by much of *The Travelling Players*, I appreciated Angelopoulos's wise instinct to place the two tragedies—one ancient and canonical, one peasant and popular—alongside each other. It is impossible to watch this film and not comprehend the moral ferocity of its indictment of the rise of fascism, even though there isn't any exploitation of violence itself. Unlike Costa-Gavras's film, the ghosts of history are continually whispering just beyond the frame. Angelopoulos first began the film during the last years of the junta, and the incorporation of the ancient Greek myths was itself a subversion, a way of putting the censors off the track. By provocatively allowing this subterfuge to become a central part of his narrative, by making the traveling actors' struggles to interpret social events—ancient, modern, *and* contemporary— part of the structure of the film, he was also challenging us as an audience to consider our own understanding of historic memory. In comparison to *The Travelling Players*, *Z*'s narrative ploys were journalistic and superficial. I was now at one with the view of the critics from *Cahiers du cinéma* that a radical take on history required a radical formalism and aesthetic.

Yet *The Travelling Players*, and my realization that formal questions were as important to understanding political cinema as narrative and intent, meant that I could elide a much more personal and troubling aspect to *Z*. I had already initiated the long-term project of coming out as homosexual by the time I saw both films. Yet I was too self-conscious back then of being accused of interpreting everything through the lens of sexuality to admit to

Marcel Bozzuffi as the right-wing thug, Vago, in *Z* (1969)

what we would now call a queer interpretation of the Costa-Gavras film. For there is a character in *Z*, Vago, that continues to disturb and challenge me at every viewing. He is the most sadistic of the right-wing conspirators, and Bozzuffi also gives the most sensual performance in the film; with his shirt unbuttoned, he is cocky and dynamically masculine. And he's a homosexual; there is no doubt of this. In a carefully coded conversation, we learn that Vago has an ongoing sexual relationship with a newspaper editor and that, whether it is from fear of blackmail or simply a desire to maintain the sexual liaison, the editor prints stories favorable to the right wing at Vago's urging. And in a long interrogation scene, it is revealed that Vago has done time in prison for "possession of a weapon, abuse and slander, theft ... and rape." When he is asked about the rape, Vago shrugs and says, "It was nothing, I was a boy scout counselor." In a film where all other references to prison have to do with activists being punished by the state for their political activities, this casual, unconcerned admission has a clear ideological purport: Vago is scum.

He is also one of the most vividly alive homosexual characters in pre–gay liberation cinema. The use of homosexuality to denote decadence and corruption was also part of the plot in Rossellini's *Roma città aperta* (*Rome, Open City*), the 1945 film key to the development of neorealist and subsequently realist socialist cinema. The homosexual Nazi officer and the lascivious lesbian collaborator of *Rome, Open City* now strike contemporary viewers as risible. Their inclusion in the plot is to function in contrast to the

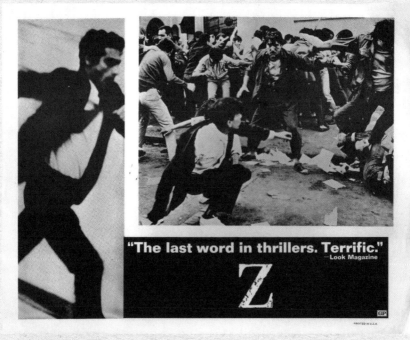

"The last word in thrillers. Terrific."
—Look Magazine

Z

US lobby card for *Z* (1969)

morally upright members of the resistance. Arguably, Vago's character is utilized in a similar way to the queer villains in Rossellini's film. He clearly is meant to represent the corrupting effects of right-wing authoritarianism on the body politic. Yet through Bozzuffi's enthusiastic and sly playing, in which strutting machismo and narcissistic preening are core elements of his persona, the retrograde conception that marks the writing of the character is subverted and ultimately undermined.

Undoubtedly, Bozzuffi's skill as an actor is key to the vividness of Vago in the film, but it isn't only performance that makes the character so compelling. Even in the writing, in the ambiguity and chilling seductive virility of his character, Vago is by far the most fascinating character in *Z*. The film's screenplay is carefully plotted, with each cumulative incident underlining the malevolence of the forces arraigned against liberalism and democracy. The characters are simplistically drawn, to emphasize either the hypocrisy and duplicity of the military and the police state or the righteousness of its liberal and socialist hero-activists. From their first appearance on the screen—whether it is a dim-witted, sanctimonious colonel, a pure-hearted activist, or a grieving widow—we know exactly who the characters are and what we are meant to think of them. Only Vago defies easy categorization.

Yves Montand as the radical deputy in *Z* (1969)

He transcends the bounds of the traditional archvillain role. Vago is depicted as a sexual outsider, but he was not written as a victim. And Bozzuffi didn't play him as one.

There is an undoubted call-and-response that was happening to me as a young queer viewer first seeing *Z*. A few years earlier, I had seen Bernardo Bertolucci's 1970 masterwork, *Il conformista* (*The Conformist*), in which Trintignant plays Marcello, a fascist assassin working for Mussolini's dictatorship. Unlike the deliberate vilifying of Vago, Bertolucci brings a greater nuance to the subterranean shadow of homosexuality in his film. In *The Conformist*, the attempted seduction of a teenage Marcello by an older man isn't a confirmation of perversion; its occurrence leads to a permanent question that hangs over the rest of the film: how much is Marcello's acquiescence to fascism a result of his need to repress the "danger" of his sexuality? I was deeply shocked and moved by my first encounter with *The Conformist*. It was the first time an artwork in any medium had posed for me the startling existential choice that still lies at the heart of "coming out": what is lost in becoming, and how does it compare to what is lost with suppression?

Of course, with Trintignant so central in both *The Conformist* and *Z*, I was inevitably comparing how each film dealt with the complication of sexuality and desire. And, of course, in such a comparison, *Z* is the more conservative film. Vago is made a fag, and possibly a pedophile, not to interrogate the complex repression which makes fascism so contradictorily attractive to those who are fearful of being denounced as outsiders, but to provide a conveniently repellent antithesis to Montand's heroic martyr. I want

to be clear on this point: unlike with Bertolucci's film, there is no empathy in
Z for Vago. *Z*'s sexual politics are as crude as those of *Rome, Open City*. The
sympathy I feel for Vago arises from my deliberately oppositional interpretation of the film's sexual politics.

In Vito Russo's groundbreaking book *The Celluloid Closet* (1987), he
argues convincingly that in much of pre-Stonewall cinema the sexual
outsider was marked as either evil or masochistic. And queer characters had
to die on-screen. *Z* doesn't kill off Vago, but he is clearly marked as malicious.
Though Russo's work remains important for theorizing how sexuality has
historically been portrayed in film, a weakness of his thesis is that he assumes
a straightforward relationship between a filmmaker's intent and the reception
that we as an audience have of these intentions. If I keep returning to Vago in
this essay, it is only in part that I am attempting to right my own fearfulness
when I first saw *Z* to raise objections to its homophobic representation. The
film's homophobia is a key element that keeps it alive to reinterpretation. If
all the other characters are embalmed in the past, Vago continues to unset-
tle us as viewers. Watching it again recently, it is impossible not to view his
character through the lens of recent global events, because of his unrepentant
machismo, his assertion of his masculinity as prerogative, and his disdain
for cosmopolitanism and the hypocrisy of the intelligentsia. What is it that
is most offensive about Vago? That he is a pervert, or that he refuses the
utopian pluralism of progressive culture? And because these reverberations
occur, it becomes possible to discern in *Z* the fracturing of left-wing politics
that found full flower in the twenty-first century. In such a reading, *Z* isn't
fascinating for what it documents about the events in Greece in the 1960s.
That history is laid out more comprehensively and with more rigorous scrutiny in *The Travelling Players*. Vago, however, is a provocative harbinger of
the tensions that arose in left-wing political and cultural thought with the
end of the Soviet Union, and our subsequent preferencing of questions of
identity over those of class.

The films of Costa-Gavras suggest that traditional narrative forms and
filmmaking techniques are not irrelevant or irredeemable for use in political
cinema. This might be the most important element of *doubt* as a critical
stance. I can criticize *Z* as homophobic and simplistic, for example, yet still
think it an admirable film. In an era in which appraisal of cinema is reduced
to a thumbs-up or a thumbs-down, this defense of ambivalence, nuance,
and doubt is crucial.

The importance of formal radical work is key to rethinking how we tell
stories of politics and engagement. Angelopoulos's work continues to inspire

and challenge filmmakers globally
to think through the ethical and
existential issues at stake when it
comes to approaching history. But
such a radical aesthetic can't be
popular. Costa-Gavras's films like
Missing (1982) and *State of Siege*
(1972) show that it is possible to use
genre forms with a thoughtfulness
that doesn't condescend to any of its
potential audiences. This remains
my main critical reservation with
Z. I understand the exigencies of
its creation, of how the filmmakers
wanted to bring the world's attention to the terror occurring in the
Greek nation-state. It did so, brilliantly and with focused energy

Czechoslovakian poster for *The Confession*
(1970)

and righteousness. Yet in foreclosing doubt—in privileging polemic over
argument—it is reductive and erases the contradictions and complexities
of history.

There is a Costa-Gavras film in which thoughtfulness is much in
evidence. It is *The Confession*, a film made in 1970 that details the arrest
and interrogation of a Soviet apparatchik in one of the last purges before
Stalin's death. Montand is again the lead actor, and he is superb. The film
is relentless in showing us the cruelty of a totalitarian regime, yet it also
uses flash-forward to interrupt our emotional immersion in the narrative, to
present complicated arguments about socialism and totalitarianism. Costa-
Gavras isn't hiding leftist rhetorical flourishes in *The Confession*, and the
film doesn't pretend that history is Manichean. And for this reason, the film
hasn't dated, and its questions about individual conscience and submission
to communal authority are still potent.

In the opening harangue in *Z*, the colonel identifies education as the
first point at which the state's uncompromising "weeding" must commence.
During the long and ugly years of the junta, as an Australian child in primary
school, I would attend Greek lessons twice a week. The year would begin with
each of us being given a Greek grammar book and a child's book on history.
Printed in Greece, each of the books would include a flyleaf that portrayed
an image of a Greek soldier with a phoenix rising haughtily above him. This

was the insignia of the colonels. I would take the books home, and both my parents would guide me in tearing up those pages. I'd follow my parents outside to a small bonfire, and we'd set the pages alight, and my brother and I would cheer as we saw the hateful insignia char and burn. I have tried again and again in watching *Z* to get a glimpse of my parents. Of their history, their conflict, their struggle. But they're not there; or if they are, they are in the dim, untrustworthy shadows cast by Vago. I've looked and I've looked, but the rural past and the working-class present are just not there.

Christos Tsiolkas

"DON'T BUY BREAD ... BUY DYNAMITE!"

Franco Solinas and the Zapata Spaghetti Westerns

When the Italian writer-director team of Franco Solinas and Gillo Pontecorvo made *La battaglia di Algeri* (*The Battle of Algiers*, 1966), they produced an arthouse documentary-like retelling of a recent anticolonialist insurrection. In Roger Ebert's interview "Pontecorvo: 'We Trust the Face of Brando'" (1969), Pontecorvo asserted that the film had been made in order to allegorically champion the dispossessed worldwide and to encourage them to fight for their rights. Given that Solinas had served as a partisan during World War II and joined the Italian Communist Party after the war had ended, it has been presumed that the same political intent was present in other works that he wrote for the screen. These further efforts sometimes adopted a different approach: a number of them were popular genre films whose narratives unfolded within much earlier historical time frames. However, the contents and themes of historical genre films often tell us more about the society and the time in which they were made than they do about their diegetic period settings, and that is surely the case with Solinas's popular film work.

His historical allegories of oppression and insurrection would seem to reflect and be intended to resonate with those sectors of Italian society—and, indeed, those members of marginalized groups worldwide—who were embroiled in bitter, violent struggles for social and political change during the late 1960s. In *The Euro-Western: Reframing Gender, Race and the "Other" in Film* (2016), I detail how the 1960s marked an increasingly turbulent time in Italy. When the country's postwar "economic miracle" came to an end in the early 1960s, it was clear that not all Italians had enjoyed the benefits of the miracle equally. Around three million poverty-stricken southern Italians had been forced to migrate north in search of work during the 1950s.

The rude reception that these dark-skinned southerners received in northern cities—along with the exploitation in the workplace that they suffered and the appalling living conditions that they endured while living in ramshackle ghettoes on the outskirts of big northern cities—resulted in the long-standing economic, cultural, and racial tensions that had traditionally existed between the north and south of Italy becoming the subject of growing public discourse as the 1960s wore on. Southern Italian workers played key roles in the mass demonstrations of 1968, alongside political activists, students, and the members of a variety of newly emergent social movements. These demonstrations were initially about employment-based grievances, such as poor working conditions and low pay, but they became increasingly violent and intensified during the *Autunno caldo* (Hot Autumn) of 1969 and were couched as demands for an end to wider social injustices too. The Piazza Fontana bombing in Milan on December 12, 1969, would result in the Hot Autumn being succeeded by the *Anni di piombo* (Years of Lead), a period in which political extremists brought devastating acts of terrorism to Italy's streets.

Whether Solinas's political parables truly connected with their intended audiences and whether they had the desired effect is open to question, but his political engagement with popular genres marks another interesting chapter in the history of Italian popular cinema. The Italian film industry had become reinvigorated during the 1950s when numerous Hollywood studios chose Italy as a prime shooting location for a series of popular historical epics. These films were primarily concerned with the histories and legends of Greece and Rome. By the end of the decade, Italian filmmakers had begun trying to cash in on the trend by producing their own similarly themed films. The box office success of one such film at home and abroad, Pietro Francisci's *Le fatiche di Ercole* (*Hercules*, 1958), set in motion a practice that was to become a long-standing convention among those who produced popular genre films in Italy.

Hoping to ride on the coattails of *Hercules*'s success, countless similarly plotted productions were initiated, which led to a cycle of *peplum* (sword and sandal) films. As Steve Neale observes in *Genre* (1980), all genre films—whether produced in Hollywood or Italy—have an element of "repetition and difference" about them. Elements of repetition are needed to assist viewers in recognizing which genre a particular film belongs to, while elements of difference work to assure viewers that they are paying to watch a suitably original cinematic product. But in Italian genre films, the elements of repetition tended to be ramped up, while the elements of difference tended to be dialed down, leading to cycles of films known as *filoni* (formula films) that have been criticized for being somewhat derivative. A quote from the Italian director Luigi Cozzi in Mark Goodall's *"Spaghetti Savages": Cinematic Perversions of Django Kill* (2016) sums up the mechanics of this practice: "In Italy … when you bring a script to a producer, the first question he asks is not 'what is your film like?' but 'what *film* is your film like?'"

When Hollywood studios began withdrawing from Italy in 1960 and the popularity of the *peplum* films began to wane, domestic filmmakers sought to initiate new *filoni* based on recent international box office hits; examples include gothic horror films in the mold of Hammer Films' output and spy movies based on the James Bond series, but these tended to be relatively short-lived trends. One *filone* that did endure beyond all others was the *Western All'Italiana* (spaghetti western). Following the success of Sergio Leone's *Per un pugno di dollari* (*A Fistful of Dollars*, 1964), Italian-made westerns would remain popular—and be produced in huge numbers—until the late 1970s.

In plotting the history and the evolution of Italian westerns in *The Spaghetti Western Genre* (2000), I argue that the genre was able to survive and grow in a fickle marketplace because its core directors were savvy enough to introduce a succession of novel cycles and subgenres that served to periodically reinvigorate the larger parent genre. This process was initially led by the success that Sergio Leone's films enjoyed. *A Fistful of Dollars* led to a number of films where lone gunmen played two villainous gangs against each other; *Per qualche dollaro in piu* (*For a Few Dollars More*, 1965) led to a number of films that featured two gunmen teaming up to take on a gang of villains; and *Il buono, il brutto, il cattivo* (*The Good, the Bad and the Ugly*, 1966) led to a number of films where numerous gunmen enter into uneasy alliances in order to pursue treasure hunts out West. The films that were made in the mold of Leone's box office smashes might be best described as cycles. However, further clusters of spaghetti westerns arose throughout the genre's lifetime that shared thematic and symbolic content that was pointedly distinct enough for them to be more readily classed as subgenres. One such subgenre was the "Zapata" spaghetti western.

The Zapata spaghetti westerns are usually set during one of Mexico's post-1900 periods of revolution. They feature government officials and soldiers who are shown to be fascistic and greedy oppressors of the people,

Screenwriter Franco Solinas   Director Damiano Damiani

while their nominal heroes tend to be exploited and downtrodden Mexican peons who eventually become politically enlightened insurrectionists. These peons are often befriended and further exploited by American or European weapons experts who are cast as meddlesome foreign interventionists or callous profit-driven mercenaries. Several personnel who were involved in the making of the films have suggested that their Mexican characters functioned as racial palimpsests that spoke on behalf of both the Italian proletariat (particularly the dark-skinned southern Italians living in—or migrating from—the rural south of the country) and oppressed "Others" worldwide; that their uniformed Federales and Rurales might be read as stand-ins for the repressive state apparatuses of any contemporary reactionary regime of choice; and that their Anglo interlopers might be read as metaphors for contemporaneous American and European interventions in South America and the Third World. Given that the films' left-leaning politics are laid open so obviously, there's little reason to discount such assertions. But at the very least, these Italian films can be said to have captured the political zeitgeist of the late 1960s and early 1970s both at home and abroad.

Franco Solinas was involved in the making of three key and influential Zapata spaghetti westerns. Indeed, it was Solinas and director Damiano Damiani who initiated the subgenre when they came together to produce *Quién sabe?* (*A Bullet for the General*, 1966). Solinas's screenplay, which was an adaptation of a story by Salvatore Laurani, details the exploits of El Chuncho (Gian Maria Volonté), a bandit who steals guns for the revolutionary forces of General Elias (Jaime Fernandez). Chuncho's nefarious activities are intensified when his gang is infiltrated by an American, Bill Tate (Lou Castel), who has a talent for planning lucrative raids on Federale armories. However, Tate is actually a contract killer in the pay of Mexican officials,

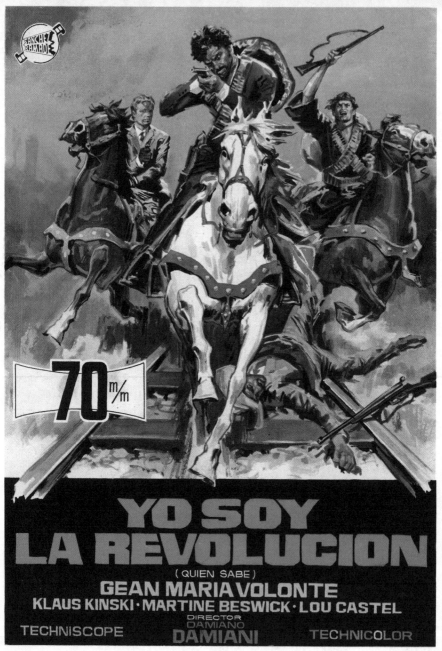

Italian poster for *A Bullet for the General* (1966)

and he eventually succeeds in assassinating Elias before sharing his blood money with Chuncho.

But Chuncho's newfound status as a wealthy sharp-dressed man idly passing time in a woefully impoverished country—and Tate's careless boasting about how he set up his subterfuge and his obvious disdain for Mexicans and Mexico—results in the bandit experiencing a political awakening that compels him to kill his American benefactor. As he makes his escape, Chuncho discards the fine clothes that threaten to constrain his newfound revolutionary spirit and leaves his ill-gotten gains to be picked up by a shoeshine boy, to whom he implores, "Don't buy bread with that money, hombre. Buy dynamite!"

A Bullet for the General is a truly remarkable film, and its convincing art direction, sets, and costumes—and Damiani's use of many ordinary-looking nonprofessional actors as extras—give it the appearance and feel of a serious arthouse production. Indeed, Damiani was adamant that his film was not a western. In Austin Fisher's *Radical Frontiers in the Spaghetti Western* (2011), the director observes that "the Western belongs to Protestant North American culture. If one leaves this culture one is not making a Western anymore. South of the Rio Grande it is not the West, it is Mexico.... To say that a film which is set in Mexico is a Western shows that you have understood nothing."

Damiani's pointed reference to the Protestant North of America here immediately prompts a vision of that industrial region's "Other," the rural Catholic "South" of Mexico. Once the rural Catholic "South" of Mexico has been conceptualized, it becomes easy to draw obvious parallels between that region and the rural Catholic "South" of Italy (which is in turn the "Other" to Italy's industrial "North"). Similarly, the industrial "North" of America and the rural "South" of Mexico can also be thought of as stand-ins for the countries located in the Global North (the developed Western capitalist countries and former colonial powers of the First World) and the Global South (the underdeveloped/developing former colonies of the Third World). The countries of the Global North and the Global South are differentiated by their distinct political and socioeconomic characteristics, and it is these very differences and the tensions they create that inform the broader politics of *A Bullet for the General* and the Zapata spaghetti westerns that followed in the film's wake.

Damiani himself was at pains to stress that his film was indeed a serious political endeavor. In Christopher Frayling's *Zapata Spaghetti: Reflections on the Italian Western and the Mexican Revolution* (2016), the director states,

"*Quien sabe?* is a film about the Mexican Revolution, set in the Mexican Revolution, and is clearly a political film." It's not hard to appreciate where Damiani is coming from. For example, in one particularly pointed scene, Chuncho's gang stay over at the town of San Miguel, whose citizens have just liberated themselves from the domination of Rurales in the pay of the town's noble head dignitary, Don Felipe (Andrea Checchi). A local man, Raimundo (José Manuel Martín), advises Chuncho that they still need to dispose of the aristocratic landowner. When Raimundo leads a band of townsfolk to Don Felipe's grand hacienda, Damiani uses the film's mise-en-scène to highlight inequality and privilege. Solinas's dialogue complements this with talk of land ownership and such like. It all boils down to Don Felipe asking, "You have then decided to murder me. Why? Is there a reason? Is it only because I'm a rich man?" Raimundo replies, "No, *señor*. It's because we are poor men. And you've done all you can to keep us that way."

Interestingly, the feudal system depicted in this scene isn't that far removed from the feudal system that persisted as a social norm in southern Italy during the 1960s, where the wealth and power wielded by landlords still allowed them to lord it over their peasant workforces. In the contemporary ethnographic article "Rural Life in Southern Italy" (1965), Gustav Schachter reveals that the southern Italian peasants still called their betters "don" (a leftover from the region's time spent under Spanish rule) while providing an illuminating quote from one of them: "*Il Barone* thinks that we are his slaves and he treats us accordingly. The only difference between us is that he has lands and money and I do not. He had the luck to inherit his father's lands, and I inherited my father's misery. He is afraid that the communists will take away his land. I am not a communist, but it is good that he is afraid." The grievances that this southern Italian peasant articulated in 1965 are remarkably similar to those that are articulated by the Mexican peon Raimundo in the scene analyzed above.

A Bullet for the General can thus be appreciated as a political art film of sorts. However, it cannot be denied that the film also pointedly incorporates elements that were readily associated with a popular film genre that was already regarded as being Italian cinema's most lucrative genre yet. Several of the film's key actors (Gian Maria Volonté, Klaus Kinski, Aldo Sambrell, Spartaco Conversi, José Manuel Martín, et al.) were instantly recognizable from their appearances in top-grossing spaghetti westerns. The film was shot on location in Spain, utilizing familiar vistas that had already served as convincing stand-ins for Mexico in a number of spaghetti westerns. And the film's music was composed and supervised by two maestros who were already firmly linked to the genre, Luis Bacalov and Ennio Morricone. Mexican characters, horseback chases, gunplay, and spectacular dynamite-induced explosions had also become staple elements of the spaghetti western genre by the time *A Bullet for the General* went into production in 1966.

A Bullet for the General was a success at the Italian box office and abroad. This success naturally meant that the film was used as a basic template for a series of Zapata spaghetti westerns, whose narratives would feature the pattern of (much) repetition and (little) difference that had become associated with popular filmmaking in Italy. Certainly the film features scenarios and set pieces that would be repeated in some form or other in nearly all of the subgenre's subsequent entries: the uneasy and dishonest nature of the relationship that binds a gringo mercenary to a Mexican peon-turned-revolutionary; the transgressive actions of a strong female gang member; the clever ruses that lead to Mexican Federales and Rurales being slaughtered en masse; the Mexican antihero being sentenced to death, only to be rescued by his gringo benefactor; incidental and at times almost documentary-like scenes of political violence and its aftermath; the fetishization of machine guns; celebratory fiestas; political prisoners being released from their cells; liberated towns being brutally retaken by the Federales; encounters with the symbols of mechanized modernity, such as automobiles; train robberies; and so on.

Solinas returned to the subgenre when he worked on the next Zapata spaghetti western of note, Sergio Corbucci's *Il mercenario* (*The Mercenary*, aka *A Professional Gun*, 1968). Producing Sergio Leone's *For a Few Dollars More* and *The Good, the Bad and the Ugly* had enabled Alberto Grimaldi to forge a lucrative working relationship with the American film distribution company United Artists. This enabled him to produce some of the biggest and best spaghetti westerns of the late 1960s, including *The Mercenary*. One of Leone's regular scriptwriters, Luciano Vincenzoni, led the film's writing team, who based their work on a story that Solinas had cowritten with Giorgio Arlorio. The film's director, Sergio Corbucci, possessed Marxist leanings, and he brings Solinas and Arlorio's work to the screen with a sense of enthusiasm and fun.

At the film's start, a socially aware peon, Paco Ramon (Tony Musante), and his fellow workers are grafting hard in the Garcia brothers' silver mine for a pittance. It's dangerous work that has cost Paco's father and brother their lives. When they break for dinner (an unedifying bowl of beans), a disappointed peon addresses an armed supervisor with the words, "On Sunday aren't they supposed to give us something extra?" Paco finds a small lizard

Compañeros (1970)

The cast of *A Bullet for the General* (1966); left to right: Lou Castel, Klaus Kinski, Martine Beswick, and Gian Maria Volonté

in his bowl and observes, "Look, amigos, they have given us the meat." The supervisor laughs and says, "It's true, no difference between rich and poor here.... After you eat that, you'll be able to stomach anything."

The supervisor's callous response works as a damning observation that sums up the plight of the poor everywhere. Paco is seen glancing at the supervisor's holstered pistol before the scene cuts to the culinary abundance of the Garcia brothers' dining room. Here Colonel Alfonso Garcia (Eduardo Fajardo) nonchalantly tells his brothers that Francisco Madero amounts to "nothing." When their main course of roast hog and chicken arrives, it is revealed that Paco has the supervisor's pistol, and he has used it to lead an impromptu revolt: the colonel is forced to eat the lizard at gunpoint, while the hungry workers devour roast chickens. The brothers soon have the revolt quashed and Paco buried up to his head, awaiting execution via the hooves of a squad of Rurales' galloping horses. Thankfully, he escapes.

A Polish weapons-expert-cum-mercenary, Sergei Kowalski (Franco Nero), is duly employed by the Garcias to transport their silver to the US. When Kowalski buys himself a machine gun for the job, the Mexican arms dealer Pepote (Franco Giacobini) exclaims, "Life is strange. Usually the North Americans sell arms, not buy them." Also introduced at this point is Curly (Jack Palance), an avaricious psychopath who learns about the silver

Franco Nero and Sergio Corbucci on the set of
The Mercenary (1968)

Giovanna Ralli as Columba in Sergio Corbucci's
The Mercenary (1968)

shipment and wants it for himself. A series of narrative contrivances result in
Paco employing Kowalski as his military adviser and Colonel Garcia recruit-
ing Curly to help him track the pair down. Paco is initially happy for his
growing gang of bandits-cum-revolutionaries to rob banks while he spouts
impromptu political platitudes. His take on the revolution at this point is to
simply "kill the bosses and take their money." However, Paco is transformed
into a fully committed revolutionary thanks to the influence of a strong and
idealistic woman, Columba (Giovanna Ralli).

The Mercenary is a rollicking and at times mildly humorous action-adventure film, but its narrative does feature a number of interesting contextual
counterpoints. For example, it's significant that low pay, atrocious working
conditions, social immobility, and related inequalities are the motivating
factors that lead Paco on his journey to becoming a revolutionary, since these
were the same concerns that were fueling the strikes and political protests
in Italy at the time of The Mercenary's release in 1968. Given that women's
groups were part of the patchwork coalition of new social and political movements that emerged in Italy during the late 1960s, it's equally significant
that it is Columba's teachings that serve to make Paco fully politically aware.

When contrasted with the Mexican revolutionaries, Kowalski is a true
Western capitalist. His contract of employment with Paco is financially
lucrative, and he routinely refuses to work until he has been paid. This suits
Paco to an extent, but Kowalski refuses to throw off the sense of privilege
that his white European heritage grants him in Mexico. His contract with

Paco also gives him access to every home comfort, while the Mexican gang members suffer increasing hardships and indignities. When Paco eventually orders Kowalski to appear before a revolutionary court, the charge sheet that Columba compiles and reads out is a catch-all affair whose content would surely have resonated with the poor and dispossessed worldwide in 1968:

The Mercenary (1968)

"For having eaten when we were all suffering from starvation, for having drunk when we were all thirsty, for having always been kept dry when we were rotting under the rain, et cetera, et cetera."

The sentence should be death, but Paco cannot bring himself to pass it immediately. By contrast, later in the film Kowalski has no problem turning Paco over to the Federales for the reward on his head, in order to recoup some of the money that the revolutionary court confiscated from him. Narrative contrivances result in both men being spared, but in Solinas and Arlorio's original story, Kowalski got his reward money and Paco was executed. Kowalski remains a true mercenary, though. He isn't bothered whose side he fights on, so long as he is paid. At the film's end, Kowalski suggests that he and Paco should set their sights further afield, advising the Mexican, "In this world, there is always someone who is making a revolution or a counterrevolution. We can work for the one and then for the other. In a few years, we'll retire with a big pile of money." Now completely radicalized by Columba and committed to the cause, Paco simply replies, "My revolution is in Mexico."

Solinas returned to the subgenre the very next year, cowriting the story and the screenplay for Giulio Petroni's *Tepepa* (1969) with Ivan Della Mea. At first glance, *Tepepa* possesses a fairly straightforward storyline. Tepepa (Tomas Milian) is a Mexican revolutionary who is due to be executed by the Federales. An Anglo interloper, Dr. Henry Price (John Steiner), rescues Tepepa from the firing squad because he wants the satisfaction of killing him himself. Tepepa outsmarts Price, takes him prisoner, and forms a community of revolutionaries, all of which infuriates the Federale colonel Cascorro (Orson Welles), who sets about bringing Tepepa and Price to justice. However, the film becomes much more interesting when Tepepa's backstory is told via extended flashbacks, as he dictates the contents of a damning letter to President Madero (Paco Sanz). At the height of the revolution in 1909, Madero

EXCELSIOR FILMS

TOMAS MILIAN · ORSON WELLES

TEPEPA

TECHNICOLOR · TECHNISCOPE

JOHN STEINER

UK quad poster for *Tepepa* (1969)

was hiding out at the young Tepepa's family home, waiting for Tepepa's father to return with a message from Pancho Villa. He duly arrives, but he has been mortally wounded. Madero urges Tepepa to deliver his response to Villa immediately, because "the revolution doesn't wait," and he does so, even though it means that he must leave his dying father.

By January 1911, Tepepa has become a fighter in the ranks of the victorious revolutionary army, and he meets Madero, who is now the president and who does not remember him, outside Mexico City. Madero is flanked by Federales who are overseeing the handing in of arms held by the revolutionary forces, which results in an irate Tepepa breaking ranks to tell him, "I took this rifle from the army to fight against the army. And now I have to give it back to the army. Who won? The revolution or the army? ... We have made a mistake, Señor President, because everything is like before." Madero tries to assure him that the army "is at the service of the state" and that new laws—enforced by that very army—will bring social change to Mexico.

But later that year, Tepepa sees firsthand that change has not come, and he starts a local insurrection, which leads to him being imprisoned and sentenced to death (taking the viewer to the point at which they entered the film). As Frayling (2016) notes, Tepepa's fractious relationship with Madero can only point toward "the need for continuing armed insurrection beyond parliament." Another strand of *Tepepa*'s narrative involves the political awakening and radicalization of Paquito (Luciano Casamonica), a small boy who Tepepa effectively adopts. Thus, it is clear that *Tepepa*'s central concern is the continuity of political ideas and devotion to the cause through three generations of the same family. Since Tepepa dies at the film's end (just like his father), the film also articulates ideas about sacrifice for the cause and political martyrdom.

The sense that a victorious armed struggle against the state had been pointless because nothing had changed, the feeling of being betrayed by political elites, the need for continuity in political activism through the generations, and a willingness to die for the cause were all ideas that were relevant to Italy in 1969 too. In *Politics of Violence* (2013), Charlotte Heath-Kelly details how some have argued that a sense of continuity links Italy's internal struggles during World War II to the terrorist violence that divided the nation during the Years of Lead. Indeed, there are accounts from members of the Red Brigades (the militant left-wing activists who brought terrorism to Italy's streets during the 1970s) that suggest they were simply continuing the struggle that the partisans began in World War II. Some of the members of the leftist extraparliamentary groups of the 1960s and 1970s were actually the sons of former partisans. Many of these partisans had been members of the Italian Communist Party, which had been a key player in the resistance movement that fought to liberate Italy from the fascists and their Nazi sponsors at the end of World War II.

After the war, the party was the second-largest political organization in Italy, but it needed to present itself as a party that could function within a democratic system, and that meant rethinking some of its central ideologies. Thus, as Richard Drake explains in *Italy in the 1960s: A Legacy of Terrorism and Liberation* (2000), Marxist-Leninism in its truest revolutionary form could only cling "to life in diverse sectors of the extra-parliamentary left movement" from which "the [insurgent] Red Brigades emerged." For the members of the extraparliamentary left, disappointment in the Communist Party's nonrevolutionary stance was compounded by the idea that the tenets of fascism still endured in Italy in spite of the partisans' victory at the end of World War II. Under these circumstances, Tepepa's question "Who won?" and his follow-up observation, "We have made a mistake ... because everything is like before," would surely have resonated with some left-leaning members of Italian society.

Interestingly, Tomas Milian (himself a Cuban) had much to say about the characters that he played in his political Italian westerns. Frayling (2016) quotes him as saying, "With my Westerns, I am trying to help my people, the Latin American people.... Latin Americans are always dirty little spics, and I'm still a spic but I've made the spic a hero." In Frayling's *Spaghetti Westerns: Cowboys and Europeans from Karl May to Sergio Leone* (1981), Milian suggests that his work in Italian westerns resulted in him becoming a recognizable "symbol of poverty and revolution" to Third World cinemagoers. Similarly, in Fisher, Milian suggests that "the Third World figure" he played in a variety of spaghetti westerns "could in some sense have also been an Italian sub proletarian." All of which suggests that the Zapata spaghetti westerns did indeed possess the will and the power to resonate with a wide variety of oppressed peoples worldwide.

Tepepa would be Solinas's final contribution to the subgenre that he had helped to create, but the cycle did endure, and it is worth giving a brief account of the key Zapata spaghetti westerns that followed. Sergio Corbucci returned to the subgenre with *Vamos a matar, compañeros* (*Compañeros*, 1970), a film that takes the idea of (much) repetition and (little) difference to a new level as it is essentially a loose rewrite (based on an idea by Corbucci) of *The Mercenary*. The key players in this tale are Yod Peterson (Franco Nero), a mercenary Swedish arms dealer working in Mexico; El Vasco (Tomas Milian), an earnest revolutionary foot soldier; General Mongo (José Bódalo), a corrupt revolutionary leader; Professor Xantos (Fernando Rey), a rival but pacifist revolutionary leader who has been imprisoned by American capitalists; John (Jack Palance), another gringo arms dealer who has been employed to kill Xantos and who has his own reasons for wanting Yod dead; and Xantos's army of loyal and idealistic students.

Another action-adventure film that is humorous at times, *Compañeros* does actually introduce a couple of contextual elements that add difference to its instances of repetition. The presence of the student army is the first. The students, who are led by the strong female Lola (Iris Berben), have come to the conclusion that "words are of no use to us anymore. The time has come to respond to violence with violence." The students' attitudes and actions would appear to be a clear allusion to the numerous, increasingly violent student protests that took place in Italy during 1968 and 1969. Indeed, Drake highlights the most prominent of these, "the legendary Battle of Valle Giulia in Rome on 1 March 1968," which resulted in "160 policemen and several hundred students" suffering injuries. He also indicates that the Red Brigades "evolved from a small group of communist students." *Compañeros*'s second contextual element of interest is the insurgent Vasco, the beret-wearing son of immigrants from the Basque Country. His Basque beret gives Vasco the look of Che Guevara, but his heritage also serves to forge a link between the historical revolutionary action depicted in the film and the contemporaneous acts of armed struggle that were being enacted by the Basque separatist group Euskadi Ta Askatasuna (Basque Homeland and Freedom, or ETA).

UK quad poster for *A Fistful of Dynamite*, aka *Duck, You Sucker!* (1971)

A similar approach can be found in two entries from 1971, Sergio Leone's *Giù la testa* (*A Fistful of Dynamite*, aka *Duck, You Sucker!*) and Duccio Tessari's *Viva la muerte ... tua!* (*Long Live ... Your Death!*, aka *Don't Turn the Other Cheek*). In *A Fistful of Dynamite*, Juan Miranda (Rod Steiger) is a Mexican bandit who is duped into becoming a hero of the revolution by a former IRA operative and explosives expert, Sean Mallory (James Coburn), who finds it hard to give up his insurgent ways while hiding out in Mexico. In *Long Live ... Your Death!*, a radical Irish newspaper reporter, Mary O'Donnell (Lynn Redgrave), makes it her business to stir up revolutionary activity wherever she goes. Her actions complicate the plans of a Mexican bandit, Lazoya (Eli Wallach), and a gringo interloper, Prince Orlowsky (Franco Nero), who are uneasy partners involved in a hunt for treasure.

Both films seek to forge a link between the historical revolutionary action depicted within their narratives and the contemporaneous acts of armed struggle that were being enacted by the IRA in Northern Ireland. Interestingly, in March 1971 details of the aborted *Golpe Borghese* (Borghese coup) were made public, and it became apparent that neofascists had been planning an armed takeover of Italy in December 1970. With thoughts of this floating in the ether, it is perhaps unsurprising that both films present their uniformed Federales as analogues of fascists and Nazis—complete with

Italian poster for *Long Live . . . Your Death!*, aka *Don't Turn the Other Cheek* (1971)

high-tech, lethal armored cars—and their revolutionaries as partisans. In both films, the Federales carry out atrocities against innocent victims who are closely connected to the films' protagonists. In *A Fistful of Dynamite*, a mass execution of civilians and political prisoners results in Juan's entire extended family being wiped out. In *Sergio Leone: Something to Do with Death* (2000), Christopher Frayling indicates that this scene is a direct reference to the Fosse Ardeatine massacre in which 335 civilians and prisoners were executed by the Nazis outside Rome on March 24, 1944. In *Long Live ... Your Death!*, Lazoya's innocent sister and nephew are executed by the Federales.

Sergio Corbucci returned to the subgenre to write (along with Massimo Franciosa and Sabatino Ciuffini) and direct *Che c'entriamo noi con la rivoluzione?* (*What Am I Doing in the Middle of a Revolution?*, 1972). The film was the last Zapata spaghetti western of significance, and Corbucci took the trends initiated by *A Fistful of Dynamite* and *Long Live ... Your Death!* to their logical conclusions. The Federales are again coded as analogues of fascist and Nazi military forces. The film's credits play over a series of mass executions that are intercut with shots of an Italian priest being readied for the firing squad. Later, a group of unarmed revolutionaries are massacred when Colonel Herrero (Eduardo Fajardo) reneges on his agreement to let them surrender peacefully. In this film, the insurgent European operating in Mexico is actually an Italian, which serves to finally forge a direct link between the historical revolutionary action depicted in the film and the contemporaneous acts of armed struggle that were being enacted by the Red Brigades in Italy.

The Zapata spaghetti western's traditional lead characters are present here, but they are not the main focus of the film. Carrasco (Leo Anchóriz) is the film's revolutionary Mexican bandit, while Peppino Garibaldi (Riccardo Garrone) is the insurgency-loving gringo. Peppino is the grandson of Giuseppe Garibaldi, Italy's greatest national hero, guerrilla fighter, insurrectionist, and foreign interventionist, and he proclaims that he is continuing his grandfather's tradition of fighting "on the side of all oppressed and tyrannized people."

While these two characters remain important to the film's narrative, much of its story focuses on the misadventures of two additional Italian characters, who do not understand or indeed care for the revolution but who must nevertheless find a way to navigate its dangerous landscapes. Guido Guidi (Vittorio Gassman) is a theater actor, while Don Albino Moncalieri (Paolo Villaggio) is a priest. The pair find themselves tossed from pillar to post in their efforts to survive multiple encounters with both Carrasco and Colonel Herrero. Guido and Albino could be Italian Everyman figures who represent the contemporaneous Italian public, caught in the crossfire between the Red Brigades and the Italian police.

There are two particular points of interest in *What Am I Doing in the Middle of a Revolution?* First, as I note in *The Euro-Western: Reframing Gender, Race and the "Other" in Film*, various political thinkers—and, indeed, numerous strands of post–World War II Italian cinema—have sought to establish symbolic and allegorical links between oppressed African Americans and the marginalized dark-skinned southern Italians, often imagining them as kindred spirits in a joint struggle for a better life that is free from prejudice and marked by equality. Corbucci explicitly manifests this link in a scene in which Guido, who is in blackface because he is on his way to a rehearsal for a production of *Othello*, is chased through a Texan town by racist rednecks who wish to kill him because of the perceived color of his skin. He manages to wash the black greasepaint from his face, but his Mediterranean skin tones result in the racists still perceiving him to be an African American.

Second, the apolitical Guido has a kind of political awakening at the film's end, and he incites an insurrection, albeit one that results in him being mortally wounded. The film's final shot of Guido dying in Albino's arms is strangely moving, and it was a suitably ambiguous note for the Zapata spaghetti western subgenre to end on. It might be that the Italian public had lost interest in films about revolutionary politics, or maybe Italian film producers felt a need to return to more escapist fare. Either way, the very next year would see the spaghetti western's creative personnel attempting to reinvigorate the genre with a new subgenre: the "East meets West" films that brought western and kung fu action together.

Lee Broughton

OUTTAKE: THE FILMS OF ELIO PETRI AND GIAN MARIA VOLONTÉ

The creative partnership between Italian director Elio Petri and actor Gian Maria Volonté—both leftist activists as well as filmmakers—remains one of the most vital in political cinema. Petri made a dozen films throughout his career, across a wide range of genres, though all bear evidence of his radical politics: themes of class tension, violence, and the horrors of capitalism and bureaucracy are ever present. With Volonté, he made four particularly important films that combine the crime thriller and political drama genres: *A ciascuno il suo* (*We Still Kill the Old Way*, 1967), *Indagine su un cittadino al di sopra di ogni sospetto* (*Investigation of a Citizen Above Suspicion*, 1970), *La classe operaia va in paradiso* (*The Working Class Goes to Heaven*, aka *Lulu the Tool*, 1971), and *Todo modo* (1976). Many of these focus on characters undergoing psychological deterioration and existential despair and share the sense that a shadowy conspiracy is always hovering in the background, manipulating people and events.

Petri was politically active from a young age; he was a member of the youth branch of the Italian Communist Party but distanced himself in the '50s. Like so many others, he was horrified to learn the truth of Stalin's legacy and was enraged by the Soviet oppression of the Hungarian Uprising. Like Volonté, he proved throughout his work as an activist and political filmmaker that his values remained unchanged, and his films—regardless of whether they fall under the umbrella of sci-fi, horror, Mafia film, or black comedy—are all concerned with political themes. He made a name for himself with unique, stylish works like *La decima vittima* (*The 10th Victim*, 1965), a postapocalyptic sci-fi satire about a government-sponsored "hunt," in which international contestants battle to the death on reality television. Even his *giallo* (horror) film, *Un tranquillo posto di campagna* (*A Quiet Place in the Country*, 1968), about an unstable artist who rents a seemingly haunted villa in the countryside, includes themes of political violence and class tension. Throughout his films, Petri speculates on more popular leftist topics like the value of protesting, the best ways to revolt against repressive powers, and the true impact of political violence, but he also fixates on the destructive effects capitalism has on everything from work and family to sexual expression and gender roles. Violence is often a focal point.

Petri and Volonté first teamed up in 1967 for *We Still Kill the Old Way*, a crime thriller about a professor (Volonté) who investigates a series of seemingly unconnected deaths in his small town and unveils a conspiracy. Like the giallo film, *We Still Kill the Old Way* follows an unlikely investigator. His real motivation to solve the string of murders is revealed to stem from his unrequited love for a widow (Irene Papas) of one of the victims. Petri also combines elements of the Italian crime film, or *poliziotteschi*, as the professor comes up against

Gian Maria Volonté and Irene Papas in *We Still Kill the Old Way* (1967)

the local Mafia, the Catholic Church, and politicians who are revealed to benefit from these killings. The deeper the professor gets into his investigation, the clearer it becomes that he has buried himself; the film's ultimate implication is that murder and assassinations are a fundamental part of the political process in Italy.

Much of the film hinges on Volonté's compelling performance, and in some ways, his debut with Petri marks a shift in his career. Earlier in the '60s, he established himself with a series of memorable roles in genre films, primarily spaghetti westerns with directors like Sergio Leone and Damiano Damiani, as well as crime movies with directors like Carlo Lizzani. He would go on to a new level of acclaim with *We Still Kill the Old Way*, but he became a sensation throughout European cinema because of his follow-up collaboration with Petri in 1970, *Investigation of a Citizen Above Suspicion*. Widely regarded as Petri's masterpiece, it stars Volonté as a perverse police inspector known as "Il Dottore" ("the doctor"). He and his mistress (Florinda Balkan) play a series of sadistic sex games in which he pretends to murder her. As he becomes more powerful in the police department, he decides to take their game to a new level: he actually murders her, convinced that he has enough clout to get away with the crime.

Sort of an inverse of the popular poliziotteschi film—where a ruthless detective pursues violent, amoral killers but is stymied by internal corruption within the government—Il Dottore becomes a blackly comic

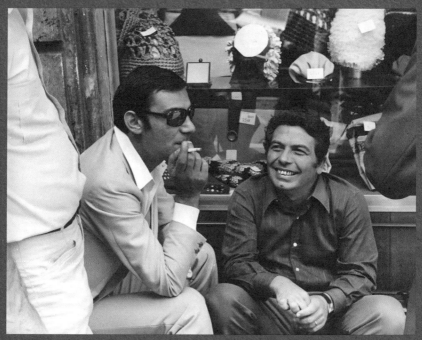

Gian Maria Volonté and Elio Petri on the set of *Investigation of a Citizen Above Suspicion* (1970)

antihero, using the corruption to become both cop and criminal. He gleefully tampers with evidence, identifies false suspects (including a leftist student), and basks in his own invincibility. But the single murder he commits, conceals, and later confesses to is revealed to be a minor affair compared to the violence breaking out around him as the city erupts in chaos. It is a scathing indictment of the political situation in Italy in the '60s but remains a satire of police brutality that is still unnervingly relevant. It would propel Volonté into more serious arthouse fare with directors like Jean-Pierre Melville, Jean-Luc Godard, and Francesco Rosi.

Japanese poster for *Investigation of a Citizen Above Suspicion* (1971)

French poster for *The Working Class Goes to Heaven*, aka *Lulu the Tool* (1971)

Gian Maria Volonté being arrested as part of a demonstration organized by workers of Coca-Cola, 1970

Volonté and Petri's third film together, *The Working Class Goes to Heaven*, cemented their creative legacy with its depiction of a worker's frustrated political awakening and ensuing struggles against the factory union, which remains harrowingly relevant. A factory worker, nicknamed Lulù (Volonté), takes pride in his ability to work rapidly, but his focus on speed results in the loss of one of his fingers. This traumatic incident forces him to see his body, his labor, and the factory around him in a new light. He realizes he is just the "tool" mentioned in the film's alternate English-language title, *Lulu the Tool*—just a cog in the machine and not a valued, respected individual—leading to a radical awakening where he joins the young leftist students protesting outside the factory.

In many ways, *The Working Class Goes to Heaven* is the ultimate expression of Petri and Volonté's highly political cinema. It is not a straightforward protest film or simple work of leftist propaganda with a heroic protagonist who revolts against his oppressors. Though it does focus on labor relations, corrupt power dynamics, and workers striking at a factory, it is deeply satirical. Through Lulù, Petri pokes and prods seemingly every aspect of Italy under capitalism but goes beyond depicting rote class tensions: everyone in Lulù's life, including the working-class people around him, are shown to be part of the system of oppression.

As a sort of working-class Everyman, Lulù is initially self-absorbed and apolitical, an unlikely figure to experience a radical political awakening. Once he begins to consider how the system exploits everyone, the people in his life, from his girlfriend (the great Mariangela Melato) to his former coworkers, refuse to entertain the idea that a more egalitarian version of society is possible. Petri suggests that this kind of capitalist-consumerist logic permeates everything from work, finance, and government to individual identity, family, sexuality, and so on. In a 1974 interview, Petri explained that he chose to focus on a blue-collar worker because the condition of the working class is representative of the capitalist system as a whole. He said, "Work on the assembly line is also exemplary of bourgeois existence: the workers are the first victims, but I think that anyone who works in the capitalist system, based on the need to produce as much as possible, suffers from the same tensions, from the same alienations; even the intellectual and the petty bourgeois, happy with their little privileges, are not aware of where they stand in this system." Notably, Petri included real factory workers from Novara—where the film was shot—as actors, giving the film a cinema verité quality. Many of them were involved in actual protests in Novara, and *The Working Class Goes to Heaven* intentionally evokes the protests that rocked the world in 1968 and the *Autunno caldo* (Hot Autumn) of 1969, when northern Italian workers held frequent, mass strikes to demand better treatment.

Their follow-up film, *Todo modo*, concerns a shady political conspiracy during a retreat held for the leaders of the Christian Democratic party, where Volonté stars as the austere leader of the party—a stand-in for real politician Aldo Moro—and comes up against a corrupt priest (Marcello Mastroianni), culminating in violence. *Todo modo* is their most arcane film together and is a historically specific product of its time and place. But in general, Petri and Volonté's films stand as some of the strongest examples of a collaborative cultural project among leftists, and it is remarkable how most of their films remain frighteningly relevant fifty years later.

Samm Deighan

"ARE YOU ASKING US TO INVESTIGATE OR OVERTHROW THE GOVERNMENT?"

Political Conspiracy and Violence in Italian *Poliziotteschi* Cinema

Stefano Vanzina's 1972 Italian/German coproduction *La polizia ringrazia* (*Execution Squad*) opens with two men being interviewed by the media. The first, former police superintendent Ernesto Stolfi (Irish actor Cyril Cusack) responds to a journalist's questions about the crime wave gripping Italy: "In my opinion, something radical has to be done if we are to restore the faith of the individual in government." The second, Bertone (Enrico Maria Salerno), head of Rome's homicide squad, comments to journalists about a man called Bettarini, who was accused of a vicious heist in which a night watchman was killed and who has just been acquitted for lack of proof, describing the decision as "criminal." Bertone is soon fronting the media again after an unsuccessful jewelry store heist leaves two members of the public dead and the criminals escape. Listening to accusations that police are not doing their jobs, he claims it is they who are under constant attack. Disillusioned, ground down by the demands of his job, Bartone is also under pressure from the district attorney, Ricciuti (Mario Adorf), who is keen to ensure that the police continue to do things by the book despite the chaos.

One of the young men involved in the jewelry store heist is soon apprehended by men in plain clothes. It is unclear who they are. They take him to a secluded spot, execute him firing-squad style, and leave the body for Bartone and Ricciuti to find. The same men are subsequently shown executing a string of people: Bettarini, a street walker, a businessman caught trying to pick up a young man, and another waiting at a train station, who we learn is a trade unionist charged but acquitted of killing a cop in a street demonstration.

Execution Squad (1972)

Amid growing police sympathy for the vigilantes, Bartone suspects the killings are the work of rogue cops he dubs "the clean-up squad," coordinated by someone "interested in showing that our system of democracy is unable to curb the underworld and [who has] got the idea to promote a clean-up job of their own." Bartone asks a friendly journalist, Sandra (Mariangela Melato), to help him uncover who is orchestrating the vigilantes in return for an exclusive. She connects the killers to a conservative journal pushing for the restoration of capital punishment, part of a wider but undefined

US poster for *Execution Squad* (1972)

far-right conspiracy. Bartone eventually confronts Stolfi, an old friend he has come to believe is involved in the killings. Stolfi tells him the killers are ex-police, backed by politicians, businessmen, and members of the clergy, with the aim of overthrowing the state and establishing a dictatorship. Bartone is shot dead by a sniper before he can arrest Stolfi. His body is dumped for the police to find, and the evidence compiled by Sandra disappears.

Execution Squad was one of over a hundred hard-boiled Italian police procedural thrillers, referred to in that country as *poliziotteschi*—a term derived from the Italian word for "police," *polizia*, and *esco*, or "esque" in English—produced from the late 1960s to the end of the 1970s. This life cycle coincides with the peak of a lengthy continuum of political conflict in Italy, stretching from the end of World War II to well into the 1980s, referred to as the *Anni di piombo* (Years of Lead). Its most intense phase in the 1970s was bookended by two major events. The first was the bombing of the headquarters of the National Agricultural Bank in the Piazza Fontana in Milan, in December 1969, which killed seventeen people and wounded eighty-eight. Initially linked to the far left, the act was soon connected to the neofascist paramilitary group Ordine Nuovo, or New Order, working with elements of Italy's secret service. The second event was the kidnapping and subsequent assassination of former Italian prime minister Aldo Moro by the far-left Brigate Rosse (Red Brigades) in 1978. Other forces contributed to the generalized sense of chaos in Italy during this time: rising crime, an economic downturn due to the 1973 oil crisis, and rapid social changes, which divided the country between the modern, sexually liberated urban centers and a more conservative agrarian society still prevalent in rural areas.

The poliziotteschi cycle was in part influenced by the international success of Hollywood movies such as *Dirty Harry* and *The French Connection*, both of which appeared in 1971, *The Godfather* (1972), and *Death Wish* (1974), as well as the work of European directors such as Jean-Pierre Melville. It also formed part of a mode of domestic film production referred to as the *filoni* (*filo* meaning "thread" in Italian), in which a successful film resulted in the proliferation of similar movies, until they ceased to become profitable, at which point the industry moved on to other subjects. While narratively they can be characterized as a grouping of hard-boiled, often ultra-violent films featuring tough, rule-breaking male police and criminal characters, according to Austin Fisher's *Blood in the Streets: Histories of Violence in Italian Crime Cinema* (2020), the poliziotteschi was in fact made up of several interrelated subgenres: the Mafia film, the vigilante film, and the police procedural. Some exhibited aspects of the Italian horror cycle, the *giallo*. Some combined more than one subgenre.

Poliziotteschi reflect the Years of Lead in many ways. Collectively, they can be viewed as embedding radical cultural artifacts in their historical, political, and economic moment: the street demonstrations and radical political iconography, graffitied slogans and Che posters on the walls of squats and student apartments, and many other signifiers of post-1968 ferment. But the Years of Lead are most pronounced in a subgenre of films that fused police procedural and hard-boiled crime tropes with attempts to uncover high-level political conspiracies and attempted coup plots, always far-right or neofascist in origin. In addition to *Execution Squad*, Fisher lists these films as: Roberto Infascelli's *La polizia sta a guardare* (*The Great Kidnapping*, 1973); Sergio Martino's *Milano trema: la polizia vuole giustizia* (*The Violent Professionals*, 1973) and *La polizia accusa: il servizio segreto uccide* (*Silent Action*, 1975); Luciano Ercoli's *La polizia ha le mani legate* (*Killer Cop*, 1975); and Michele Massimo Tarantini's *Ploiziotti violenti* (*Crimebusters*, 1976). To these, I would add Martino's poliziotteschi/giallo hybrid, *Morte sospetta di una minorenne* (*The Suspicious Death of a Minor*, 1975), Francesco Rosi's *Cadaveri eccellenti* (*Illustrious Corpses*, 1976), and Damiano Damiani's *Lo ho paura* (*I Am Afraid*, 1977). The latter two titles are usually differentiated from the poliziotteschi because of their higher-status directors and better production values. But while they may lack the poliziotteschi's frenzied violence and often gratuitous nudity and sex, they arguably have more in common with their so-called lower-brow cinematic cousins than not. As academic Brian Brems argues in a 2019 piece on the Vague Visages site, the poliziotteschi adopted many aspects of neorealist filmmaking, including "using real locations and cinematic signifiers meant to resemble the documentary approach." They also represent "a cynical extension of neorealism's sympathies with the victims of an unjust society."

Crucially, all these films exhibit the same basic genre formula. Each features a lone individual, always male and working as a cop or an investigator. These individuals are alerted to the existence of a far-right political conspiracy or attempted coup, which they then seek to root out, unmask, and neutralize. The protagonists are tough and cynical but essentially decent, distrustful of authority even though they represent it, and prepared to bend or break rules to further their investigation, sometimes in ways that seem almost as brutal as those of the criminals they oppose. Crucially, in all the films above, while the conspiracy has some public manifestation, for the most part it remains shrouded in secrecy. The protagonist encounters its foot soldiers—the flunkies, assassins, and hitmen—but those who give the orders remain veiled, their aims articulated only through code words and phrases. The protagonist's efforts to give corporeal form to the conspiracy are matched by its efforts to silence him and eliminate anyone who can point to its existence. The protagonist must also contend with more senior policemen or judicial officials who believe in the integrity of the Italian state's political and legal system and insist on enforcing its rules.

The only assistance the protagonist usually receives is from a journalist, which mirrors events in Italian history. Neofascists in the military staged a failed coup in 1964, details of which only became public when the story was broken by journalists in 1967. Investigative reporters were also instrumental in exposing far-right involvement in the Piazza Fontana bombing. And, like the gradual dissipation of the Years of Lead, what victories the protagonists may have achieved at the end of each film are pyrrhic or inconclusive and usually come at the cost of career destruction or, as in the case of *Execution Squad*, death.

In his 2003 book *The Dark Heart of Italy: Travels Through Time and Space in Italy*, Tobias Jones calls the Years of Lead a "low intensity civil war." Approximately fifteen thousand political acts of violence occurred, in which 491 people were killed and thousands wounded. For all the very real political violence, the period exhibits a strange incorporeal sense, at least in terms of identifying those responsible. In relation to Piazza Fontana, Jones writes,

"The extraordinary thing was that nowhere was there anything resembling a consensus about the most simple facts. Everyone agrees that the Piazza Fontana bomb changed forever the direction of Italian history, but thereafter the country's left and right diverge irreconcilably." The subsequent investigation went on for years after and was ultimately inconclusive. The lack of culpability for this and other acts of violence was partly due to tactics of far-right sympathizers in politics, the media, the police and judiciary, and the intelligence services to deliberately muddy the waters to prevent clearer outcomes.

The politically opaque nature of the Years of Lead is also part of a much longer contested history dating back to the conflict between communist partisans and the remnants of Italy's fascist regime in the closing stages of the war. According to English historian John Foot, this was immediately followed by a period in which an estimated twelve to fifteen thousand people were killed across Italy as old scores were settled and former fascists were hunted down and killed. Occupying Allied forces made efforts to purge Italy's institutions of fascist elements, until the far right was replaced by communism as the key international enemy and many former fascists were rehabilitated and reinserted in positions of influence. Washington was particularly concerned by the popularity of the Italian Communist Party (PCI), which emerged from the war as the largest Western European leftist party due to the significant role it played in the resistance against the Nazis. With the support of the Catholic Church and the United States, Italy's second postwar election in 1948 saw the center-right Christian Democrats defeat the PCI. They retained unbroken power for thirty years, during which time the unspoken rule of Italian politics was that the left, particularly the PCI, was not to be admitted into national government. An accommodation was made in 1963, when the Christian Democrats under Aldo Moro brokered a coalition with the Italian Socialist Party (PSI). Lasting until 1966, this aroused concern among the far right that it might lead to wider openings through which the communists might enter government, and was the catalyst for what has been referred to as the "strategy of tension": a coordinated far-right attempt to spread chaos and instability in the hopes it would lead to public weariness and acquiescence to a neofascist takeover.

Despite its influence, the far right seldom appeared on the screen during the Years of Lead as anything other than one-dimensional villains. Examples include: Mario Monicelli's *Vogliamo i colonnelli* (*We Want the Colonels*, 1973), a black comedy that focuses on the efforts of a far-right politician to put together a coalition of disgruntled military veterans, conservative clerics,

Polish one-sheet for *Slap the Monster on Page One* (1972)

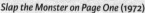

Slap the Monster on Page One (1972) Italian poster for *The Violent Professionals* (1973)

business leaders, and various political opportunists to overthrow the state, and Renato Savino's 1976 film *I ragazzi della Roma violenta* (*The Children of Violent Rome*), which depicts a neo-Nazi youth gang as bored, violent, spoiled offspring of the postwar boom and draws a strong link between their fascist tendencies and sexual depravity. A more sophisticated depiction is the 1971 film *Sbatti il mostro in prima pagina* (*Slap the Monster on Page One*), helmed by a director with close ties to the PCI, Marco Bellocchio. It begins with a left-wing demonstration that turns into a series of running street battles with police and fascist counterdemonstrators. Much of this was taken from archival footage of the Milan funeral of publisher-turned-militant-communist-activist Giangiacomo Feltrinelli. Fearing a looming far-right takeover of the country, Feltrinelli set up the Gruppi di Azione Partigiana (Partisan Action Groups), Italy's second-largest militant left organization, and went underground. He was killed in March 1972, most likely when an explosive device he was planting near an electrical pylon on the outskirts of Milan went off. Leftist demonstrators shout, "Let's burn the master classes' press," as they attack the offices of a right-wing Milan newspaper, *Il Giornale*. No sooner have police dispersed the attackers than the editor, Bizanti (Gian Maria Volonté), is on the phone to the paper's owner to strategize about how they can use the attack to their advantage.

The film centers on Bizanti's efforts to pin the murder of a young woman on the left, to deflect from media reports that *Il Giornale*'s owner is funding neofascist squads and to undermine communist candidates in upcoming elections. Bizanti identifies a suitable left-wing student as the killer and puts his photo on *Il Giornale*'s front page. He also manipulates an elderly, disillusioned former radical to help smear the student. But the plan comes unstuck when it emerges that the woman's killer is a right-wing religious zealot. Bizanti is portrayed as the acceptable face of fascism. A bully and misogynist, he is also suave and charismatic. Most importantly, Bizanti knows how to use his newspaper to maximum impact. He also has a developed sense of political praxis, telling one of the journalists who voices disquiet about his methods, "We need to be protagonists, not observers. We are at war! We do class struggle too. Marx and Lenin didn't invent it!"

For many on the left, Piazza Fontana was proof the country was on the brink of far-right rule, a view not totally without foundation. By the late 1960s, Italy's Mediterranean neighbors, Greece, Portugal, and Spain, were all under military dictatorships, and in September 1973 the Chilean military, covertly backed by the United States, overthrew the elected socialist government of Salvador Allende. In response, the PCI adopted the so-called Historical Compromise, an accommodation with the Christian Democrats. Others, drawn from student movements and the PCI's own youth wing, turned to more extreme forms of Leninism and talked of taking up arms against the increasingly repressive state. Several far-left groups were established, the best known of which was the Red Brigades, founded in 1970.

The Red Brigades planted their first bomb in 1972 and undertook a wave of sabotage, bank robberies, shootings, and kidnappings. This continued into the 1980s, when the group fizzled out due to political differences, an official crackdown, and the end of Soviet support. The Aldo Moro kidnapping was the Red Brigades' most daring and high-profile act. Moro spent fifty-five days in a "people's prison" before he was shot and his body dumped in the boot of a car parked on a street. The kidnapping was part of a "spring campaign" of around forty actions that the Red Brigades believed would trigger revolution, but it only led to a more intensive police crackdown on the extraparliamentary left. Moro was literally on his way to finalizing an agreement with the PCI to support the Christian Democrats in a government of national unity when he was snatched. In his book *The Moro Affair* (1978), Sicilian writer and intellectual Leonardo Sciascia alludes to the desire to derail the political union as being one factor behind the decision of senior Christian Democrat leaders not to negotiate an exchange of jailed Red Brigades members for Moro's release. Sciascia's book was the basis for the 1986 film *Il caso Moro* (*The Moro Affair*), directed by left-wing filmmaker Giuseppe Ferrara and starring Volonté as

The Violent Professionals (1973)

Moro. Filmed in a semi-documentary style, using snippets of news broadcasts and parliamentary debates, it implies Italy's intelligence services also played a part in frustrating the search for the kidnapped politician.

The sense, articulated by Neil Belton in his introduction to Sciascia's book, that these "were years in which paranoid conspiracy theories were the subject of everyday conversation in Italy and often referred to something real," is clearly captured in conspiracy poliziotteschi. According to Fisher, these films take the culture as it was in Italy in the 1970s, the political violence and corruption, the swirling miasma of rumor and innuendo, and the general air of paranoia "as an accepted and assumed starting point and therefore offer little pretense toward complex analysis or investigation into its precise political motivations." Reinforcing this was the fast-moving, repetitive *filone* production model, "a concentrated schedule that necessitated the efficient anticipation of their target audiences' level of prior [political] knowledge."

Some conspiracy poliziotteschi contain only vague allusions to the existence of right-wing plots. *The Great Kidnapping* focuses on a syndicate kidnapping the children of wealthy families, the ransom funds from which are being used to pay off political parties on both sides, part of a wider, undefined conspiracy to make the country ungovernable. In Martino's *The Violent Professionals*, poliziotteschi regular Luc Merenda plays a hardworking maverick Milanese cop, undercover in a criminal organization linked to a far-right conspiracy dedicated to destroying democracy and building a new nation. A rare departure from the smut films that comprised most of director Tarantini's output, *Crimebusters* includes another lightly sketched far-right plot. Henry Silva is a paratrooper commander who teams up with a tough, Magnum-revolver-wielding cop (Antonio Sabato) to investigate criminals trafficking the army's latest-model machine gun in an apparent attempt to sow chaos and thus create public support for an unspecified far-right seizure of power.

Other poliziotteschi evince a much more overt take on the Years of Lead. Martino's *Silent Action* begins with the death of several current and retired former senior military officials. Meanwhile, maverick police inspector Giorgio Solmi (Merenda) and his partner, Lieutenant Luigi Caprara (Michele Gammino), are investigating an unrelated murder, a man bludgeoned to death in his living room. Solmi and his partner track down a female witness, a sex worker, Giuliana (Paola Tedesco), and find her on kitchen floor of her apartment with her wrists cut in an apparent suicide attempt. They also find evidence linking her to the bludgeoning death. Straight-shooting district attorney Mannino (Mel Ferrer) believes it is a robbery gone wrong and wants to prosecute the woman, but Solmi is not convinced. He discovers the dead man was a private investigator who, while working a divorce case, taped a conversation between one of the murdered military men, General Stocchi, and a lawyer named Rienzi, in which the general refused to be involved in some unspecified plot. Solmi confiscates the recording as evidence, but it is mysteriously wiped before Solmi can play it to Mannino.

Silent Action's winding, complex plot leads to a far-right oil baron and an officer in the "Special Information Branch" of the Rome police, Captain Mario Sperli (Tomas Milian). The conspirators start eliminating anyone who can assist the police, while the oil baron flees the country and a car bomb, obviously meant for Solmi, kills another policeman. Refusing to give up the case, Solmi turns to his journalist girlfriend, Maria (Delia Boccado), who uncovers links to international gunrunning and the existence of a neofascist training camp in the mountains. A full-scale gun battle erupts as Solmi leads a helicopter assault on the camp. He captures one of the key leaders, the man Reinzi, who turns out to be Sperli, for once providing a concrete link between the coup plotters and Italy's intelligence community. Sperli is arrested and charged but is then murdered en route to being interrogated. The killer is Solmi's assistant and friend, Caprara, who has been in on the conspiracy the whole time. Solmi is then gunned down in front of Maria. *Silent Action* includes several nods to reality. Solmi's discovery of a rural para-military training camp is a reference to the discovery of a fascist training camp in the aftermath of a bomb-ing in May 1974. His drive-by murder mirrors the assassination of a senior police commissioner at the hands of left militants in 1972.

Proof, perhaps, of just how absorbed the Italian psyche was by shadowy political conspiracies threatening Italy's body politic in the 1970s, the trope of far-right plots even influenced Martino's horror output. Appearing the same year as *Silent Action*, his giallo/ poliziotteschi fusion, *The Suspicious*

Italian poster for Luciano Ercoli's *Killer Cop* (1975)

Death of a Minor, sees another unorthodox cop, Germi (frequent Martino collaborator Claudio Cassinelli), investigate the death of a young prostitute in Milan. He uncovers a prostitution ring linked to a powerful industrialist. The film contains standard giallo touches, including a black-gloved killer in aviator shades hired by the industrialist to eliminate any witnesses who can implicate him, and plenty of action, the highlight of which is an innova-tive shoot-out on a rollercoaster. The conspiracy, which Germi cannot prove, involves a kidnapping operation backed by powerful businessmen to raise money for an unspecified far-right political agenda. Ferrer reprises his *Silent Action* role as a by-the-book police superintendent who is skeptical of talk of a wider conspiracy and will not consider prosecuting the industrialist until he is given firm proof. "Are you asking us to investigate or overthrow the government?" he demands of Germi at one point.

Ercoli's *Killer Cop* is a thinly veiled rendering of the Piazza Fontana bombing. Cassinelli plays Matteo Rolandi, a Milanese cop investigating drug trafficking who happens to be visiting a large hotel hosting a conference of developing-nation representatives, when a bomb goes off, killing twelve people and injuring many more. Investigating judge Armando Di Federico (American actor Arthur Kennedy) immediately comes under pressure from politicians to act fast and identify the culprit. But Federico, who believes absolutely in the rule of law, demands concrete evidence before he will move on any suspects. As he puts it: "This time there will be no suicides at an opportune moment. There will be no disappearing tapes or tapes that have been tampered with, and after two or three years of inquiries, I will not be replaced suddenly by another judge."

It emerges that the hotel bombing was a bungled operation by a low-level operative with poor eyesight called Altieri (Paolo Poiret), who was seen trying to warn hotel staff about the bomb moments before it exploded and who is spotted trying to escape the scene. Rattled, the conspirators start eliminating all potential links between themselves and the bombing. A radical young female student, Papaya Girotti (Sarah Sperati), tips Rolandi off about Altieri's location, a down-at-heel boardinghouse. Rolandi arrives, only to be knocked unconscious by the same assassin who has been killing other suspects, who then throws Altieri out the window and disappears. Rolandi wakes to find he is the chief suspect in Altieri's murder. Girotti subsequently confesses to Rolandi that she works for the intelligence services before she too is killed. Rolandi eventually corners and kills the assassin, but his death shuts down the case, as there are no further leads or evidence. In the final scene, Rolandi stakes out Judge Federico's assistant, Bodi, who it has been implied was in league with the conspirators. The film ends with this script on the screen: "The body of prosecutor Bodi was found eight days later, riddled with bullets, in a ditch near Lugano. The first to arrive on site was commissioner Matteo Rolandi." In many poliziotteschi, Fisher writes, "vigilantism is the only rational response to a bloodthirsty criminal organization too powerful for the law, rendered absurd by the police's inability to enforce it."

Based on another Sciascia book, *Illustrious Corpses* boasts an all-star cast, including Lino Ventura, Marcel Bozzuffi, Fernando Rey, Max von Sydow, Renato Salvatori, and Luigi Pistilli. Rome police inspector Amerigo Rogas (Ventura) is assigned to investigate the murder of a prominent Sicilian judge, viewed as an anti-Mafia hero by some and a pawn of organized crime by others, particularly the island's younger, more radical inhabitants. Two other judges are killed in quick succession in different parts of Italy, all with bullets from the same gun. Initially believing the deaths are a vendetta on the part of a mysterious convicted killer, Rogas starts to suspect political involvement. There are two other key characters: Cusan (Pistilli), a childhood friend of Rogas, now a well-known communist journalist, who believes the killings are bound up in a broader far-right political conspiracy, and a fiercely conservative chief judge, Riches (von Sydow), who may be the next target. Discovering he is under surveillance by the country's intelligence services and that his own life might be in danger, Rogas confides his fears to Cusan,

Above: Lino Ventura (left) in a still from Francesco Rosi's 1976 film *Illustrious Corpses*
Left: Francesco Rosi and cinematographer Pasqualino De Santis on the set of *Illustrious Corpses*

the only person he trusts, and urges immediate action by the Communist Party to head off a far-right coup. But Cusan says he must talk to Amar, the party's head, before anything can be done.

Riches is indeed killed, and both Rogas and Amar are assassinated as they meet in Rome's National Gallery, shot by a sniper like the judges. Tanks and soldiers are shown waiting on Rome's outskirts as communist crowds pour into the streets to mourn Amar's death. Interspersed with these images is a news report that both Rogas and Amar were shot with the same weapon, the pistol which we saw the investigator get for his own protection earlier in the film, and which the chief of police states Rogas used on Amar and then turned on himself. At communist headquarters, Cusan and a senior party functionary discuss how to respond to what is obviously a far-right plot, an exchange that is worth quoting in full:

> CUSAN: They felt so confident they went the whole way. And now they have created the ultimate provocation.
> FUNCTIONARY: Even if that is so, what do you want? A civil war and confrontation?
> CUSAN: But we won't be accomplices.
> FUNCTIONARY: What accomplices? What would we be if we took part in their game? Incite the people in the square? Is that what they want?
> CUSAN: So the people will never know the truth?
> FUNCTIONARY: Truth is not always revolutionary.

Italian poster for *Illustrious Corpses* (1976)

Illustrious Corpses depicts Italy as mired in political conflict and blighted by poverty and substandard development. Cheaply built concrete apartments dot the outskirts of major cities, a graphic depiction of the link between organized crime and real estate speculation. This was a theme Rosi explored in more detail in his 1963 film *Le mani sulla città* (*Hands over the City*), which followed the political aftershocks of the collapse of a poorly constructed residential building in Naples. *Illustrious Corpses* also contains a prescient take on Italy's near-future political trajectory, when the country's

Spanish poster for *I Am Afraid* (1977)

security minister (Rey) tells Rogas that while the Christian Democrats have continuously ruled the country for three decades, he can see the time when they will be forced to rule with the communists. Until then, he concludes, they should keep harassing the left but with the veneer of the rule of law as a shield.

Arguably the most pessimistic of the films examined in this chapter, Damiani's *I Am Afraid* opens with the assassination of an anti-Mafia judge and the cop assigned to protect him. Against this backdrop, a grizzled police detective, Graziano (Volonté), is assigned as a driver and bodyguard for an old judge, Cancedda (Swedish actor Erland Josephson). Graziano is progressive but profoundly disillusioned with politics. He is also recovering from a wound received during a political demonstration that has left him psychologically and physically damaged. It is not specified what side of politics was responsible. Initially insistent he does not need a bodyguard, Cancedda warms to Graziano as he investigates the death of a shopkeeper. The case soon becomes linked to the trafficking of arms and explosives, some of which were used in a recent far-right train bombing in which twelve people were killed. The involvement of members of the intelligence service is soon apparent. The judge, intent on exposing the conspiracy but doing so strictly by the book, swears Graziano to secrecy about the intelligence service link. For his part, Graziano becomes convinced Cancedda's life is in danger, as well as his own. *I Am Afraid* is a complex thriller, and Volonté delivers a powerhouse performance as a man almost driven to the edge of his sanity by the violence, lies, and secrets of the Years of Lead. Damiani injects the film with added verisimilitude by using footage from the aftermath of an actual train bombing, possibly what is referred to as the Italicus Express massacre in August 1974, in which twelve people died and forty-eight were wounded. New Order claimed responsibility. Several of the films examined in this chapter take a similar approach to breathe realism into their stories and give them a ripped-straight-from-the-headlines feel, including *Violent Professionals*, *Illustrious Corpses*, and *Killer Cop*, the latter using footage from funerals following the Piazza Fontana bombing. It is also one of the many ways that these poliziotteschi films can be viewed as an unofficial archive of the political violence of Italy's Years of Lead.

Andrew Nette

ANDRE GÉNOVÈS présente

NADA

un film de
CLAUDE CHABROL

avec **FABIO TESTI** et **MARIANGELA MELATO**

écrit par JEAN-PATRICK MANCHETTE
d'après son roman (EDITIONS GALLIMARD) série noire

MAURICE GARREL • MICHEL DUCHAUSSOY • DIDIER KAMINKA   MICHEL AUMONT • LOU CASTEL

avec la participation de VIVIANE ROMANCE   Une coproduction Franco-Italienne LES FILMS LA BOÉTIE (Paris) VERONA PRODUZIONE (Roma) Distribution LES FILMS LA BOÉTIE
Diffusée par CINEMA INTERNATIONAL CORPORATION

Interdit aux moins de 18 ans

Nada (1974)

OUTTAKE: *NADA* (*THE NADA GANG*, 1974), CLAUDE CHABROL, FRANCE/ITALY

A far-left group, referring to themselves as the Nada Gang, snatch America's ambassador to France during his weekly assignation in an exclusive Parisian brothel, leaving one policeman dead and several people injured. The kidnappers are a politically disparate collection of individuals: Buenaventura Diaz (Fabio Testi), a professional revolutionary and the leader; Épaulard (Maurice Garrel), a former communist partisan during the war and militant in support of Algerian independence, who has just returned to France after nearly a decade away; Meyer (Didier Kaminka), involved more to escape an unhappy marriage to a mentally ill woman than for any ideological considerations; D'Arey (Lou Castel), an alcoholic hothead and the group's wheelman; Treuffais (Michel Duchaussoy), an embittered sociology lecturer and the gang's resident intellectual; and Cash (Mariangela Melato), a cynical libertine rebel.

"My cool and chic exterior hides the wild flames of a burning hatred for a techno-bureaucratic capitalism," Cash says at one point. Whether she is joking or not is unclear, but she has brought her own Sten submachine gun, a family "heirloom," as she puts it, dating back to the days of German occupation. The gang hide with the ambassador in a dilapidated farmhouse while they wait to see whether the authorities will accede to their ransom demand. Meanwhile, a brutal right-wing cop, Goemond (Michel Aumont), heads up the search for the kidnappers. The question is very obviously when, not if, the police will find them and whether the Nada Gang can keep from exploding internally in the meantime.

Claude Chabrol's 1974 film was adapted from the book of the same name, published the previous year by French crime writer Jean-Patrick Manchette. *Nada* was one of ten novels penned by Manchette between 1971 and 1981, all of which blew a large hole in what had traditionally been seen as French crime fiction. "Manchette essentially launched an industry of left-wing thrillers," writes critic Lucy Sante in a 2019 *Crime Reads* article, by fusing hard-boiled crime narratives with radical politics in a deliberate attempt to use the genre to undermine capitalism.

Born in Marseille, Manchette had been a member of the French Communist Party's youth wing and was active in the domestic opposition to France's war in Algeria. He wrote crime fiction criticism for French newspapers and journals, an unknown amount of pulp under other names, dabbled in script work, and translated American hard-boiled crime fiction into French, all before focusing his creative energies and politics on his literary career. This was influenced by a mix of left-wing communism and the writings of the Situationist International, including the work of Guy Debord, author of *La société du spectacle* (*The Society of the Spectacle*, 1967).

Manchette's first solo novel, *L'affaire N'Gustro* (*The N'Gustro Affair*), appeared in 1971. A thinly veiled take on the kidnapping and murder of Moroccan opposition leader Ben Barka by King Hassan II in Paris in 1965, carried out with the covert assistance of the French security services, it is largely told from the point of view of a dissolute far-right paramilitary agitator who is made a scapegoat for the crime. *Nada*, Manchette's third book, is structured like a caper novel but, writes Sante, is "adapted to the single most newsworthy leftist-terrorist scenario of the 1970s: the symbolic abduction. The casual reader, unburdened by dates, might think that *Nada* was inspired by the kidnapping of Hanns Martin Schleyer by the Red Army Faction in Germany, or that of Aldo Moro by the Red Brigades in Italy, but those events would not occur until 1977 and 1978, respectively."

Like most crime capers, no sooner have the Nada Gang embarked on their plan than it starts to unravel. Unbeknownst to the kidnappers, the brothel from which the American ambassador was snatched is under surveillance by French counterintelligence as part of a routine operation to collect blackmail material on its VIP patrons. The gang members are captured on film and, with the help of the brothel madam, Diaz and Épaulard are quickly identified. This leads to the group's weak link, Treuffais, who got cold feet and pulled out of the kidnapping plot. Soon the police have the location of the farmhouse where the kidnappers are holed up. An adviser to the French interior minister intimates to Goemond that his minister would not be displeased were the police to go in hard against the kidnappers, forcing them to kill their hostage, and thus generating public antipathy against the far left. With these unofficial riding instructions, the police launch a major assault on the farmhouse. Some of the gang members are killed in the resulting gun battle. The survivors surrender and are executed in cold blood by Goemond. Diaz kills the ambassador and escapes. The same Interior Ministry adviser then lambasts Goemond for using excessive force and informs him that in response to the public and media outcry over the excess of the farmhouse siege, he is going to be posted to a remote part of France's empire in Africa. But using

Lou Castel, Mariangela Melato, and Maurice Garrel confront the police in *Nada* (1974)

the academic, Treuffais, as bait, Goemond sets up a final confrontation with Diaz.

Chabrol helms a faithful adaptation of Manchette's book, one of eight of the author's novels to be adapted for the French screen. Chabrol was a leading member of the French New Wave but was also one of its more commercially minded directors, mixing films featuring sharp social criticism of the moral and sexual proclivities of the French bourgeoisie with a steady stream of genre output, everything from Eurospy fare to crime tales. He thus captures the action and political thriller aspects of Manchette's source novel, but fares less well in translating to the screen Manchette's depiction of the internecine politics of the French far left. The Nada Gang are depicted as dilettantes and political amateurs, except for Diaz and Épaulard, the latter of whom thinks the kidnapping idea is "politically dumb" but goes along with it anyway to recapture some sense of the ideological fervor of his youth. Which is to some degree how they are treated in Manchette's novel and, one could argue, not that far removed from Chabrol's own political identity.

What *Nada* does capture brilliantly is the desperation of a group of far-left activists who realize that despite everything that they threw at it in May 1968 in Paris and immediately after, France's social order is not going to crumble. And it prefigures with uncanny accuracy how such intense political frustration would coalesce into France's own experience of far-left political violence, Action Directe (Direct Action). Formed in 1979, Direct Action espoused libertarian communist politics and considered itself in alliance with other urban guerrilla groups in Western Europe and far-left liberation movements overseas. It undertook various bombings, kidnappings, and assassinations of capitalist targets. One of the most prominent of these occurred in January 1985, when its so-called Elisabeth Van Dyck branch—named after a second-generation member of West Germany's Red Army Faction shot by police in May 1979—assassinated a French army general. Individuals affiliated with the group also attacked Jewish targets to protest what it saw as Paris's pro-Israel foreign policy. It continued to be active until around 1987, but it never gained much of a political foothold among the French public and was effectively crushed by French authorities by the end of the 1980s.

Nada shows the political futility of such actions. Surveying the ruins of its operation while he hides in a house in the country, Diaz records his thoughts about what went wrong, a passage which is also in Manchette's novel: "Leftist terrorism and state terrorism, even if their motivations cannot be compared, are the two jaws of the same mug's game," he says. "The state hates terrorism but prefers it to revolution."

Andrew Nette

OUTTAKE: *7 DÍAS DE ENERO (SEVEN DAYS IN JANUARY*, 1979), JUAN ANTONIO BARDEM, SPAIN

The "strategy of tension" undertaken by Italy's far right in the late 1960s and 1970s had a parallel elsewhere in Western Europe: in Spain after the downfall of the thirty-six-year-long fascist dictatorship of Francisco Franco. Not happy with the transition to a constitutional democracy following Franco's death in late 1975, a faction of hard-right fascist loyalists in the country's business, military, security services, and political elite, known as the *búnker*, staged various political provocations to sabotage the shift and bring about a return to fascist rule. The most high-profile of

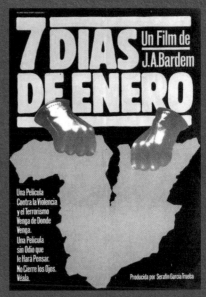

Seven Days in January (1979)

these provocations, the "Atocha massacre," is the subject of Juan Antonio Bardem's 1979 film *7 días de enero* (*Seven Days in January*).

On January 24, 1977, three armed members of the Spanish far right entered the offices of an independent transport workers trade union in central Madrid, which was affiliated to the then still illegal Spanish Communist Party (PCE). They opened fire, murdering five labor activists and seriously wounding four others. The intended target was the union's general secretary, who was leading a citywide transport strike. The strike was part of a larger wave of industrial action that rocked Spain throughout 1976 and peaked in January 1977, during which independent unions emerged in open defiance of official Francoist-controlled labor organizations. The attack was designed to provoke the Spanish left into a violent counterresponse, thus providing the fascists with a pretext to stage a coup d'état. But it had the opposite effect, unleashing widespread public revulsion against the far right and solidifying support for the move

VOTAR COMUNISTA
S VOTAR DEMOCRACIA

Director Juan Antonio Bardem (wearing glasses, foreground left) at a Spanish Communist Party
meeting, date unknown; party leader Santiago Carillo is standing at center

to democracy and the PCE's legalization, which occurred two months later.
Several men were put on trial and jailed for the Atocha massacre—the
first Francoists to be publicly and legally held to account for any of their
actions during the transition to democracy. There were also claims, never
conclusively established, that the perpetrators had links to the Italian far
right and to individuals active in illegal death squads established by the
security services to combat Basque separatists.

Seven Days in January depicts the events leading up to and
immediately after the Atocha massacre, mainly through the eyes of an
impressionable young fascist, Luis (Manuel Ángel Egea). Luis is the scion
of an influential family that hates communism and venerates its political
past fighting on the fascist side during the civil war and with the Nazis in
World War II. Bardem shows the family's patriarch and Luis's stepfather,
Don Thomas (Jacques François), and his steely mother, Adelaïda (Madelaine
Robinson), increasingly concerned by the strike wave gripping Madrid.
Faced with what he views as a growing wave of secular Marxist influence
in Spain, Don Thomas and his fellow fascist sympathizers embark on a
strategy of tension, mentioned by name in the film, to demolish democracy
before it has a chance to take hold. Having been politically groomed by his
far-right friends and family, Luis volunteers to take part in the attack on
the labor union's office. The actual killings are not shown at first, but we
see the shock on Luis's face when he views the bodies. The massacre—but

again, not the actual killings—is also depicted from other points of view: a survivor of the attack, as well as a group of trade unionists in a nearby bar who are first on the scene afterward.

But not only does the left-wing backlash fail to materialize, the PCE is lauded as a responsible political player and a restraining influence following the massacre. Don Thomas tells Adelaïda that to protect the movement's senior leadership, those who took part in the killings, including Luis, must be abandoned to their fate. Bardem shows the actual perpetrators of the massacre dealing with the aftermath in different ways. While Luis struggles with the implications of what he has been part of, the leader of the attack, Antonio (José Manuel Cervino), does not even bother to hide his face, such is the impunity with which he is accustomed to operating. He and others who carried out the killings, including Luis, are soon identified by another survivor, a young woman, and arrested. It is via her flashback that the viewer is finally shown the cold-blooded massacre of the unionists. The film's political message is underscored in the final scenes, with newsreel footage of mass demonstrations by pro-democracy supporters and the left in the aftermath of the crime.

Seven Days in January was one of nearly twenty films made by Bardem, an outspoken critic of the Franco regime and PCE member. It is made in the semi-documentary style that seemed to be favored by European leftist directors making political thrillers at the time. The production was bankrolled by "red millionaire" and PCE supporter Teodulfo Lagunero. Lagunero, who made his fortune in real estate investment and construction, was the unofficial contact for controversial PCE leader Santiago Carillo during his exile while Franco was in power. Lagunero helped smuggle Carillo back into Spain after the dictator's death and was instrumental in negotiating the PCE's legalization.

Seven Days in January is among a loose grouping of Spanish films made in the second half of the 1970s and early 1980s that dealt with themes relating to the struggle against fascist dictatorship, the country's transition to democracy, and the political violence that took place around it. Foremost is the 1979 Italian/Spanish-coproduced drama-documentary directed by Gillo Pontecorvo, *Operación Ogro* (*Ogro*), about the 1973 assassination by the ETA of the then Spanish prime minister and chief henchman and successor to Franco, Luis Carrero Blanco, nicknamed "the Ogre," discussed in more detail earlier in this book. Other entries include: Manuel Gutiérrez Aragón's *Camada negra* (*Black Litter*, 1977), about a young man who joins an extreme right group who present themselves as singers, led by an

Confessions of a Congressman (1978)

Exit Dead End (1981)

influential older woman; Eloy de la Iglesia's *El diputado* (*Confessions of a
Congressman*, 1978), a drama about a leftist politician during the transition
to democracy who is blackmailed by fascists over his secret homosexuality
and his affair with a street hustler; *La patria del "rata"* (*Exit Dead End*, 1980),
directed by Francisco Lara Polop, the story of a man released from prison
after serving a sentence for political crimes under the Franco dictatorship,
who turns to robbing banks due to the lack of alternative ways to earn
a living; and *La fuga de Segovia* (*The Escape from Segovia*, 1981), Imanol
Uribe's depiction of the real escape of approximately thirty ETA political
prisoners from Segovia prison in the dying days of the Franco regime.

Andrew Nette

THE RED ARMY FACTION

Radical Violence in West German Cinema in the 1970s

eginning in the mid-1960s, West Germany was rocked by increasing acts of political violence. While the government labeled these acts as terrorism, their young perpetrators considered them to be part of a necessary campaign of resistance. Though there were several left-wing urban guerrilla organizations operating at the time, the most famous of these is undoubtedly the Rote Armee Fraktion (Red Army Faction, or RAF), commonly referred to by the media as the Baader-Meinhof Group. The RAF loosely formed in West Germany in 1970 and quickly became an influential, fearsome force, responsible for kidnappings, bombings, assassinations, plane hijackings, shootouts with the police, and more, spread across decades. In addition to fighting capitalist greed and oppression, the communist RAF members sought to violently resist what they saw as growing totalitarianism in West Germany.

The early RAF members were the children of the World War II generation and were filled with both guilt and horror that their parents didn't do enough to stop the tide of fascism. They explicitly saw the West German government in the '60s and '70s as a continuation of the country's Nazi past. Several high-ranking politicians and businessmen in the '70s had earlier served as Nazi Party members—and some as SS officers—during the war. Whether these elders were literal Nazis or just enabled fascism, the young radicals of the '70s demanded resistance. In Stefan Aust's *Der Baader Meinhof Komplex* (1985), he writes, "The moment you see your own country as the continuation of a fascist state, you give yourself permission to do almost anything against it. You see your action as the resistance that your parents did not put up." But as hard as the RAF and associated guerrilla groups fought what they saw as fascism, the government tried to destroy them on all fronts, including through the media and propaganda.

A lot of the conflict between the RAF and the government relates to representation and the question of who was allowed to have a voice in West German society. Originally, leftists and student protesters sought to speak up for impoverished minorities and workers and speak out against the Vietnam War and Western militarism. After the country rebuilt itself in the wake of World War II, West Germany experienced a boom in the middle class during a period of growth known as the *Wirtschaftswunder* ("economic miracle"). Directors like Rainer Werner Fassbinder, for example, explored the unpleasant truth behind this rosy facade of bourgeois prosperity and the oppression and exploitation some experienced under the *Bundesrepublik Deutschland* (BRD, or Federal Republic of Germany). But when leftist groups sought more open discussion about the country's various social issues in the late '60s, they were largely silenced by the conservative press, who more or less had a media monopoly supported by the government. The government's response has many parallels to American McCarthyism in the '50s: the attempted suppression of left-wing ideals, particularly communism, through blacklisting, surveillance, arrests, and state-sanctioned violence. This was enabled by the passing of certain laws seen to be in violation of civil liberties, like the *Radikalenerlass* (Anti-Radical Decree) of 1972, which legalized the firing of leftists from public service work.

Thus, it is no surprise that screen depictions of the RAF and leftist political violence were particularly fraught during the height of their activity in the '70s. The government and mainstream media sought to portray the RAF as an aberration in West German society: violent, antisocial outsiders determined to disrupt German democracy—and prosperity—at any cost. But leftist and left-leaning filmmakers were more sympathetic to the RAF's cause, if not downright supportive of it. The work of directors associated with *Neuer Deutscher Film* (New German Cinema), like Fassbinder, Volker Schlöndorff, or Margarethe von Trotta, can be seen as an extension of the RAF's mission to overthrow government oppression and resist what they saw as the increasingly totalitarian impulses of the BRD. While early films made about or alluding to the RAF tend to be more sensational, satirical genre fare, films made later in the decade increasingly question how individuals are driven to violence, particularly politically motivated violence.

Though the RAF wasn't founded until 1970, the activities of their earliest members coincided with the global protests of 1968. Founding members like

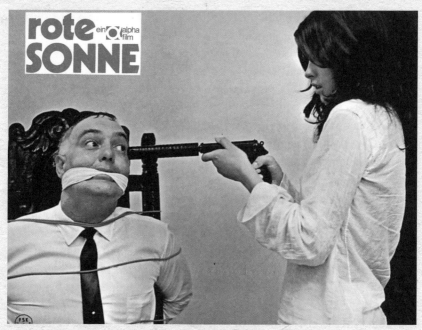

Red Sun (1970)

Ulkrike Meinhof, Gudrun Ensslin, Andreas Baader, Horst Söhnlein, Jan Carl Raspe, and Horst Mahler—often referred to as the "first generation"—were all involved in various forms of activism that became increasingly Marxist and increasingly violent. Some of these events quickly found their way into film. Early examples include a 1968 department store bombing in Frankfurt by Ensslin and Baader, which was the inspiration for Klaus Lemke's made-for-TV film *Brandstifter* (*Arsonists*, 1969). Future director Margarethe von Trotta stars as a student activist who plans to burn down a department store. Though Lemke personally knew Baader, *Arsonists* feels like a youth revolt film as equally concerned with style as it is with substance. Similar examples include the slightly earlier *Tätowierung* (*Tattoo*, Johannes Schaaf, 1967), whose star Christof Wackernagel would go on to join the RAF later in the '70s.

But there were also some early films made in response to this movement—and to the tumultuous protests and violence wracking West Germany since 1968—by more mainstream directors. These films are often more satirical, with depictions of young radicals as degenerate hippies. Director Rudolf Thome's little-seen *Rote Sonne* (*Red Sun*, 1970) falls squarely into this category. The opportunistic Thomas (Marquard Bohm) runs into his ex-girlfriend Peggy (Uschi Obermaier), sweet-talks her into taking him home, and proceeds to freeload off Peggy and her politically active roommates. But he soon realizes the house full of women all have a dim view of men—and a particularly radical solution to the problem.

Communes were a recognizable and influential aspect of left-wing politics in the late '60s, particularly in West Germany, where they sprang up around the country. Experimental artists, Situationists, student protesters, communists, hippies, and other marginalized young people came together in an attempt to conceptualize a new kind of society. They created art, which merged into political actions, attempted to reject capitalist notions of property ownership, and practiced "free love." The focus on reimagining romantic and sexual norms and, to a lesser degree, conventional gender roles was a major component of radical politics, particularly in the late '60s and early '70s. Communes represented an abandonment of the conservative, nuclear family so central to the '50s narrative of capitalistic growth and prosperity.

Though Thome's film essentially focuses on a feminist commune, *Red Sun* often feels more like an eerie satire of leftist movements and their forays into radical violence. Thome was part of the loosely defined *Neue Münchner Gruppe* (New Munich Group), which included directors like Klaus Lemke, May Spils, and Eckhart Schmidt. In many ways, they were the opposite of more experimental, confrontational New German Cinema directors. The New Munich Group sought to create accessible, relatively mainstream cinema that played with Hollywood movie tropes, familiar subgenres like the crime thriller, and elements of pop culture. While some, including Thome himself, were influenced by arthouse directors like Jean-Luc Godard, their films were generally lighter and more playful, with a focus on sex and romance. *Red Sun* flirts with hot-button themes, such as revolution and sexual freedom, without exploring them in any meaningful way. And while it was likely Thome's intention to present a parody of issues like feminism, commune life, and the use of political violence, *Red Sun* transcends these aims to become something stranger and more surreal. This is largely due to the casting of the hypnotic Uschi Obermaier. She began working as a model in 1968 and soared to popularity. By 1970, she was a countercultural icon associated with radical politics. Around this time, she joined influential krautrock band Amon Düül. Though they are most frequently remembered for their psychedelic music, they began as a Munich-based art commune heavily involved in leftist politics. Obermaier lived at the commune and played percussive instruments for some of their sprawling performances and early recordings. She soon moved on to the Highfisch-Kommune, also in Munich, before settling into Berlin's Kommune 1.

In Kommune 1, she was in a highly publicized relationship with radical Rainer Langhans, who became one of its leading organizers. Obermaier and

Uschi Obermaier at a political rally in West
Germany, circa 1970

Uschi Obermaier in *Red Sun* (1970)

Langhans served as inspiration for a more famous counterculture couple who followed their example, John Lennon and Yoko Ono, and musicians like Fleetwood Mac and Jimi Hendrix visited Highfisch and Kommune 1. Though Obermaier claimed indifference to politics, she became a sex symbol thoroughly associated with the protests of 1968, thanks to her modeling work and alleged affairs with Hendrix, Mick Jagger, and Keith Richards. In this sense, she is a notable symbol of the tension between the desire for real political action and the desire to be seen in association with leftist political groups because of optics—wanting to appear cool and trendy—a theme that emerged in many European arthouse films during the period.

And as a sex symbol, Obermaier can be seen in *Red Sun* as an embodiment of the sexual revolution and the dangers associated with it. The apartment in *Red Sun* seems like an obvious jab at the kind of commune life Obermaier participated in. The women seem to share everything: finances, food, a car, and a central bedroom, where they take turns sleeping. Kommune 1 was notorious for having one bedroom shared by all its members. The alleged rule was that anything was permitted, as long as it was done in front of the commune. In *Red Sun*, the women have a pact that heterosexual trysts can only last a few days before the women must murder the male partner in question, which can be seen as a satirical twist on the policy of many communes against private ownership, including possessing other people.

But while sexual revolution and free love was a key focus of many communes at the time, it was often a more complicated endeavor in reality.

Certain films from the period, like *Red Sun*, suggest or overtly depict that this arrangement was not always idyllic, particularly for women. *Red Sun* essentially focuses on how women are tired of being treated badly by men, so, as a group, they vow to take violent action. They turn this into a well-oiled operation, and it is implied they have killed dozens of men. Thomas, the film's loose protagonist, is an ideal victim for Peggy's commune. He is immediately shown to be selfish and manipulative; he is obviously using Peggy for sex, housing, food, alcohol, and seemingly anything he can exploit from her.

Though Thome's film is satirical, it unintentionally taps into the feminist themes that would dominate West German films about political violence in the '70s. Thomas is similar to the aimless male protagonist type found all over European cinema at the time: a deeply immature man and selfish manipulator who demands to be coddled and cared for by the begrudging women around him. There is a similar recurring figure in West German cinema, such as May Spils's *Zur Sache, Schätzchen* (*Go for It, Baby*, 1968), and especially in the films of Fassbinder. His 1971 films *Rio das Mortes* and *Pioniere in Ingolstadt* are two examples out of many Fassbinder films that feature a manipulative, selfish grifter (often played by Harry Baer) who takes advantage of a woman in love with him and drives her to madness and ruin.

Women frustrated to the point of violence by relationships with men—and by misogyny rampant in society—became a recurring theme in European films of the period more broadly, coinciding with the rise of feminist movements. While women are more often the victims rather than the perpetrators of violence in cinema, the movies of the '70s suggested radical alternatives were possible. Many of these films about women driven to violence feature horror movie and crime thriller tropes, and *Red Sun* must be considered alongside some of these. Examples include *Die Weibchen* (*The Females*, 1970), a French/Italian coproduction from Czech director Zbyněk Brynych, which is a more explicit exploration of *Red Sun*'s themes: a woman learns that a health clinic is run by a cabal of feminist cannibals who kill and eat men. In Tonino Cervi's *Le regine* (*Queens of Evil*, 1970), an opportunistic young motorcyclist ingratiates himself at the remote country home of three beautiful women. He attempts to use his charms to take advantage of them, unaware that they are witches.

Parallels can also be drawn between *Red Sun* and Rolf Olsen's *Blutiger Freitag* (*Bloody Friday*, 1972). Both are essentially crime genre films that satirize elements of the RAF while intentionally or unintentionally raising questions about West German society. *Bloody Friday* focuses on a bank robbery planned by escaped convict Heinz (Raimund Harmstorf), his

Bloody Friday (1972)

US poster for Bloody Friday (1972)

Italian friend Luigi (Gianni Macchia), and Luigi's pregnant girlfriend, Heidi (Christine Böhm). The heist becomes predictably violent, resulting in several unintended deaths, and ends on a tragic, blood-spattered note. But Olsen's portrayal of their motivations—and the public's reaction to this—adds a more political layer to the film. Heinz is presented as something of a modern-day swashbuckler: he is motivated by greed, but also genuinely seems to find crime and violence, and the idea of living beyond the law, exciting. He is essentially a negative caricature of how mainstream German media viewed young leftists: Heinz looks like he's just rolled out of a commune and into a photo shoot for a rock magazine. There is no suggestion that he has a regular job, and he views women as possessions. He is also eager to exploit the perception that the bank robbery is an act of political terrorism. Luigi and Heidi, on the other hand, are sick of living in poverty and tired of struggling at their thankless, often exploitative jobs. They are somewhat reluctantly joined by Heidi's brother Christian (Amadeus August), an army deserter who becomes a convert because he's also fed up with daily life.

Olsen was known for his early exploitation films and mondo movies. Bloody Friday similarly has pseudo-documentary sequences in which journalists interview the crowd outside the bank as the heist is in progress. Some subjects express criticism of the robbery and espouse a more conservative viewpoint, but increasingly people seem to sympathize with the trio, admitting that they are also frustrated with BRD's idea of democracy. Both Red Sun

Italian poster for *Bloody Friday* (1972)

and *Bloody Friday* depict bored, frustrated young men driven to take advantage of those around them, especially the women in their lives. And both portray women as capable of planning and carrying out acts of politically motivated violence. This echoes and anticipates the violence perpetrated by women throughout the '70s and '80s in the service of a global revolution. Many of the key New Left organizations had women as leading members, including the RAF: Ulrike Meinhof and Gudrun Ensslin were two of its founding leaders, both of whom died in prison under suspicious circumstances. Women also helped lead the Japanese Red Army, the Italian Red Brigades, and the Black Panthers and Weather Underground in the US. So even though *Red Sun* and *Bloody Friday* function on different levels as loosely satirical, somewhat nihilistic crime films, there is a clear message that women are sick of inequality and misogyny and are taking dramatic steps to strike back.

This message would be further emphasized by New German Cinema figures like Margarethe von Trotta. Von Trotta and her then husband and filmmaking partner Volker Schlöndorff explored this theme much more explicitly in *Die Verlorene Ehre der Katharina Blum oder: Wie Gewalt entstehen und wohin sie führen kann* (*The Lost Honor of Katharina Blum, or How Violence Develops and Where It Can Lead*, 1975). An adaptation of the novel from radical writer Heinrich Böll, it is one of several films from later in the '70s to explore leftist political violence from a seemingly impartial, somewhat oblique viewpoint. The film follows Katharina Blum (Angela Winkler), the reserved young housekeeper for a corporate lawyer (Heinz Bennent). After a one-night tryst with a suspected criminal (Jürgen Prochnow), Katharina is arrested and interrogated by the aggressive local police. They are so eager to apprehend a terrorist that they don't seem to care whether the suspect is actually guilty or if Katharina has any real political connection to him. Her arrest is spun into a sensational story by tabloid reporter Werner Tötges (Dieter Laser), who paints her as a terrorist, invades her personal life, and twists the words of anyone he interviews about her into outright lies to turn the public against her.

The Lost Honor of Katharina Blum notably doesn't explore political violence from the viewpoint of a character who is already a radical leftist; Katharina's lover on the run is barely on-screen, and his politics are unclear, though their relationship is shown to be deeply romantic. Instead, the film reveals how an average, innocent person is gradually turned toward violence by the authoritarian state. At the end of the film, Katharina shoots the reporter Tötges, who is ironically remembered as a hero at his funeral. She is driven to this desperate act of violence after enduring abuse and mistreatments at

The Lost Honor of Katharina Blum (1975)

the hands of the police, district attorney, journalists, and even people in her life, as well as brutal—and often inherently sexual—harassment from the public. It is revealed that Katharina often receives unwanted attention from the men around her; when she names this behavior as negative and stresses that it is one-sided and utterly undesired, several characters are shocked. Their outrage suggests Katharina is expected to tolerate or even enjoy this behavior. But this is shown to be only a small piece of the overall puzzle, the ultimate ruination of a person's life by an invasive, overzealous police force and irresponsible journalism enabled by the government itself. As Amy Taubin notes in a 2003 essay for the film's Criterion release, it captures a time "when the anxiety about terrorism eroded basic democratic values"—and as a result remains frighteningly relevant.

The focus on a sympathetic woman as protagonist—and her experiences living in a fundamentally misogynistic world, which drives her to violence—is also central to von Trotta's first solo directorial effort. *Das zweite Erwachen der Christa Klages* (*The Second Awakening of Christa Klages*, 1978), which followed a few years later, is like a feminist inversion of *Bloody Friday* with the crime genre elements stripped away. The titular Christa (Tina Engel) has robbed a bank to keep her children's day care center afloat after funding falls through. The film takes place in the aftermath of the robbery, showing it only in brief flashbacks. Instead, the focus is on the difficulties Christa encounters trying to find someone to help her get the stolen money to the day care center. Though many characters she encounters sympathize with her plight, they are reluctant to be associated with criminal activity.

Both *The Lost Honor of Katharina Blum* and *The Second Awakening of Christa Klages* implicitly connect capitalism, authoritarianism, and misogyny and tacitly cast all three as the root causes of left-wing political violence. Both films also focus on a social issue key to the mid to late '70s: the demonization of "sympathizers," anyone who took part in, supported, or understood the RAF's urban guerrilla warfare. Both films are stories about how and why an individual is radicalized or at least driven to politically motivated violence, but while Katharina is sent to prison, Christa is more optimistically shown to radicalize characters around her, namely other women. This includes her friend and later lover (Silvia Reize), an unhappy housewife effectively trapped at home by her absent but domineering husband, and a bourgeois bank teller (Katharina Thalbach) who witnessed the robbery but becomes determined to learn more about Christa and eventually tracks her down. Notably, the film closes with the bank teller insisting to the police that Christa is innocent, a tacit approval of the bank robbery. Unlike the pulpy *Red Sun* or the barrage of content produced by the mainstream German media, which depict leftist radicals as violent extremists, the women of *Bloody Friday*, *The Lost Honor of Katharina Blum*, and *The Second Awakening of Christa Klages* show how the average person is inevitably radicalized and emphasize how seemingly mundane domestic stressors are related to political oppression. This would also be the theme of von Trotta's 1981 film *Die bleierne Zeit* (*Marianne and Juliane*), about two radical sisters, inspired by the lives of Gudrun and Christiane Ensslin.

The Second Awakening of Christa Klages must also be seen as a response to the explosive, tragic events of 1977, when clashes between the conservative government and RAF reached their bloodiest. Earlier in the year, members of the so-called second generation of the RAF murdered the West German attorney general and a prominent banker. In September, the RAF kidnapped leading industrialist and former SS officer Hanns Martin Schleyer. When the government refused to exchange Schleyer for the freedom of several imprisoned RAF members, the RAF and Popular Front for the Liberation of Palestine hijacked Lufthansa Flight 181 in retaliation on October 13. On October 18, known as the Stammheim "Death Night," RAF leaders Andreas Baader, Gudrun Ensslin, and Jan-Carl Raspe were found dead in Stammheim high-security prison: allegedly Baader and Raspe shot themselves and Ensslin hanged herself. Another imprisoned RAF member, Irmgard Möller, attempted stabbing herself to death but survived. Schleyer was murdered later on October 18 by the RAF, whose members and sympathizers believed the Stammheim deaths were not suicides, but government-sanctioned murders.

The shockwave that spread through the German left-wing movement deeply impacted several films released later in 1978 and 1979. As a response to the events of October, a group of primarily leftist filmmakers associated with New German Cinema collaborated on an anthology film, *Deutschland im Herbst* (*Germany in Autumn*, 1978). Film distributor Filmverlag der Autoren approached Fassbinder and Schlöndorff, who contributed segments alongside Alexander Kluge, Edgar Reitz, Bernhard Sinkel, and several others. Filmverlag der Autoren was hoping for a film more sympathetic in nature. As is suggested years earlier in *The Lost Honor of Katharina Blum*, there was an ironclad media bias against the RAF: all press channels were virulently unsympathetic and painted them as deranged killers out to obstruct democracy at every turn. In Martin Blumenthal-Barby's 2007 essay "Germany in Autumn: The Return of the Human Author(s)," he writes that the filmmakers questioned "what could be done in light of the univocity of all television channels, radio stations and the press. There Schleyer was established as 'demi- saint,' as 'martyr,' whereas the RAF members were depicted as 'subhumans' and 'the scum of humanity.' Thus they agreed that a more eclectic counter-public sphere needed to be constituted."

Germany in Autumn is a eulogy for Baader, Raspe, and Ensslin. The film is bookended by funerals and raises questions about who can and should be mourned and how acts of political violence can be perceived as positive or negative based on state propaganda and historical shifts. The film opens with the elaborate funeral of Hanns Martin Schleyer, attended by state, business, and church dignitaries, and ends in stark contrast with the stripped-down, joint outdoor funeral of Ensslin, Raspe, and Baader, attended by what looks like students, other leftists, and average working-class people. *Germany in Autumn* is made up of three types of scenes: pseudo-documentary fictional sequences, historical footage of political assassinations and government-sanctioned violence, and interviews with notable figures from the period. One of the lengthiest segments follows the opening funeral and features a series of Fassbinder's "private" conversations. These take place either in his apartment with his lover (Armin Meier, also a regular actor in his films at this period), at a table with his mother (Lilo Pempeit, who he also cast in his films), or over the phone with his former wife (frequent collaborator Ingrid Caven, though she remains off-screen). This segment sets the tenor for the film: Fassbinder learns of the deaths of Baader, Ensslin, and Raspe and displays disbelief and despair. This serves as somewhat of a satire of Fassbinder's own life and his more grotesque, transgressive qualities; he buys drugs, quarrels with and is abusive to Armin, vomits, sits naked, and ultimately weeps.

His fear of surveillance from the police—which he mentions in the film but also struggled with in life—adds to the aura of paranoia. Fassbinder knew Meinhof and Baader from his earlier years in the experimental Aktion-Theater in the late '60s and believed his phone calls were being monitored because of that association. Wiretapping was certainly a common practice during this period. Over the phone, Fassbinder discusses how the government encouraged citizens to report on each other and compares this to life under Nazism. Later segments similar in tone include a history teacher exploring the more

Germany in Autumn (1978)

nuanced realities of key events in German history—for which she is repri-manded—and historical footage of political violence during World War I and World War II; generally, the film is closely concerned with how the issues that caused World War II have gone unresolved and led directly to the present situation. A major component of the second half of the film features scenes from a fictionalized made-for-TV version of Sophocles's tragedy *Antigone* from director Schlöndorff and writer Heinrich Böll, featuring much of the cast of *The Lost Honor of Katharina Blum*. Much of the play is concerned with the question of who deserves burial rites and mourning; after a civil war in which two of Antigone's brothers, leaders of opposing sides of the battle, are killed, the new king declares that one brother will be given a funeral and the other will be unburied, left to rot. These scenes from *Antigone* are debated by a panel of TV producers, who discuss whether the play adaptation should be allowed to air on television given its themes of violence, sacrifice, and resistance. Ultimately, they decide to cancel the screening.

The palpable sense of defeat and despair in *Germany in Autumn* becomes even more bitter in two final films from the decade: Reinhard Hauff's *Messer im Kopf* (*Knife in the Head*, 1978) and Fassbinder's own *Die dritte Generation* (*The Third Generation*, 1979). *Knife in the Head* opens with a police raid on a commu-nity center known as a gathering point for revolutionaries. A biogeneticist, Berthold Hoffmann (Bruno Ganz), is shot in the head, barely survives, and loses his memory. The police paint him as a terrorist, though his estranged wife (Angela Winkler) insists he was only at the community center to meet her and had no real political affiliations. During Hoffmann's time in the hospital, relearning how to talk and write, he attempts to learn the truth. Hoffmann is effectively a blank slate driven to investigate the right-wing police, the left-wing radicals, and his own possible involvement with both groups. The political clash of the period is essentially treated as the subject of a murder mystery plot. Ultimately, it becomes clear that the police are violent bullies who nearly murdered Hoffmann in cold blood and are attempting to place the

Knife in the Head (1978)

blame on him. But the radicals are not painted in a particularly flattering light either; Hoffmann is used as a pawn by the revolutionaries, namely his wife's lover, Volker (Heinz Hoenig).

In many ways, *Knife in the Head* hits a lot of the same plot beats as *The Lost Honor of Katharina Blum*, and notably Reinhard Hauff regularly collaborated with Schlöndorff. Both films follow an isolated protagonist who is romantically associated with radicals, is harassed and victimized by the police, is accused of being a terrorist, and essentially has their life ruined. While *Knife in the Head* doesn't address any feminist issues, it also deals more overtly with characters who are radical leftists. Hauff frequently explored political themes throughout his work, namely the impact an oppressive state has on individuals and how it can drive them to acts of violence. *Die Verrohung des Franz Blum* (*The Brutalization of Franz Blum*, 1974), about a man who is radicalized because of the brutality he experiences in prison, is an important earlier example of this. Hauff would make this even more explicit later in the '80s with the historical drama *Stammheim: Die Baader-Meinhof-Gruppe vor Gericht* (*Stammheim: The Baader-Meinhof Gang on Trial*, 1986).

While *Knife in the Head* falls somewhere between political thriller and downbeat psychological drama, *The Third Generation* is more of an experimental black comedy and goes even further with its critique of the current

ICH
WERFE
KEINE
BOMBEN
ICH
MACHE
FILME
R.W.F.

Der neue Rainer Werner Fassbinder-Film

mit
VOLKER SPENGLER
BULLE OGIER
HANNA SCHYGULLA
EDDIE CONSTANTINE
HARRY BAER
GÜNTHER KAUFMANN
VITUS ZEPLICHAL
UDO KIER
MARGIT CARSTENSEN
I SA LO
RAUL GIMENEZ
HARK BOHM
CLAUS HOLM
LILO PEMPEIT
JÜRGEN DRAEGER

DIE DRITTE
GENERATION

Buch, Regie und Kamera Rainer Werner Fassbinder
Eine Gemeinschaftsproduktion der Tongo-Film, Berlin, mit der Pro-ject Filmproduktion im Filmverlag der Autoren, München.

**FILMVERLAG
DER AUTOREN**

wave of left-wing radicalism. In
the film, an industrialist (Eddie
Constantine) concocts a plan to
boost his company's tech sales by
instigating and secretly funding
a group of largely middle-class,
middle-aged revolutionaries. Their
leader, August (Volker Spengler),
is actually a double agent working
with the industrialist. Their plans
become increasingly chaotic and
violent as they succumb to the
machinations of August and the
industrialist. If *Knife in the Head*
is skeptical of the leftists' actions,
The Third Generation paints many
of them as selfish, lazy, inept, and
even stupid. Like *Knife in the Head*,

West German police wanted poster for the
Baader-Meinhof Group, 1972

there is a sense of real defeat to the film. This is partly due to the implication
that the leftists are so desperate that they have lost sight of the first generation's original goals. Both *Knife in the Head* and *The Third Generation* show
how easily individuals can be manipulated, even those on the left.

This harsh critique of radical West German groups came at a time when
many, including Fassbinder himself, believed the battle that had begun with
1968 had failed and the left had effectively lost. Yet, like Nagisa Oshima in
Japan, Fassbinder can be described as a leftist filmmaker who used cinema
to explore and criticize the effectiveness of the left. Fassbinder's earlier film,
Mutter Küsters' Fahrt zum Himmel (*Mother Küsters Goes to Heaven*, 1975),
has a similar, if softer critique: an older, working-class widow gets swept
up into radical politics after her husband commits suicide because of the
oppressiveness of his job; ultimately, she is little more than a symbol for
bourgeois communist activists, and she dies a sacrifice for their cause. As
Meagan Day writes in "Fassbinder and the Red Army Faction" for *Jacobin* in
2021, "It's admittedly difficult to see *Mother Küsters* as anything other than
the story of how members of a crazed left neglect and exploit a grieving
working-class woman and ultimately get her killed."

Clearly as early as 1975, Fassbinder was exploring the motives of leftist
groups, the effectiveness of their actions, and what impact they really had
on struggling working-class people. *The Third Generation* leaves viewers

with the sense that actions that could be considered fruitful from earlier in the decade—bank robberies, political kidnappings, and so on—had lost all meaning and had been reduced to yet more fuel for the capitalist agenda in the wake of October 1977. But, as Day notes, the film is not critical of the radical revolutionary movement as a whole, more where it wound up at the end of the decade: "*The Third Generation* is not an oblique reference to the student left, nor even to those disposed to political violence who emerged from it. It's about 'come-lately West German terrorists' who were active at the end of the 1970s and who, according to Fassbinder, knew little of what had motivated their forebears of his generation."

Though the RAF were active into the '90s and filmmakers continued to depict them on-screen, the guerrilla war started by Fassbinder's generation around 1968—the "first generation" of the RAF—reached its peak in 1977. By the early '80s, much of that first generation was dead, including Fassbinder himself, who died of a drug overdose as he was preparing another film concerned with radical politics, a biography of Rosa Luxemburg. Key members of the "second generation," who were most active in the mid to late '70s, were in prison or exile. The "third generation" that Fassbinder targets in his film was technically only emerging on the scene in the '80s. His film can be seen as the disappointing conclusion of a period when the genuine hope for revolution was alive. It can also be seen as a warning to future revolutionaries not to be taken in by manipulation and corruption, and to remain true to the cause of improving life for underprivileged communities around the world.

Samm Deighan

PLASTIC JESUS IN THE LAND OF THE PARTISANS

The Black Wave and the Subversion of the Socialist Yugoslavian National Mythos

On August 3, 1969, the readers of *Borda* (*Struggle*), the official ideological mouthpiece of the League of Communists of Yugoslavia, woke up to the first salvo in what soon became a broad attack on the nation's *Novi Film* (New Film) movement. The eight-page article, penned by the president of the Serbian branch of the party's Ideological Action Committee, Vladimir Jovičić, warned readers of a Black Wave (*Crini Talas*) that was infecting Yugoslav cinema. Jovičić's article explicitly attacked a series of films created by primarily young, ethnically Serbian filmmakers for their depiction of Yugoslavian society in an overly negative light. The filmmakers were accused of the "systemic distortion of reality with improper images of violence, moral degeneracy, misery, lasciviousness, and triviality."

Both Jovičić's article and the films he was attacking need to be viewed within the context of the extreme paradox that was postwar Yugoslavia. Ever since the ideological break between Josip Broz Tito and Stalin in 1948, Yugoslavia had embarked on a radically different model of "Actually Existing Socialism." "Workers Self-Management" (*Samoupravljanje*) coupled with the genuine openness to influences from the First, Second, and Third Worlds made Yugoslavia a true outlier in comparison to other Marxist-Leninist states. Simultaneously, however, the ruling League of Communists of Yugoslavia still maintained an almost complete hegemony over most facets of political and cultural life. Dissent and criticism had its limits, and the coercive institutions of state power were still very much a feature of Yugoslavian reality. Taboo topics that were either closely censored or off-limits included certain

"Everyone grab onto your weapons": propaganda poster made by Yugoslavian partisans during World War II

aspects of the "People's Liberation War" (World War II), the uneven progress of the nation's postwar socialist reconstruction, and the uncomfortable (yet rather obvious) parallels between the "cult" of Josip Broz Tito and similar cults of personality in the more Stalinist nations of the Socialist Bloc. Postwar Yugoslavia can be seen as an extremely liberal variant of the other "people's democracies" in Central and Eastern Europe. More open than East Germany or even Poland, it was still a byproduct of the Soviet-Stalinist model in some ways.

It was in this strange incubator that the Yugoslav Black Wave took root, flourished, and ultimately drowned in a sea of reaction. The openness of the post-1948 cultural and economic policies meant that Yugoslav artists operated without the kind of draconian state censorship that their comrades in other Socialist Bloc states had to contend with. Direct exposure to foreign films (particularly American, French, and Italian) gave Yugoslav filmmakers a tool kit to challenge the formal constraints of state-sanctioned aesthetics.

In addition, the Titoist state openly propagated the idea of citizens' engagement with ideology and, in its own words, sought to apply "Marxism in a creative context." This is a critical facet in our understanding of the Black Wave. Even though these filmmakers openly challenged some critical components of the postwar Yugoslavian mythos, they were always doing so from a Marxist perspective. Like other strands of the international counterculture, the Black Wave critiqued aspects of the system to ideally foster a more humanist, less repressive version of the socialist system. In this sense, the Black Wave grew out of the postwar Yugoslavian critique of both Stalinism and capitalism: the stated return to Marx, and the project of developing Marxist philosophy as a tool in the construction of a socialist society.

Of course, these visions of dissent had very real limitations. Again, the paradoxical nature of the Yugoslavian system meant that criticism was valid only insomuch as it did not upset the existing order of things. Titoism was always a state-making ideology. And it is that respect, the Black Wave's critique of several of Yugoslavia's core national myths, that eventually brought the full weight of the state upon these artists.

When speaking of political violence in this context, it is important to define our terms. The directors associated with the Black Wave did not simply expose the very real violence within Yugoslavian society, such as wartime atrocities committed by the partisans or the coercive power of the Titoist state. Rather, the truly radical, dangerous component of these films was that they challenged the violence embedded within the fabric of postwar Yugoslavia. Borrowing from Slavoj Žižek in *Violence* (2008), "Objective

Student protests in Belgrade, Yugoslavia, 1968 (Photo credit: Stevan Kragujević, Museum of Yugoslavia War)

violence is precisely the violence inherent in the seemingly 'normal' peaceful state of things." It is the everyday violence that maintains and sustains systems of power through institutions, myths, memorialization, etc. In that respect, the films of the Black Wave challenged the inherent practices of violence that both sustained and defined the Titoist experiment.

On the night of June 2, 1968, students at the University of Belgrade went on a seven-day strike. Demanding a rollback of the recent economic reforms and framing their demands in the language of both Marxism and the international counterculture, the students were met with the full force of the local police. These events were followed by demonstrations in Zagreb, Sarajevo, Ljubljana, and other major cities. On the barricades, (mostly young) workers and prominent cultural figures joined the students, including the director Dušan Makavejev. Calm was only restored after Tito appeared on state television on the night of June 9, promising to meet some of the students' key demands and telling the nation that "the students are right."

Although partially inspired by the larger wave of global student-worker protests in the spring and summer of 1968, the unrest in Yugoslavia had particularly domestic roots. Yugoslavia's own unique brand of socialism created the conditions for a culture of dissent. For Tito's "baby boomers," the state had given them both the space and the ideological tool kit to voice their dissatisfaction with certain elements of the system. Indeed, the same applied for directors like Makavejev and other artists associated with the Black Wave. Only by understanding the specific context of Yugoslavia's "socialist '60s" can we fully appreciate how the filmmakers of the Black Wave were able to thrive and survive for as long as they did.

Postwar Yugoslavian cinema was set up along the already established Soviet model. The industry was at first highly centralized and, following Lenin's own axiom on the importance of cinema as a "weapon in revolutionary struggle," was seen as a medium for propaganda. Socialist realism was the order of the day, and filmmakers were explicitly directed that film should "reflect a distinctive socialist art based upon the principles of nationalist realism conceived by Stalin-Zhdanov." State censors carefully monitored what could or could not be screened, and the film industry operated along the lines of a highly centralized bureaucratic machine. Much like Yugoslavia's initial postwar economic planning, the nation's cinema was following the Soviet model in both its form and content.

The Stalin/Tito split of 1948–49, however, changed all of this. Arguing that the Soviet model of development had become bureaucratic and had deviated from the path of authentic Marxist-Leninism, Yugoslavia embarked on a drastic campaign of decentralization. Under the label "Workers Self-Management," workers in all fields were organized into workers' councils and effectively became trustees of socially owned property. In 1952, a new series of laws formally encoded these reforms, and the ruling party changed its name to the League of Communists (LCY) as an attempt to redefine its role as a social animator.

The ideological playing field also dramatically opened. Free from the constraints of Stalinism, the newly rebranded LCY dedicated time and resources to "rediscover" the "real" Marx. Although this change was designed to justify the country's new foreign policy, these relatively open debates on ideology had a profound impact. Unlike in the Soviet Union and Central and Eastern Europe, Yugoslavian Marxism was dynamic and never truly devolved into a purely performative exercise. Equally important was the fact that the Titoist state and its educational institutions explicitly taught people to think in ideological terms. This, coupled with the various mass mobilization campaigns initiated to help speed up the country's modernization drive, gave ordinary people the sense that they were ultimately the arbiters of the revolution. Socialism could not be constructed, nor would societal contradictions be overcome without their active participation in the project. This was in stark contrast to other Socialist Bloc nations, whose young people increasingly started to check out of the public sphere after discovering the limitations of the Khrushchev-era reforms of the mid-1950s.

Unlike in the Soviet Union and most of the other "people's democracies" in Central and Eastern Europe, ordinary Yugoslavian citizens also had access to both foreign consumer goods and cultural commodities. In 1960 alone, Yugoslavia imported forty-five American films, forty-nine from Western European nations, and forty-one from the Socialist Bloc. Tito's non-aligned foreign policy also meant that this cultural exchange extended into the emerging Third World. In particular, the regime engaged in a kind of cinematic diplomacy designed to win "hearts and minds" in the decolonizing world and to frame national liberation movements as the ideological heirs to the World War II–era partisans. Travel was also largely unrestricted and was up to a point even actively promoted by the state itself. This movement of ideas, goods, and people over Cold War frontiers was singled out by Dušan Makavejev as one of the critical conditions responsible for the rise of the Black Wave. In the words of Makavejev, "In Yugoslavia every citizen can get a passport and travel wherever he wishes."

The impact of this uniquely Yugoslavian brand of socialism on both the film industry and domestic filmmakers cannot be underestimated. Although still state owned and operated, by the early 1960s Yugoslavia's film industry had already been thoroughly decentralized. Direct state subsidies were replaced by a system of taxes and self-financing. The industry slowly began to engage in foreign coproductions, with a special emphasis on cooperation with Western or Third World producers. Film criticism became livelier and more sophisticated, due to exposure from outside sources. Censorship was reduced, and the strict ideological guidelines of the immediate postwar era were rescinded. Yugoslavian filmmakers therefore enjoyed an extremely privileged position in comparison to their comrades in other Socialist Bloc states. This privilege, however, was always conditional. Although the state had created an environment where everything seemed possible, there existed certain critical lines that could not be crossed.

But 1968 was not only the year of unrest. It was also the twenty-fifth anniversary of the establishment of the Federal Socialist Republic of Yugoslavia. A year of public pageantry that celebrated Tito's wartime partisan movement in what was officially dubbed the "National Liberation War." Not unlike the Soviet cult of the Great Patriotic War, World War II became the key historical event that the Yugoslavian state chose to anchor its legitimacy. The official narrative of the war, however, was a somewhat distorted retelling of events.

Far from being a straightforward conflict against foreign occupiers, the war in Yugoslavia was a complex and brutal ethnonational and socioeconomic civil war. Although Tito's partisan movement emerged victorious and possessed a genuine degree of popular support, the conflict (and its memory and memorialization) in many ways served to divide as opposed to unify the nation. Nor did the war have a particularly clean endpoint. The slow pace of Yugoslavia's economic recovery and the chaos of the crash collectivization of agriculture in the immediate postwar years contributed to mass homelessness and social vagrancy. A brutal counterinsurgency campaign was waged against remnants of both the anticommunist Serbian nationalist Chetniks and the genocidal Ustaše Croatian movement in the mountains of Bosnia. The Department of People's Protection (OZNA) targeted wartime collaborators, members of the prewar ruling classes, and "enemy nationalities" (ethnic German *Volksdeutsche* in the Serbian Banat, Hungarians in Vojvodina, and Italians in the area around Trieste). In Serbia alone, over fifty-five thousand noncombatants were killed following the republic's liberation in autumn 1944.

The official narrative of the war presented by the Yugoslavian state was largely sanitized and devoid of any uncomfortable topics. This can clearly be seen in the form of the genre of partisan films that soon became the primary cultural medium used to convey the sanctioned version of war to the population. Beginning with Vjekoslav Afrić's *Slavica* (1947), the Yugoslavian film industry produced a steady stream of films conveying the official narrative of the "National Liberation War." Indeed, throughout the forty-three years of Yugoslav cinema, partisan films were commercially the most successful, ideologically the most representative, and culturally the most typical of all film genres in Yugoslavia. Offering an uncomplicated version of the war ("good" partisans versus "evil" Axis occupiers and their ideologically fanatical collaborators) and plenty of on-screen action, these films resembled the pre-counterculture Hollywood westerns.

By the early 1960s, however, this sanitized version of war was openly challenged by a host of young Yugoslavian filmmakers. Operating in an environment that was both genuinely ideologically liberal and decentralized, many of the early experiments of Black Wave cinema can be considered counterpartisan films. Rejecting the heroic Romanticism of the early partisan films, these young directors focus their attention on topics and taboos outside the mainstream of revolutionary history. In particular, the films presented a darker and more nuanced vision of both the war and the role of Tito's partisans.

Examples of counterpartisan cinema include Croatian director Vatroslav Mimica's *Kaja, ubit ću te!* (*Kaya, I Will Kill You*, 1967), which openly explored

Three (1965)

The Morning (1967)

the difficult motivations involved with collaboration. The same year saw Serbian filmmaker Đorđe Kadijević's truly brutal semi-gothic *Praznik* (*The Feast*, 1967), which forced audiences to examine the participation of ordinary men and women in wartime atrocities. Finally, 1967 also saw former-partisan-turned-director Puriša Đorđević's *Jutro* (*The Morning*, 1967). The first Yugoslavian film that addressed the issue of mass shootings conducted by Tito's forces, *The Morning* was met with heavy criticism from both the state-controlled press and veteran organizations. Although the film was not banned, Đorđević was "disciplined" by the state censor.

There are, however, two Black Wave films dealing with the war years that truly stand out: Aleksandar Petrović's *Tri* (*Three*, 1965) and Mića Popović's *Delije* (*Tough Guys*, 1968). Petrović's film essentially kicked off the wave of counterpartisan films. It also had the distinction of being the first Yugoslavian film to receive a general release in the US. Centered on three separate stories involving ordinary Yugoslavs, the film's tone and style owed more to the French New Wave and Italian neorealism than Yugoslavian national cinema. Indeed, Petrović attacked the Yugoslav-dominant cinema as falsified history and objected to what he termed the "primitive directing" of partisan filmmakers.

What makes *Three* so transgressive is less its style than the way it frames the war. Unlike previous partisan films that promoted and celebrated a heroic

UN FILM DI PURISA DORDEVIC

L'ALBA DI UN GIORNO
(JUTRO)

CON MILENA DRAVIC - LJUBISA SAMARDZIC - NEDA ARNERIC - MIJA ALEKSIC

Una produzione
DUNAV FILM BELGRADO

Esclusività
CORMONS FILM

COPPA VOLPI PER LA MIGLIORE
INTERPRETAZIONE MASCHILE
ALLA XXVIII MOSTRA INTERNAZIONALE
D'ARTE CINEMATOGRAFICA
DI VENEZIA

French poster for *The Morning* (1967)

narrative of antifascist resistance, Petrović's film is important for its complete lack of heroes. His protagonists are ordinary people faced with a host of extremely difficult, morally ambiguous choices. Shot almost totally in POV and with little actual dialogue, this is a deeply individualistic examination of war and its impact on everyday life. Gone are the larger-than-life partisan heroes that had grounded earlier films. Taking their lead from Stalinist Soviet epics, many of the early partisan films not only featured ridiculous, almost superhero-like heroes, but also Tito himself. Like the cult of Stalin in the Soviet Union, cinematic Tito was very much the "rock star dictator," guiding and inspiring literally everything. In contrast, *Three* is a starkly grim antiwar piece stripped of any ideological polemics, larger-than-life heroes, or patriotic messages. There is a particularly striking scene in the final story that is focused on a partisan hit squad's assassination of a young female collaborator. The young woman in question, although clearly from a bourgeois background, is fully humanized. Her death is not valorized as a righteous act of revolutionary justice, but rather as simple murder.

Mića Popović's *Tough Guys* meanwhile aims its critique at the violent and chaotic immediate postwar period. Filmed and released during the student protests of 1968, the narrative follows two unemployed war veteran brothers (actors Jovan Janićijević Burduš and Danilo "Bata" Stojković) as they attempt to reintegrate themselves into civilian life. The pair are profoundly damaged from their wartime experience. However, the film clearly problematizes the neat and tidy borders between war and peace. Much like Yugoslavian society itself, liberation does not mean an end to the violence for our protagonists. Unable to find meaningful work and with their home village destroyed, the two wander the barren countryside. Keeping a machine gun in the trunk of the car, the pair are constantly reminded that the war is not truly over. As the brothers are increasingly pushed to the margins of society, they eventually turn their pent-up rage on each other.

Popović's grim portrayal of the immediate postwar years directly challenged some essential pillars of the established Yugoslavian war mythology. His protagonists are not the lionized soldiers of the revolution. Rather, they represent a generation of young men who were lost after the war. Lacking education and employment and emotionally damaged, many of these veterans resorted to criminal behavior. Indeed, the film's opening scene introduces the two brothers with mug shots. Not surprisingly, the film was not received well by the authorities. Popović, a painter whose work had already come under heavy criticism, was, not unlike his film's protagonists, pushed to the margins of the Yugoslavian artistic community. When he reemerged in the

Tough Guys (1968)

Dragan Nikolić as Stiv in *Young and Healthy as a Rose* (1971)

1980s, it was as one of the cultural godfathers of the Greater Serbian nationalist movement.

In Jovan Jovanović's *Mlad i zdrav kao ruza* (*Young and Healthy as a Rose*, 1971), a gang of hippies, junkies, sex workers, and unemployed youth occupies the hotel "Yugoslavia." This not-so-subtle satire of both the student occupations of 1968 and the myriad of social issues that plagued contemporary Yugoslavian society was subsequently banned by the state censors. Unemployment, which was almost unheard of during the 1950s, suddenly became a real issue after the neoliberal economic reforms of 1965. Especially hard hit was the country's younger workforce, which increasingly began to immigrate to Western Europe as "guest workers" in the early 1970s. By this point, the young artists of the Black Wave were critiquing not just the Yugoslavian past, but also the contradictions of the nation's present. Raised in a relatively liberal ideological environment that promoted both engagement and activism, the children of the Titoist state had been inadvertently provided with the tools to criticize the failings of the system. However, following the events of June 1968, the Yugoslavian state's tolerance for open dissent became increasingly narrow.

Like Jovanović's film, Makavejev's *W.R.: Misterije Organizma* (*W.R.: Mysteries of the Organism*, 1971) was savagely attacked by the state's cultural apparatus. Makavejev's film comprises two main intersecting themes: a

Orgasmterapi. Milena Dravic. Jagoda Kaloper. Ivica Vidovic. Tull Kupferberg. Zoran Radmilovic. Jackie Curtis. Miodrag Andric. Sexpoligatrop. Författare. Regissör. Dusan Makavejev. Foto. Pega Popovic. Aleksandar Petkovic. NEOPLANTA FILM. Novi Sad. TELEPOOL. München. Medarbetare. Bojana. Probst. Ivanka. Sarlo. Speciell gäst. Stalins vålnad. WR. Wilhelm Reich. WR. Världsrevolution. WR. Livsglädje. WR. Socialism med kroppen. Vad gör du med din kapacitet på 4.000 orgasmer under din livstid? WR. Kör igång din egen hämningslöshet med den här filmen. Frihet och kärlek är outtömliga. Var skitförbannad men sluta inte andas. Den som väljer sitt eget slaveri — är han fortfarande slav?

WR KROPPENS MYSTERIER
LES MYSTÈRES DE L'ORGANISME
DIE MYSTERIEN DES ORGANISMUS
THE MYSTERIES OF ORGANISM

FÄRG

W.R.: Mysteries of the Organism (1971)

Director Dušan Makavejev with actress Milena Dravić (right) and her prop head on the set of his 1971 film *W.R.: Mysteries of the Organism*

documentary about the controversial Austrian Marxist psychoanalyst Wilhelm Reich (W.R.) and the tale of a sexually and ideologically liberated Yugoslav woman named Milena (Milena Dravić). Directly linking sexual fulfillment with revolutionary politics, Makavejev's criticism was aimed at Yugoslavian socialism's inability to live up to its own radically emancipatory, humanist ideals. In a scene directly parodying Tito's own public speeches, Milena proclaims to her fellow communal apartment dwellers, "Socialism must not exclude human pleasure from its program." This reference to Reich's theories connecting sexual repression and authoritarian politics is clearly implying that the Yugoslavian experiment had gone stale and was at risk of descending into "red fascism."

The extraordinary thing about Makavejev's critique of contemporary Yugoslavian society, however, is how firmly rooted it was within the ideological coordinates of the system itself. Yugoslavian socialism made a point to deliberately define itself in opposition to both Western capitalism and Soviet-style socialism. In the film, both the United States and the Soviet Union are critiqued for misdirecting sexuality into power politics and militarism. These two oppositional systems are symbolized by characters of both the Soviet ice-skating champion Vladimir Ilych (Lenin) and an unnamed American

Vietnam veteran who wanders the urban landscape jerking off an assault rifle. Makavejev's thesis, however, is that if the Titoist system fails to live up to its stated goals, it runs the risk of regressing into what it purports to despise. The choice of the filmmakers to juxtapose Yugoslavian patriotic songs with American advertising jingles, along with the fact that our damaged American veteran is wearing a standard-issue JNA (Yugoslavian People's Army) helmet, clearly hammers this point home to the audience.

In contrast to Makavejev's somewhat sympathetic vehicle of dissent, Lazar Stojanović's *Plasticni Isus* (*Plastic Jesus*, 1971) presented a full-frontal assault on the Titoist state. Making no attempt at a linear narrative, the film relies on music and images to convey its messages. Deeply problematic and dangerous messages, as far as the state was concerned. Stojanović openly takes the system's stated critique of Stalinism to task by subverting the omnipresent cult of Tito. Over the course of the film, images of the nation's violent past (World War II–era atrocities, the Nazi occupation, etc.) are paired with the seemingly peaceful present. For Stojanović, there is no clearly defined temporal break between the two. This is where *Plastic Jesus* is truly transgressive. Tito (the title's "plastic Jesus") is directly equated to Hitler and the partisans to their wartime ultra-nationalist opponents. The film also utilizes music, pairing the popular Titoist propaganda ballad "Comrade Tito, Our Fair Violet" with the popular German wartime song "Lili Marlene."

According to Stojanović, his film was a "victim of the calendar" that was conveniently used as a proof of antisocialist cultural politics in the early 1970s. This reading of the situation is not without some merit. *Plastic Jesus* was in many ways the culprit that finally brought the full weight of the state down upon the Black Wave. However, the tide of cultural reaction had been brewing since at least the events of June 1968. Perhaps because Stojanović's film is the most outwardly subversive, its importance has been somewhat exaggerated. Both the League of Communists and its associated cultural organs were already engaged in their own ideological counteroffensive by the time *Plastic Jesus* appeared before the state censor.

At the end of *W.R.: Mysteries of the Organism*, the severed head of Milena utters the line "I am not ashamed of my communist past." In a very real sense, this piece of dialogue could be used to sum up the ethos of most of the directors associated with the Black Wave. Their films, although providing a violent critique of both the Yugoslavian past and present, were ultimately speaking "Yugoslav." Forged and nourished by the country's unique brand of state socialism, these filmmakers did not set out to violently destroy the existing system. Rather, as historian Jeremi Suri has argued about the global

Plastic&Jesus

screenplay by,
directed by &
montage: **Lazar Stojanovic**

cast: Tomislav Gotovac, Svetlana Gligorijevic, Vukica Djilas, Kristina Pribicevic, Zivojin Gligorijevic,

Melanija Bugarinovic, Mida Stevanovic, Ljubisa Ristic, Zorica Sumadinac, Josip Broz, Adolf Hitler, Benito Musolini,

Ante Pavelic, Josif Visarionovic Staljin, Miljenko Zuborski, Darinka Gajic, Bozidar Borjan, Mikan Marinovic

director of
photography: Branko Perak sound: Bata Pivnicki & Marko Rodic light: Borislav Blagojevic produced by: CENTAR FILM & FDU Beograd

 ЕКСПРЕС   BASF

designed by: mirko beokovic printed in "beograf"

UK poster for *Plastic Jesus* (1971)

Cold War–era counterculture more broadly, their dissent was concerned with turning the theory of Titoism into practice.

Starting in the early 1970s, a red wave descended over Yugoslavian cinema. Experimentation and critique were out. Revolutionary epics, comedies, and big-budgeted international coproductions became the order of the day. The Yugoslavian cultural industry became like their counterparts in Central and Eastern Europe, a closed shop in terms of ideas. Although Yugoslavia remained the most liberal example of existing socialism until its violent collapse, the openness of the 1950s and 1960s had given way to their own version of what Václav Havel referred to as post-totalitarianism. There was no return to the state terrorism of the regime's early years, but the security services were once again empowered to crush dissident voices. The Titoist state's legitimacy was increasingly predicated on its ability to deliver cheap and plentiful consumer goods to its citizens. As for ideology, that became a largely performative exercise devoid of any real content.

The fates of the various Black Wave filmmakers varied during this period. Some stayed on and continued to work in the new, more restricted cultural environment. Others, like Makavejev, emigrated west. Mića Popović, who was always the most strident critique of the regime, is a notable outlier. He morphed into an ultra-nationalist, becoming a champion of the Serb cause in Kosovo and an early supporter of Slobodan Milošević's so-called Antibureaucratic Revolution. In the context of the violent ethno-nationalism of the 1990s, the vision of humanist Marxism presented by the filmmakers of the Black Wave became even more out of place. The films were both too Marxist and too culturally liberal for the new state builders of the various independent republics. Despite Makavejev's fears that Titoism would degenerate into red fascism, Yugoslavia ultimately descended into several very real variants of fascism. Although highly regarded internationally, the voices of the Black Wave continue to sit uncomfortably within postsocialist Yugoslavia society.

Matthew Kowalski

OUTTAKE: *DIABEŁ* (*THE DEVIL*, 1972), ANDRZEJ ŻUŁAWSKI, POLAND

In 1970, the political situation in Poland was particularly fraught. Władysław Gomułka, leader of the Polish People's Republic, had introduced more liberal reforms when he took office in the mid-'50s, but restrictions gradually returned throughout the '60s and became increasingly oppressive. By 1970, Poland had sunk into poverty and was heading toward an economic crisis. During that year, widespread riots broke out in which over a thousand were injured and dozens killed. The government cracked down on religious, intellectual, and artistic freedoms. It was this environment

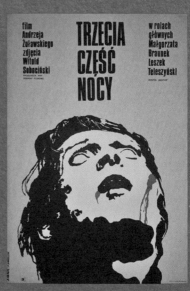

The Third Part of the Night (1971)

in which the young Andrzej Żuławski developed his first two feature films, *Trzecia część nocy* (*The Third Part of the Night*, 1971) and its follow-up, *Diabeł* (*The Devil*, 1972), which would soon force him to leave Poland.

On the surface, the two films have much in common, including numerous horror genre elements and a surreal, nightmarish quality. Notably, both films are set during times of German invasion (the 1940s in *The Third Part of the Night* and the 1790s in *The Devil*). The popular Polish World War II war films of the '50s, particularly those by Żuławski's mentor, Andrzej Wajda, largely presented simplified narratives focused on the courage of resistance fighters. But by the '60s and into the '70s, younger directors like Żuławski sometimes used these accepted war themes as a stand-in for protests against the repression of totalitarian Soviet rule. As Antonin and Mira Liehm write in *The Most Important Art: Soviet and East European Film After 1945* (1977), "The occupation and the war were used as a package to smuggle in contemporary themes: films about the recent past became a disguise for contemporary commitments."

DIABEŁ

SCENARIUSZ & REŻYSERIA:
ANDRZEJ ŻUŁAWSKI

ZDJĘCIA MACIEJ KIJOWSKI

W ROLACH GŁÓWNYCH:

WOJCIECH PSZONIAK

LESZEK TELESZYŃSKI

MAŁGORZATA

BRAUNEK

PRODUKCJA:

PRF ZF · ZESPÓŁ

FILMOWY X ·

1972

WALKUSKI · 87

The Devil (1972)

Though it is essentially a surrealistic horror film, *The Devil* often brazenly explores themes of political dissent. During the Prussian invasion of 1793, a mysterious man in black (Wojciech Pszoniak) rescues Jakub (Leszek Teleszynski) from a squalid prison overseen by nuns. Jakub is an alleged organizer of some political conspiracy, and the man in black frees him in exchange for the eventual promise of a list of Jakub's collaborators. Jakub's chaotic journey home is disrupted by political turmoil and the aftermath of a violent battle. But he finds his home life is even more devastating, and corruption within his own family sets him on a path of madness and psychotic violence, encouraged by the devil in black.

The Devil was banned in Poland due to its layered themes of resistance and dissent. While historically set films were typically considered safe content to get past the censor boards, it is impossible not to read the late-eighteenth-century setting of *The Devil* as a barely concealed metaphor for contemporary turmoil in Poland. The period from the late eighteenth century through the nineteenth century was marked by wars of succession known as the Partitions of Poland. The French and American revolutions were countered by absolute monarchies in Prussia, Russia, and the Ottoman and Austro-Hungarian Empires. Poland was then part of the Polish-Lithuanian Commonwealth, a relatively democratic government situated directly among warring neighbors. The commonwealth dealt with regular assaults from Sweden, Russia, Austria, France, and Prussia, among others. These conflicts—along with attempts at government reform that resulted in one of the first constitutional monarchies in European history—led to united attacks from Russia and Prussia. This ultimately resulted in the conquering and partitioning of Poland, which began in the 1770s when Russia, Prussia, and Austria claimed they were acting in Poland's best interests. By the Second Partition of the Commonwealth in 1793, the country was reduced to a protectorate, stripped of territory and political and financial independence, a situation that would not change for over a century.

While this is the backdrop of *The Devil*, it is important to note that the real threats to the country in the film's narrative come from within Poland itself—from its own people, who are consumed by greed, misplaced patriotism, opportunism, and widespread corruption. Michael Goddard argues that Żuławski used the period of the partitions as yet another way to disrupt the "sacred" myths about Poland and Polish history: "While it seemed that Żuławski had gone as far as possible in overturning everything that was sacred in Polish political and cinematic history, this tendency would be carried, at least in censorship terms, beyond acceptable limits" in *The Devil*.

This was further emphasized by Żuławski's use of literary references, namely to Adam Mickiewicz's epic poem *Dziady* (often translated as *Forefathers' Eve*, 1824) and Shakespeare's *Hamlet* (1601). Both references would have been understood by Polish audiences—and censors—as allusions to resistance against corrupt governments

Wojciech Pszoniak channeling Hamlet as the titular devil in *The Devil* (1972)

and occupying forces. While *Dziady* has become one of Poland's most important literary works, Mickiewicz and the type of nineteenth-century Polish Romanticism he represented were directly associated with political resistance. Mickiewicz's dramas and epic poems frequently served as the inspiration for wide-scale protests from the nineteenth century on; for example, the beginning of student protests in Poland in 1968 related to the government banning a theatrical performance of *Dziady*.

A four-part Gothic drama, *Dziady* features various tales of suffering and includes ghosts seeking redemption, tragic love, suicide, and so on. One of the recurring characters, Gustaw, has returned from death by suicide to lament his unrequited love and bears much in common with Jakub. The unnamed antagonist of *The Devil* is also like a spirit out of *Dziady*, and it is unclear if he is a ghost, demon, or madman. His aim to rescue Jakub from prison evokes the third part of *Dziady*, where the protagonist is a revolutionary, rotting away in prison. Likewise, *Dziady* functions as a morality play, with symbolic figures representing the journey to salvation and the struggle with God's seeming indifference. This is echoed in *The Devil*, in which Jakub wanders a cruel and chaotic universe populated with figures like courtiers, nuns, and theatrical players adapting *Hamlet*.

Żuławski undoubtedly knew that *Hamlet* has often been interpreted as a play with strong themes of political dissent, particularly within the Soviet Union and its satellite states: it is fundamentally about a prince who conspires to murder a king. As in *Hamlet*, Jakub was prepared to sacrifice all to assassinate the king, but comes to learn that his sacrifice may have been for nothing because of the corruption in his own family. And like Konrad, the vampiric prisoner hell-bent on revenge in *Dziady*, he is monstrous, yet also heroic. The titular devil encourages him to perform a ritual "cleansing," which comes to mean blood-spilling and throat-slitting.

The film's correlation between deranged murders and political liberators, cleansing the world of injustice one slit throat at a time, enraged the Polish government. The film's vitriol against oppression emerges most clearly in this final act, and if there is a central thesis, it is in a telling line of dialogue from Jakub's nameless fiancée: "Deprivation is when people live by ideals that are not their own. An even worse deprivation is when they stop protesting. And the worst deprivation is passive consent."

In my interview with writer and Żuławski collaborator Daniel Bird (2016), he notes that "officially, the film was banned for upsetting Catholics. Unofficially, it was because the film alludes to the role of the minister of the interior in the student riots of March '68 which resulted in a purge of Jews from the Polish Communist Party." This refers to General Mieczysław Moczar, minister of the interior, who used the demonstrations in defense of *Dziady* as an excuse to begin a largely antisemitic but also anti-intellectual attack. It forced thousands to emigrate from the country, seriously depleting a Jewish population that had nearly been wiped out two decades earlier.

These protests continued with events like the December 1970 Gdańsk shipyard riots, a chaotic scene straight out of *The Devil*. In *Poland Under Communism: A Cold War History* (2008), Anthony Kemp-Welch writes, "About 10,000 people went on the rampage. Looting took place, particularly of luxury items such as furs. Symbols of privilege and status, such as cars parked in front of the Hotel Monopol, were set on fire. Twenty militiamen were hospitalized, five with serious injuries. No figures for civilian casualties were recorded. The militia announced 16 arrests 'for vandalism and petty theft.' This figure was rightly disbelieved. Secret reports to Warsaw reported 330 arrests." It later came to light that in these riots close to fifty people were killed, more than one thousand were wounded, and more than three thousand arrested. It is no wonder that with the treatment faced by *Dziady* and the harsh crackdown on censorship, *The Devil* was rapidly banned and Żuławski was forced to relocate to France. He wouldn't release another film in Poland for twenty-five years.

Samm Deighan

OUTTAKE: *IDI I SMOTRI* (*COME AND SEE*, 1985), ELEM KLIMOV, SOVIET UNION

Elem Klimov's devastating Иди и смотри (*Come and See*, 1985) is one of the most important, affecting war films in cinema history, a project Klimov fought to create for nearly a decade. Set in Belarus in 1943, the film follows the young Flyora (Aleksey Kravchenko), who digs up a cache of guns and sets out to join partisan resistance fighters but finds himself lost in a surreal, apocalyptic hellscape. This deceptively simple narrative presents a transgressive contrast to the majority of Soviet cinema. While it is one of the last great films of the Soviet Union, it is also

Russian poster for *Come and See* (1985)

the culmination of a rare, subversive branch of Soviet war films that share the central thesis that human suffering is the only possible outcome of war. This message is in direct defiance of the Communist Party's mythologizing the Soviet Union's role in the war as fundamentally victorious, just, and heroic.

Soviet directors were generally expected to conform to the tenets of socialist realism and produce films with optimistic, propagandistic narratives. Historical period settings were popular, particularly World War II movies featuring heroic Soviet partisans fighting evil Nazis and their capitalist collaborators, though these rarely exhibited any nuance or explored the horrific reality of war. Certain rebellious figures were occasionally able to push beyond the bounds of acceptable cinematic content. The unexpected success of Mikhail Kalatozov's downbeat Летят журавли (*The Cranes Are Flying*, 1957)—which focuses on how one young woman's life is devastated by the war—slowly encouraged filmmakers in

Partisans gathering around the skeleton of a German soldier in *Come and See* (1985)

the '60s and '70s to explore more realistic depictions of World War II and its impact on ordinary people.

Come and See developed out of such cracks in the system, particularly building on the themes explored in films like Andrei Tarkovsky's Иваново детство (*Ivan's Childhood*, 1962), a haunting antiwar polemic that follows a child's nonlinear journey through war-torn Russia. An even more crucial—and personal—influence was Larisa Shepitko's grueling Восхождение (*The Ascent*, 1977), a brutal rejection of socialist realism that follows two partisan fighters struggling to survive in Belarus. Shepitko, Klimov's wife, battled with the censors for years to complete and release her harrowing and surprisingly spiritual film about the sacrifice inherent in war. Shepitko utterly discards the expected character trope of heroic Soviet partisans and instead depicts men decimated by violence, willing to do anything to survive. She was only able to release the film intact because a high-ranking Soviet official and former partisan fighter was moved at the premiere and intervened on her behalf.

Shepitko tragically died in a car accident in 1979, and in many ways, *Come and See* can be seen as Klimov's continuation of her project to smash the Soviet myths about its role in World War II; it takes the surreal elements and profound despair of *The Ascent* to the ultimate extremes. Instead

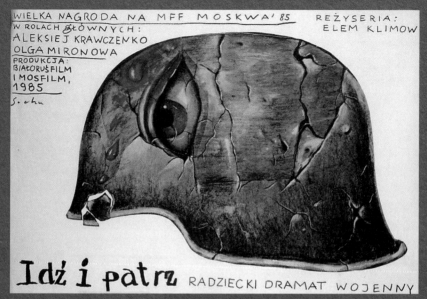

Polish poster for *Come and See* (1985)

of focusing on experienced, hardened partisan fighters, it follows two children. Flyora, a boy in his early teens, encounters the equally young and innocent Glasha (Olga Mironova), who accompanies him on his journey home, where they discover that his entire village has been massacred. Ultimately, they encounter a Waffen-SS Einsatzgruppen unit. Flyora watches as they force the members of a village into a church and set the building on fire; Glasha is gang-raped.

Evoking both a war documentary and experimental arthouse cinema, *Come and See* presents an incredibly visceral record of events in Belarus that is largely historically accurate. Klimov witnessed the horrific siege of Stalingrad as a child—allegedly fleeing the city with his family while the Volga River burned—and his cowriter, Ales Adamovich, was a Belarusian partisan fighter. The Nazi unit Flyora and Glasha come across was likely meant to evoke the notorious SS Special Commando Dirlewanger, run by a convicted pedophile. While they were ordered to target Jews and partisans, they indiscriminately tortured, raped, and slaughtered unarmed civilians throughout Belarus and were responsible for the deaths of tens of thousands of people in the region. Though the modern perception of World War II is that most of its victims died in Nazi concentration camps and death camps, the reality is that vast numbers of people were killed in Central and Eastern Europe in Soviet and Nazi massacres—particularly in

Poland, Belarus, and Ukraine—where entire communities were shot and dumped in mass graves or slaughtered in their towns.

The Soviet tendency to rewrite history is mirrored in many Soviet war films, where the atrocities committed by both Nazi and Soviet forces were downplayed, falsified, or erased. *Come and See* is so harrowing not only because of the atrocities it depicts, but in the way Klimov explores the meaninglessness and depravity of total war. Guilt is a major feature of the film, as Flyora struggles to process the horrors he has witnessed and make sense of his place in such an apocalyptic universe. *Come and See* is an important counterexample not only to the majority of Soviet war films, but to mainstream war films in general, where violence is often given a moral justification. Klimov presents it as ultimately senseless, without meaning or purpose. Following Flyora's nightmarish, highly sensory experiences, the audience becomes culpable and Klimov seems to suggest that such violence permeates the world, leaving behind a miasma that spreads through generations.

Samm Deighan

CRUEL STORIES OF YOUTH

Japanese Leftist Politics from the New Wave to the Pink Film

From roughly 1959 to 1971, Japan faced a tumultuous political period marked by a series of widespread revolts of increasing intensity. This began with the Anpo protests from 1959 to 1960, when Japan was set to renew the United States–Japan Security Treaty. Originally established in 1952 and meant to be renewed every decade, the treaty allowed for a US military presence within Japan. Left-wing student organizations kicked off a series of protests around the country that often involved daily actions at universities and government buildings. Thousands were involved in what became one of the largest protests in Japanese history. Increasingly violent clashes with police resulted in the death of a student activist in 1960.

These ongoing Security Treaty protests—which recurred in 1970—were a reaction against the American military occupation and perceived American consumerist, imperialist influences on Japanese society. But these protests also represented the fear held by many students and young leftists that the Japanese government would return to a prewar, feudalistic type of conservatism. They were also just the beginning. As Isolde Standish writes in *Politics, Porn and Protest: Japanese Avant-Garde Cinema in the 1960s and 1970s* (2011), "Three opposition movements converged at this time: the anti-Vietnam movement intensified its struggle between 1968 and 1969 in anticipation of Japan's right to terminate the US-Japan Joint Security Treaty in 1970; the movement for the return of Okinawa to Japanese sovereignty which abated with the Sato-Nixon Communiqué of 1969 in which the United States agreed to return Okinawa to Japan in 1972; and the university struggles (zenkyōtō) of 1968–1969."

As young leftists became increasingly frustrated and disappointed by the outcomes of these protests, some found alternate means to exercise their political beliefs. A handful of young directors—several of whom started out as radical student protesters and most of whom were active leftists—took political action to the screen, particularly throughout the '60s and early '70s. This group, which includes directors like Nagisa Oshima, Shohei Imamura, Yoshishige Yoshida, Hiroshi Teshigahara, and Masahiro Shinoda, became known as the Japanese New Wave. Though this should be considered more as a loose movement than a unified school, the films in the Japanese New Wave generally share a series of recurring themes, beginning roughly in 1959 with Oshima's *Ai to kibô no machi* (*A Town of Love and Hope*): bitter criticism of Japanese society, depictions of youth crime and youth culture, explicit sexuality, violence, leftist politics, and a focus on poverty and class issues.

As David Desser notes in his seminal study *Eros Plus Massacre: An Introduction to the Japanese New Wave Cinema* (1988), "Certain Japanese filmmakers used cinema as a tool, a weapon in a cultural struggle." Many of these films posit that sexual liberation can lead to political or social freedom, and likewise equate sexual repression with social repression. Because of their growing personal frustrations with the perceived failure of leftist protest movements, their increasingly violent films came to suggest that sexual violence was the result of political repression. For example, Oshima's films frequently focus on young adults who are utterly alienated from Japanese society but who are unable to find purpose or solace in radical politics. This frustration with political activism is often directly stated to stem from past disappointments. Instead, they turn to nihilistic expressions of crime and violence, as well as hedonistic descents into sexuality—and sexual violence.

But transgressive sexuality was not only the purvey of New Wave arthouse cinema. In the '60s and especially into the '70s, there was an explosion of *pinku eiga* (pink film), or softcore sex films, which led to the "pinky violence" subgenre in the early '70s. Awash with escaped convicts, rebellious students, and violent gangs, both the softcore and pinky violence films provide a parallel example of explicit, often shocking sexuality as an outlet for political dissent. This chapter will explore the connection between transgressive sexuality and radical politics in Japanese cinema of the '60s and early '70s, beginning with the work of key New Wave directors like Oshima and continuing through the explicit pink films of radical leftists Koji Wakamatsu and his collaborator Masao Adachi, into the pinky violence films of the '70s from directors like Norifumi Suzuki and Teruo Ishii.

It is important to note that the similarities in explicit sexual content between New Wave arthouse films, softcore sex movies, and cheap grindhouse fare resulted from a relatively unique set of circumstances. Much of this has to do with the somewhat singular development of the Japanese New Wave. In some ways, it can be compared to other "New Wave" or left-leaning cinematic movements in other countries throughout the twentieth century: Soviet cinema of the '20s, Brechtian theater in the '20s and '30s, the French New Wave of the '50s and '60s, and the Czech New Wave in the '60s. Like these movements, the Japanese New Wave sought to criticize both government and society. Desser writes, "The Japanese New Wave movement, while it did not necessarily define its concrete ends, may be said to have been concerned with creating a film content and form capable of revealing the contradictions within Japanese society and with isolating the culture's increasingly materialist values and its imperialist alliances."

But unlike most of the other leftist film movements, Japanese New Wave emerged out of the commercial studio system. In this way, it is something of a paradox. Due to plummeting box office revenues, the formerly traditional, conservative major studios in Japan were desperate to attract new audiences. Partly, studios wanted younger talents to create bolder, edgier films aimed at younger generations. So in a break with established studio system structure, inexperienced filmmakers like Oshima and Yoshida were promoted early to the role of full director by Shochiku, one of the "big four" studios in Japan at the time, along with Toho, Toei, and Kadokowa.

This shift in hiring practices was meant to accommodate the growing need for youth culture films, at least in part. The 1956 hit *Taiyō no kisetsu* (*Season of the Sun*, 1956), about a group of carefree, somewhat hedonistic high school boys, resulted in a craze known as the *taiyozoku* (sun tribe) series—loosely equivalent to Hollywood's youth revolt melodramas like *Rebel Without a Cause* (1955). This led to other wildly popular subgenres like biker movies and yakuza gangster films. This is likewise how other big-name studios like Nikkatsu came to focus on pink films and Toei later churned out pinky violence movies by the dozen. Studios were desperate to find directors who could accommodate the popular demand for an increasing number of cult movie subgenres about disaffected, sex-obsessed teens and young adults. But several of the young Shochiku directors were—or had recently been—students, and nearly all of them had ties to left-wing political organizations and protest movements. So instead of delivering a series of more lighthearted movies like *Season of the Sun*, the early New Wave directors provided a harsh, often nihilistic critique of Japanese society. Particularly scathing of the American military occupation, they also skewered gender norms, traditional social values, and conservative politics and grappled with Japan's violent history. Cinema became the most viable form of political action for many of these young, angry film-makers, who were frustrated that protesting didn't achieve their aims.

Dry Lake, aka *Youth in Fury* (1960)

While all the New Wave directors made films about issues within Japanese society, Nagisa Oshima and Yoshishige Yoshida explored political violence most overtly. For example, Shohei Imamura's films focus primarily on the bleak despair of postwar Japan, particularly the impact this has on the lives of women and the ways in which families exploit one another. Masahiro Shinoda often used historical settings and genre themes—like samurai and yakuza movie tropes—to focus on how tormented outsiders function in society. But there are a few notable early exceptions, particularly Shinoda's 1960 film *Kawaita mizuumi* (*Dry Lake*, aka *Youth in Fury*). Like Oshima's early work, the film essentially bridges the carefree taiyozoku film with grittier, more nihilistic themes as it follows a young man drawn to political protests, though he doesn't seem to engage with them fully because he's obsessed with looking and seeming cool. Another important example is Susumu Hani's *Mitasareta seikatsu* (*A Full Life*, 1962). Though Hani, who got his start as a documentarian, is not generally considered one of the main New Wave directors and his work has not been as internationally celebrated as theirs, he was an important early influence on the younger directors. *A Full Life* is a continuation of these themes with a decidedly feminist angle. When a young woman (Ineko Arima) becomes dissatisfied with her life and especially her marriage, she is willing to try anything, including joining a politically radical theater troupe, and has a political awakening that draws her into the Anpo protests.

But the most important film of the early '60s to begin to explore these themes is undoubtedly Oshima's *Seishun zankoku monogatari* (*Cruel Story of Youth*, 1960). The young Makoto (Miyuki Kawano again) hitchhikes to get

Cruel Story of Youth (1960)

a ride home, but the driver tries to assault her. She is rescued by Kiyoshi (Yūsuke Kawazu), and there is an immediate attraction. He takes her on what is presumably a date: first to the Anpo protests and then to a picturesque river, where he rapes her. Despite this, they fall in love and Makoto moves into the hovel Kiyoshi shares with a roommate. They find money to live on—and presumably entertainment—by developing a scheme that is a reenactment of the circumstances in which they met: Makoto hitchhikes and flirts with older male drivers who pick her up, then Kiyoshi accuses them of molesting her and demands money. Their relationship spirals further into crime, but after she becomes pregnant and is coerced into having an abortion, Makoto begins to have doubts about their future.

Many of Oshima's characters are young adults who embrace nihilism, hedonism, and crime as a rebellious way to reject political activism. As in *Nihon no yoru to kiri* (*Night and Fog in Japan*, 1960), Kiyoshi and Makoto are contrasted with an older generation, Makoto's sister Yuki (Yoshiko Kuga) and her ex-boyfriend (Fumio Watanbe), who were once politically active but have abandoned their radicalism for lives that are revealed to be dull and disappointing. As Desser notes, *Cruel Story of Youth* substitutes a kind of nihilistic desire "in place of political action and in place of dreams." The older generation of activists live in squalor and misery; Watanabe's character was once a passionate leftist but has become an abortionist in a back-alley clinic. The defiant teen generation represented by Makoto and Kiyoshi seems determined to avoid the heartbreak and disappointment of the failure of political protest—and having political ideals in general—by any means necessary.

Desser notes that "youth, sex, violence, and politics" are "the essence of the New Wave and the essence of the '60s." Many of the early New Wave films, particularly those directed by Oshima, focus on the problem of young adults attempting to establish their own identity—inextricably connected to expressions of sexuality and political awareness. Desser explains, "To change society, one first had to define society; to change one's self meant first defining this self." Oshima's films grapple with how the young, emerging self is a product of society and how it seeks to be separate, distinct from society.

This theme—and the tension between different generations of protesters—is even more overt in *Night and Fog in Japan*, one of the most important early films of the New Wave. Two different generations of student radicals come together at the wedding of a former student protester, Nozawa (Fumio Watanabe), to the younger radical Reiko (Miyuki Kuwano). As in real life, these leftists were part of the Zengakuren—the student protest association—who demonstrated loudly and sometimes violently at the

Anpo protests in 1950 and 1959–60. The confrontation at the wedding is between these two generations a decade apart; the younger radicals accuse the older group of abandoning their principles. This is further complicated when one of Nozawa's friends becomes a Stalinist and another commits suicide. This death that rocks their community refers to a real-life event: in 1960, a young student, Michiko Kanba, was killed on the most violent day of clashes between students and police over the Security Treaty. *Night and Fog in Japan* references this loss and particularly reflects a sense of anxiety about whether the sacrifices made by the older generation of leftists was worth it, or whether it even amounted to any social progress. Many of Oshima's early films express this sense of bitterness and frustration—which was clearly very personal to him—with the Japanese leftist movements to accomplish any positive changes.

Night and Fog in Japan was a sensation at the time, not only because of its experimental, expressionistic stylistic elements and theatrical, layered quality with voice-overs and numerous disorienting flashback sequences. Though Shochiku gave its new generation of directors more creative control, the studio thought Oshima went too far with the film. Its release also coincided with the assassination of Inejirō Asanuma, a socialist politician, by a radical, right-wing student. In horror, Shochiku pulled the film from theaters, and Oshima was outraged by what he viewed as political censorship. But several of the young directors of the emerging New Wave would gain further support from the Art Theatre Guild (ATG), another important influence. ATG began as an independent film distribution company, with the aim of bringing European arthouse films to Japan, but the company soon added a film production branch. ATG became a major force in producing and promoting the films of the New Wave directors, as it hoped to foster an avant-garde arthouse movement within Japan to rival radical European cinema. This allowed directors like Oshima to go much further than they would have with the backing of Shochiku alone.

Oshima's films of the '60s and early '70s reflect this freedom. Several of his films to follow use instances of sexual violence to criticize the government and explore issues of guilt, personal responsibility, and social causes of crime. For example, *Hakuchū no tōrima* (*Violence at Noon*, 1968) follows a housemaid, Shino (Saeda Kawaguchi), whose mistress is raped and murdered by Eisuke (Kei Satō). It's revealed that he and Shino are from the same village and that Shino was also raped by Eisuke after she inadvertently survived a double suicide attempt with her lover at the time. The women in Eisuke's life, including his wife (Akiko Koyama) and Shino, protect his identity and shield

Do-yun Yu as the character R in *Death by Hanging* (1968)

him from the police. It is suggested throughout the film that they don't want Eisuke punished, because his violent, criminal behavior is not his own fault but is an inevitable result of factors like World War II, postwar poverty, and the American occupation of Japan.

Kōshikei (*Death by Hanging*, 1968) provides an even more overt, incendiary exploration of this thesis that if social misery, poverty, and widespread alienation cause crime, it is unjust to punish individual criminals. *Death by Hanging* follows the execution of R (Do-yun Yu), an ethnic Korean convicted of the rape and murder of two Japanese girls. When R survives his execution—or returns to life after death—with no memory of his crimes, the question arises whether this is the original R or a different person entirely. The prison officials go to absurd lengths to reenact his crimes and trigger his memory, to prove that he is still the same person, guilty of murder and deserving of punishment. Debates break out among the officials whether it is legal to execute a person twice, and whether it is ethical to execute the young man who was once R if R's soul left the body during the first execution. Oshima uses numerous Brechtian performance and editing techniques to reveal that the prison guards and officials have their own criminal pasts and to ultimately suggest that the very audience watching the film is culpable in R's crimes.

Like most of Oshima's films, *Death by Hanging* states—quite explicitly through a line of dialogue—that crime and violence are direct products of Japanese state imperialism and postwar collusion with the American government. Oshima's use of intimate, sexual violence as a symbol for the state's oppression and exploitation of its own people is a key hallmark of the types

Yûko Kusunoki as Itsuko Masaoka in *Eros + Massacre* (1969)

of political themes in Japanese New Wave cinema, which would also, perhaps naturally, extend into Japanese pink films. As Isolde Standish notes, "Male sexual impotence is a powerful metaphor for the human failures of postwar Japanese society" in Oshima's films and also in those of his colleague Yoshishige Yoshida (also frequently known as Kiju Yoshida). Like Oshima, Yoshida got his start with Shochiku but likewise left after they interfered with one of his films. Following in Oshima's footsteps, he formed his own film company and would partner with ATG to make increasingly radical projects in the late '60s and early '70s.

Like Oshima, many of Yoshida's films of the '60s focused on fraught sexual relationships, particularly the affairs of married women, which are often described as "anti-melodrama." Like director Shohei Imamura, Yoshida and his spouse and key collaborator from this period on, accomplished performer Mariko Okada, used the difficult lives of women in Japan as a platform to explore larger social injustices. After Yoshida and Okada's anti-melodramas of the mid-'60s, they merged those domestic themes with a labyrinthine exploration of leftist politics in *Erosu purasu gyakusatsu* (*Eros + Massacre*, 1969). Inspired by the life and assassination of anarchist Sakae Osugi, Yoshida's lengthy film cuts back and forth between past and present. The past narrative follows Osugi (Toshiyuki Hosokawa) in the 1910s and his complicated open marriage and his relationships with his lovers, one of whom wants to die with him (Okada) and one of whom attempts to kill him (Yûko Kusunoki). The intersecting present narrative follows two students, Wada (Daijirô Harada) and Eiko (also Okada), researching Osugi's political radicalism and his approach to free love. They are also fascinated by other revolutionaries, particularly those who have died violently.

Similar to the way many of Oshima's films express a frustration with the organized left, *Eros + Massacre* explores the myriad effects of Osugi's radical political beliefs. While *Eros + Massacre* and its focus on female protagonists suggests that Yoshida supports sexual freedom for women and a break from restrictive traditional gender norms, the film also shows how Osugi's form of free love is selfish and destructive. It results in his attempted murder and ultimately his assassination by the military. In a 1970 *Cahiers du cinéma* interview,

Eros + Massacre director and cowriter Yoshishige Yoshida at the film's French premiere in 1969

Yoshida said, "The fundamental theme is: how to change the world, and what is it that needs to be changed? Reflecting on the present situation through the medium of an era already past, I came to believe that Osugi's problems continue to be ours.... Osugi was oppressed by the power of the state in his political activities. But most of all, he spoke of free love, which has the power to destroy the monogamous structure, then the family, and finally the state. And it was this very escalation that the state could not allow."

Eros + Massacre has a confrontationally avant-garde, even psychedelic style, replete with windows, mirrors, reflections, and dissolves from past into present, ultimately folding the two time periods into one another. Like the later work of Jean-Luc Godard, it can be seen as a filmic essay that explores the effects of the past on the present. Yoshida shows Osugi's impact on Japanese political thought in the 1900s—when he was ultimately executed for his radicalism—into the late 1960s, where he is shown to be no less incendiary. And as with Oshima's films like *Death by Hanging*, Yoshida uses acts of violence— particularly sexual violence or sexually motivated violence—to explore how individual identity is not unique but is made up of a series of determinants: society, family, government, tradition, history, etc. Yoshida would continue with these themes in what became a loose trilogy that includes *Rengoku*

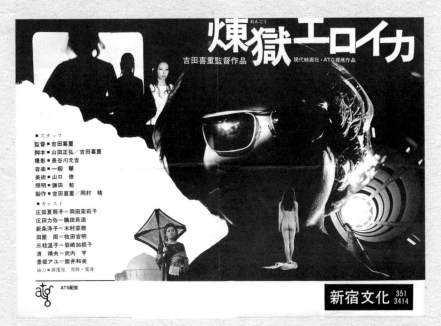

Heroic Purgatory (1970)

eroica (*Heroic Purgatory*, 1970), about a man who thinks back on his radical youth and a planned assassination, and *Kaigenrei* (*Coup d'État*, 1973), about an attempted right-wing coup and the resulting violence.

Though Oshima and Yoshida explored the intersection of leftist politics and transgressive sexuality the most overtly of all the New Wave directors, pink film master Koji Wakamatsu has many thematic similarities, particularly to Oshima. After allegedly starting out in a branch of the Tokyo yakuza, Wakamatsu found his way into film with Nikkatsu studios in the early '60s. He gravitated toward exploitation movies and pink films, such as *Kabe no naka no himegoto* (*Secrets Behind the Wall*, 1965), about a young voyeur driven to sado-sexual violence in an apartment complex where many of the residents explore their own sexual fantasies. This includes a politically relevant sex scene between a repressed housewife and a scarred communist—directly in front of a portrait of Stalin. Isolde Standish writes, "*Secrets Behind the Wall* makes complex connections through sexual 'deviances' and male inadequacies between the alienating effects of the modern urban housing estates (*danchi*), the high pressure education system, Hiroshima bomb victims and the Anpo struggles."

The apartment complex can be seen as a microcosm of postwar social decay in Japan. It was particularly offensive to mainstream critics because, through the perverse characters he depicts, Wakamatsu portrays a darker, more scandalous side of Japan, divorced from the conventional stereotypes of hardworking businessmen and their obedient wives. This emphasis on the "real," darker, sado-sexual side of Japan would become a major focus of his films, along with an interest in adapting real-life stories of violence to the screen. When *Secrets Behind the Wall*—and Wakamatsu's intention to treat it as a serious art film meant to be shared with an international audience— proved too much for Nikkatsu, he broke off and formed his own film company, much like the other New Wave directors. There he was free to produce and direct pink films with far more subversive agendas and extremely confrontational sexual violence.

Wakamatsu's key collaborator from this period was Masao Adachi, a fellow leftist and film director in his own right, who wrote many of Wakamatsu's radical pink films. This includes *Taiji ga mitsuryô suru toki* (*The Embryo Hunts in Secret*, 1966); *Okasareta hakui* (*Violated Angels*, 1967), based on Richard Speck's infamous massacre of student nurses in California in 1966; and *Yuke yuke nidome no shojo* (*Go, Go Second Time Virgin*, 1969). Wakamatsu and Adachi were the most politically radical out of all the directors associated with the Japanese New Wave. They would go on to direct *Sekigun-P.F.L.P.: Sekai sensô sengen* (*Red Army/PFLP: Declaration of World War*, 1971) together, a newsreel film about the Palestinian liberation movement. This would result in Adachi joining the Japanese Red Army; he moved to Lebanon and left filmmaking behind for two decades, though he would return to the medium in the mid-2000s. Wakamatsu was penalized in Japan and refused entry into the US for his own time spent in Palestine.

Adachi also directed several sex films in his own right, including *Jogakusei gerira* (*Female Student Guerrilla*, 1969). This sexualized tale of teenage student delinquents turned radicals depicts some Zenkyōtō-like activities but takes things much further with a story about a group of students who steal weapons for guerrilla warfare to disrupt a school ceremony. Adachi was one of few directors to confront the sexism inherent to the protest movements of the period, which is largely the theme of *Female Student Guerrilla*. His persecuted and violent schoolgirls would prefigure the girl gangs to come in the pinky violence films of the early '70s. *Female Student Guerilla* also predicted the 1972 Asama-Sansō incident. In the film, the girls use a mountain hideout as their base. The radical leftist group the United Red Army turned a mountain lodge into a massacre after a violent internal purge that left fifteen people dead and resulted in a hostage standoff with the police, which lasted over a week.

Adachi and Wakamatsu's work in this period confronts this rupture in leftist movements that led to their decline in Japan later in the '70s. The failures, the disagreements, and the general boredom of waiting around for revolution to happen—and the violence that breeds—was the subject of several of their films. Wakamatsu's *Seizoku* (*Sex Jack*, 1970), written by Adachi, contains similar subject matter and focuses on a small group of male leftist revolutionaries. This somewhat futuristic film follows their activities as they hide out in a tenement apartment. While they wait, they take turns having sex with a

Female Student Guerrilla (1969)

woman who seems to be tolerating this in the spirit of supporting the revolution they all hope is impending. Standish writes that this is "based on the actual successful hijacking of a Japan Airlines plane in March 1970 to North Korea by a militant faction of the Japanese Red Army; the fictitious characters of the film, ostensibly in hiding from the police, are the second group waiting their turn to hijack another plane."

Wakamatsu's bigger-budget, more ambitious *Tenshi no kōkotsu* (*Ecstasy of the Angels*, 1972)—with another script from Adachi—serves as a loose sequel to *Sex Jack* and a response to the Asama-Sansō incident. The film effectively reenacts the violent few weeks leading up to the slaughter and hostage incident; it follows a group of revolutionaries who descend into an orgy of violence after their mission to steal weapons from a US army base. The vision of revolution presented by *Ecstasy of the Angels* is thoroughly nihilistic, even morally reprehensible. It can be seen as the death knell of Japanese New Wave films that blended sexual transgression and leftist politics. If anything, it resembles the violent spectacles of blood, swords, and bullets often found in the yakuza films of the early '70s and represents a dissolution of the New Wave into genre cinema.

Around 1970–71, sexualized depictions of youth resistance were largely relegated to exploitation films made for the grindhouse market, like the pinky violence subgenre. While this is a nebulous subgenre that implies a

Japanese student protesters with bamboo spears and their iconic helmets, Tokyo, October 1971

Members of the Japanese Red Army

combination of sex and violence on-screen, it generally refers to films where teen girls and young women form gangs and the protagonists overcome both internal violence from other women and external violence from authority figures who are usually male (prison wardens, heads of yakuza gangs, and school superintendents). In all of them, the female characters are generally tough and violent, but also very sexual, often defiantly so.

The type of pinky violence films most aligned with New Wave political films are known as *sukeban* (or girl gang) movies, as seen in series like the *Kyōfu joshikōkō* (*Terrifying Girls' High School*). This run of four films made between 1972 and 1973 loosely takes the structure of the women-in-prison film and transports it to a Japanese girls' high school; the school is a competitive, violent place where there is no escape for many of the girls. Young women are preyed upon by their peers, their teachers, their gangster boyfriends, and especially school principals and superintendents, who are often shown to sexually exploit and rape their students. Norifumi Suzuki's *Kyōfu joshikōkō: bōkō rinchi kyōshitsu* (*Terrifying Girls' High School: Lynch Law Classroom*, 1973) is a key example: rival gang leaders (pinky violence queens Reiko Ike and Miki Sugimoto) put aside their differences at a corrupt high school to take down an out-of-control student discipline unit who tortures and murders students, the repressive administration that gives them power, and a corrupt politician trying to cover it all up. The film ends with the girls occupying and destroying the school, then having a violent standoff with the cops.

Films like *Terrifying Girls' High School: Lynch Law Classroom* can be seen as a reflection of the student protests of the period, which were partly a reaction to the university acceptance process. Students realized some preferential individuals, like children of businessmen and politicians, were being admitted without the proper qualifications. As Desser writes, "The highly competitive entrance exams to all colleges, and the relatively few high school graduates who attend four-year colleges and universities, make admission

Terrifying Girls' High School: Women's Violent Classroom (1972)

to any school a significant achievement. Thus, the understandable outrage at admissions based on political or economic favoritism. The protests blossomed into a nearly full-fledged revolt against the school authorities who, in typical administration shortsightedness, felt a crackdown on students was better than negotiation."

A real-life record of these protests can be found in the documentary films of Shinsuke Ogawa, like *Assatsu no mori: Takasaki Keizai Daigaku toso no kiroku* (*Forest of Oppression: A Record of the Struggle at Takasaki City*, 1967), and Michiko Sasaki later in the '70s. But the growing cultural association between teen angst and political revolt can be seen as a way to discredit legitimate leftist politics. The early '70s were a particularly fraught period in leftist political history in Japan. In general, radical groups disbanded or became far more violent, as in the case of the Japanese Red Army. Standish writes, "By the late 1960s, those who were intent on pursuing a leftist agenda were pushed further towards a radical politics which culminated in the formation of the Japanese Red Army Faction in 1969 and the violent uprisings known as the Tokyo, Osaka and Kobe wars."

Within cinema, there were increasingly fewer arthouse examples to compare to the films of the '60s. Exceptions include Kaneto Shindo's *Hadaka no Jukyu-sai* (*Live Today, Die Tomorrow!*, 1970), about a young man driven to violence by the extreme poverty of his surroundings. Oshima was not to be deterred and released his poetic, existential mystery *Tôkyô sensô sengo hiwa* (*The Man Who Left His Will on Film*, 1970) before turning to more controversial subject matter later in the decade—with Wakamatsu's help. And though directors like Oshima, Yoshida, and Wakamatsu had long careers making films that continued to express their political values, 1972 represents the end of an era in many ways. It effectively closed the book on the political protest movements that began in 1960 with the Anpo Security Treaty protests, surged with the global protests of 1968, and waned with the rise of the Japanese Red Army. As Gavin Walker writes in *The Red Years: Theory, Politics, and Aesthetics in the Japanese '68* (2020), these films capture "the isolation of the cell, the melancholia of defeat, the sexual micropolitics of the sect, the tragic efforts to pierce through the frozen landscapes of power into a sense of historical action." Wakamatsu's focus on what Walker describes as "the cruel blockages of revolutionary politics" represents not a stopping point, but a pause to be resumed by future generations of leftist filmmakers.

Samm Deighan

OUTTAKE: *DI YI LEI XING WEI XIAN (DANGEROUS ENCOUNTERS OF THE FIRST KIND, 1981)*, TSUI HARK, HONG KONG

In Tsui Hark's 1981 film *Di yi lei xing wei xian* (*Dangerous Encounters of the First Kind*), four disaffected youths set out on a spree of stochastic violence. Using bombs and Molotov cocktails as their weapons of choice, high school friends Paul (Albert Au), Lung (Tin Sang Lung), and Ko (Paul Che), along with antisocial misfit Pearl (Chen-Chi Lin), randomly attack

Dangerous Encounters of the First Kind (1981)

moviegoers in a theater and public bathrooms and take a bus of tourists hostage. Eventually, they get embroiled with local gangsters, international gunrunners, and the Royal Hong Kong Police. It is a bleak film, brimming with confused anger and a brand of violent teenage angst that can almost be described as anarchistic. The level of violence against an innocent populace (as well as animals) makes the reason for its eventual censorship apparent, but when you watch the version that Hark was forced to reshoot—which turns its four leads into hit-and-run thrill killers instead of amateur bomb makers—it is in many ways just as violent and disturbing. So why was the original cut of this film deemed to be so *dangerous*?

In 1967, a wave of strikes and labor disputes spread across British-occupied Hong Kong. The most violent of these initial clashes occurred on May 6, when fully armored riot police were called in to quash a protest at an artificial flower factory in New Kowloon. Several strikers were beaten and arrested, and when union leaders and picketers showed up to the police station to protest the arrest, they too were beaten and taken into custody. The following day, a mass of people took to the streets, belting out communist slogans and wielding Mao's Little Red Book. Hundreds of arrests were made, and in the weeks following, at least ten protesters were reported to have been beaten or shot to death by members of the police.

As the summer of 1967 began to heat up, so too did the tactics of the radicals. The initial throwing of stones and bottles at riot police soon gave way to hurling makeshift bombs. Police stations and bourgeois strongholds

Dangerous Encounters of the First Kind (1981)

(such as banks, money lenders, and right-wing newspapers) soon had to undergo intense fortifications to withstand these assaults. Police violence and repression also increased, but the general population at this point continued to be mostly sympathetic to what was turning into an open rebellion. This goodwill began to waver, however, when the onslaught of bombings became increasingly indiscriminate. The anticommunist scholar Christine Lo writes in her book *Underground Front: The Chinese Communist Party in Hong Kong* that police defused upward of eight thousand homemade explosive devices during the summer of 1967, but about 70 percent of these bombs were "pineapples"—the local expression for harmless decoys. While the city was gripped by this terror, leftist newspapers and meeting sites were raided. "Red schools," where these explosive tactics were alleged to have originated, were forcibly disbanded by armed authorities representing the British Crown. The outcry against these raids was muted due to the real and present fear of dying in an explosion while out in public, and after a pair of young children (ages eight and two) were killed by a bomb outside their apartment complex, true panic took hold and the initial righteous reasons that led to the uprisings were suddenly harder to recall. After the Chinese premier addressed Hong Kong rioters with an appeal to stop all bombings, the violent historical moment came to a close.

The initial strike wave that led to this prolonged bombing campaign was inspired by two factors: the first and most obvious was the Cultural Revolution taking place in mainland China; the second, but perhaps most important, was the successful general strike in Portuguese-occupied Macau. This strike directly led to massive concessions from the Portuguese authorities to cede manufacturing and labor power to a board of workers who were believed to be directly represented by the Chinese Communist Party in Beijing. Workers and artisans in Hong Kong were inspired by the successful movement in Macau and saw their subsequent attempt to shift power away from Britain as an inevitable consequence of history. The speed at which their righteous anger turned to wanton violence through a campaign of bloody bombings and terror changed the calculus on the ground. What started as an organic outcry against unfair working conditions and colonial rule was soon overshadowed by the gruesome horror of exploding bombs. In the end, over fifty people were dead (although most of these deaths were at the hands of the police) and nearly a thousand were injured.

With the memory of this violence still relatively fresh in Hong Kongers' minds, and when a fresh round of labor protests began in 1981, the release

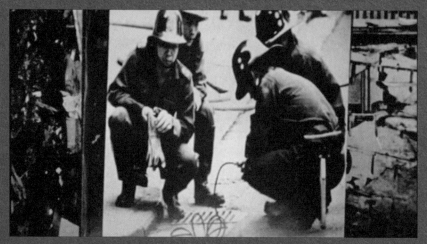

Hong Kong police investigating a "pineapple," the local term for one of the hundreds of harmless decoy bombs planted by radical protesters in 1967

of *Dangerous Encounters of the First Kind* was seen by the ruling elite as an existential threat. Tsui Hark's film—as he initially envisioned it—was a nihilistic thrill ride that would potentially remind a new generation of the destabilizing possibilities planting bombs can have during times of economic and labor strife. The exhibition of the film in its original form was deemed illegal. Everything that had to do with making bombs, planting bombs, setting off bombs, or even mentioning bombs had to be removed. In an early scene that was cut from the film, Paul shows his friends in stark detail how to put together a basic explosive: first, he drills a small pinhole into a wristwatch and attaches the necessary wiring to build the timer, then stuffs a smooth tube of volatile mercury fulminate into a pipe to create a proper initiator (also known as a fuse cap). Perhaps most shocking, splayed out on a nearby worktable is an assortment of keys, nails, and other dangerous pieces of shrapnel. The protagonists are not shown adding this material to their bombs, but the implication of its inclusion on the table is obvious.

What makes this film so hard to grapple with is the fact that none of its lead characters seem to be motivated by anything remotely political. Some are poor, some rich; Pearl, the lone female member of the group (and seeming ringleader), who baits the three male students into increasingly more harrowing attacks, is treated abysmally at work and home, but her way of passing the time involves torturing caged mice with pins and needles. This nonsimulated cruelty is hard to watch, making it difficult to fully sympathize with her class-based plights, and it forces the audience to grapple with the ever-present question: Is she a product of her harsh environment, or is she herself causing the environment to be harsher, more violent? Having no clear answer to this question makes their acts of violence seem pointless and cruel. But is this not precisely how the 1967 Hong Kong riots would have appeared to a teenager who may not have been well-versed in the political motivations behind the terror gripping his city? At seventeen years of age, Tsui Hark probably saw the wave of bombings as irrational terror writ large, not as the natural culmination of various historical forces and political actors attacking an oppressive colonial-based system impoverishing millions. The fear of suffering a fiery death is far more immediate and sensory than the fear of a lifetime of wage slavery and living in overcrowded slums.

It is important to note that many Hong Kong films in the '80s and '90s deal with political issues with varying degrees of subtlety. Extreme crime and horror films that were handed a Category III rating, equivalent to a hard R or NC-17 in the US, often depicted corruption in the courts and brutality by police. In many of these films, the police in mainland China were shown to be brutal and inept country bumpkins, while the Royal Hong Kong Police were easily bribed but often bogged down by bureaucracy. You could get away with a lot during this era before the 1997 handoff when Hong Kong ended its colonial tenure as a British protectorate, which is why the censure of a film like *Dangerous Encounters of the First Kind* is so fascinating. Here is a film that shows precisely where the line in the sand is drawn. The limitations of cinema as a vehicle for political transgression and artistic protest are laid bare, and Tsui Hark's willingness to play ball and reshoot half the movie is likely what ensured his lengthy career in the Hong Kong film industry. Many of the films he would go on to direct (or produce, or write, or appear in as an actor) are considered to be highly influential. But influential to what? Influential to whom? Beyond impacting filmmakers and other artists, *Dangerous Encounters of the First Kind* could have been a lit match when mixed with the volatile labor struggles and civil unrest bubbling up in 1981, so it stands to reason that it was snuffed out so soon. Hark's goal was merely to reflect and interpret the world, not necessarily to change it—and yet, whether he (or anyone else) knows it or not, he came very close to something truly radical.

Charles Perks

THE RELUCTANT GANGSTER IN HINDI CINEMA

Under a bridge at night, gangster Vijay meets his brother, police inspector Ravi. Their conversation is tense, pained. Vijay is a powerful Bombay don; Ravi has been tasked with bringing him in. "We rose from the same footpath," Vijay thunders. "Look at where you are today, and look at me. I have buildings, properties, wealth, a bungalow, a car. What do you have?" Ravi replies: "*Mere paas maa hai*"—"I have mother." It's one of the most famous scenes in Hindi cinema. The film is Yash Chopra's *Deewaar* (*The Wall*, 1975). The actors are Amitabh Bachchan, the biggest star in Hindi cinema then, as Vijay, and dreamboat Shashi Kapoor as Ravi. The writers are Salim Khan and Javed Akhtar, responsible for Bachchan's breakthrough film, Prakash Mehra's *Zanjeer* (*Shackles*, 1973), along with most of his iconic lines over two decades. It's Hindi melodrama at its purest: brother pitted against brother, a mother's love divided, tragedy underscoring everything. And there's another, unspoken layer of tragedy: Vijay never wanted to be a gangster. After their father is framed for theft and killed, Vijay and Ravi have to leave their village for Mumbai. There, Vijay becomes a shoeshine boy, then a dockworker, supporting his younger brother and daily-wager mother. With no prospects and nothing to offer except his explosive anger, he joins a crime ring and quickly rises to the top.

In an earlier scene, as familiar to Indian audiences as the meeting under the bridge referenced above, Ravi asks Vijay, in the presence of their mother, to sign a confession to his crimes. With cold fury, Vijay asks him to first get signatures from those who forced a false confession out of their father, and who threw their mother out of her home and tattooed "*mera baap chor hai*"

The Wall (1975)

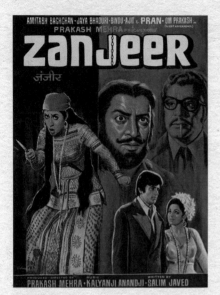

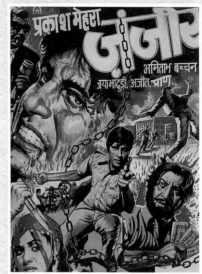

Shackles (1973)   *Shackles* (1973)

(my father is a thief) on his arm. He wins this exchange, just as Ravi wins the later one. The righteousness of Vijay's anger derives from his miserable circumstances, his helplessness in the face of destiny. He didn't choose this life, but he'll see it all the way to its tragic conclusion.

Any shortlist of landmark essays on cinema—Manny Farber's "White Elephant Art vs. Termite Art," Pauline Kael's "Trash, Art, and the Movies," Laura Mulvey's "Visual Pleasure and Narrative Cinema"—will likely include a 1948 piece by Robert Warshow published in *The Nation*, "The Gangster as Tragic Hero," which was written on the back of two decades of American gangster films, enough for Warshow to conclude that the genre was, essentially, a tragic one: "At bottom, the gangster is doomed because he is under the obligation to succeed, not because the means he employs are unlawful." Much of what he wrote still holds today; it's surprising how consistent genre rules remain over time while taking in changes in attitudes and moral standards. Warshow's gangster echoes the city's "queer and dishonest skills and its terrible daring," carrying "his life in his hands like a placard, like a club." Yet, until well into the 1990s, gangsters in Hindi films showed no such exuberance. These were the real gangsters as tragic heroes. And they were tragic because they were reluctant.

Henry Hill in *Goodfellas* (1990) says he wanted to be a gangster from as far back as he can remember. In Hindi films, they didn't want to be gangsters at all. No other national cinema had this hardwired into their films. This was not the reluctance of a Michael Corleone, who, once he lays aside his misgivings, takes to the business with a lethality even his father lacks. It's not the world-weariness of Max in *Touchez pas au grisbi* (1954). It's definitely not the one-last-job reluctance of the great '60s yakuza films from Japan. Hindi film gangsters were genuinely, deeply unhappy to be doing what they did. For thirty-odd years, antagonists were played by the biggest heroes of the day, who retained every bit of the audience's sympathy. Life made them gangsters. Society made them gangsters. They would play the cards they'd been dealt, but there was no pleasure to be had in it. It was a tremendous sleight of hand: audiences got to root for violent outlaws, yet also feel like they were watching something akin to moral redressal.

The Hindi film gangster had its origins in a series of noir-inflected films from the 1950s, made by a number of studios. The most influential was Navketan Studios, run by brothers Chetan, Dev, and Vijay Anand, which pioneered the musical-thriller-comedy-noir hybrid with *Baazi* (*Gamble*). This 1951 film, directed by Guru Dutt (before his seminal 1957 film *Pyaasa* [*Thirsty*]) and starring Dev Anand, was a big hit. They followed up with *Taxi Driver* (1954), another hit, again starring Dev Anand and directed by Chetan Anand. The same year, Dutt directed himself in his own production, *Aar-Paar* (*This or That*), playing a tough but sympathetic cabbie, just as his friend Dev had done in *Taxi Driver*. He also produced and lent his masterly cinematographer, V.K. Murthy, to Pramod Chakravorty for *C.I.D.* (1956), a delightful cops-and-gangsters film starring Dev Anand.

These films were shot in black and white, with aesthetics and attitudes borrowed from pre- and postwar Hollywood cinema. But Hindi cinema didn't have the appetite then to center films around violent mobsters. Unlike America in the 1930s and '40s, Bombay didn't have larger-than-life mobsters for filmmakers to draw on. The criminal activity in Hindi films then was nothing alarming: mostly cardsharping, con man games, and pickpocketing. I describe some of the light criminality of those early antiheroes in my book, *Bullets over Bombay*: "Kismet (1943, Ashok Kumar as a pickpocket), *House No. 44* and *Pocket Maar* (1955 and '56, Dev Anand as a pickpocket), *Sangram* (1950, Kumar as a casino owner), *Awara* (1951, Raj Kapoor as a small-time thief), *Shree 420* and *Baazi* (1955 and '51, Kapoor and Anand as cardsharps)." Yet we see in most cases a reluctance to commit even these minor crimes. In *Baazi*, Dev Anand only takes up as a cardsharp to earn money to pay for his ailing sister's treatment. Raj Kapoor may "sell his humanity" in *Shree 420*, transforming from a Chaplin-like bumpkin to a suave hustler in a suit, but it just takes a good scolding to bring him from riches to (happy) rags.

Taxi Driver (1954)

This or That (1954)

House No. 44 (1955)

While the '50s produced excellent noirish dramas and the '60s some stylish crime capers, it was in the '70s that a more consequential Hindi film gangster emerged. The crimes were serious now: smuggling, drug trafficking, murder. The emotional fallout was accentuated too, with guilt and unhappiness reducing the hero to a tortured mess. Most often, this turmoil was visited on Amitabh Bachchan, whose morally conflicted characters reflected the anxieties of a nation now well over the euphoria of independence: an upright cop turned vigilante in *Zanjeer*, the most reluctant of dons in *Deewaar*, a coal miner on the run from his past in *Kaala Patthar* (*Black Stone*, 1979).

Robert Warshow writes, "Usually, when we come upon him, he has already made his choice or the choice has already been made for him, it doesn't matter which: we are not permitted to ask whether at some point he could have chosen to be something else than what he is." "It doesn't matter which …" is the sort of fatalism that hangs over the sad, angry men played by Bachchan in the '70s. But there's one deviation from Warshow's thesis. We do not come upon them only after they've become gangsters. Instead, we're nearly always shown a time before crime, before oppression and crushing responsibility force them off the path of good. You can see why Hindi cinema insisted on unhappy childhoods for its gangster antiheroes. It was easier to root for someone you'd seen as a miserable kid at the start of the film, even if that person was now a killer. It was a moral safety net in a country with a lot of film censorship. And it was a useful source of future conflict: the ones responsible for wrecking the protagonist's childhood were usually the ones who paid when he grew up.

Lobby card for *Shakti* (1982); the film's lead, Amitabh Bachchan, is on the right

In film after film, writers and directors located the source of adult malaise in childhood trauma. This was a staple of Hindi films, gangster and otherwise, from the '50s till well into the '90s. We see this especially in a number of Bachchan films in which his character suffers hardship as a boy. In *Zanjeer*, he's traumatized by the killing of his parents; though he grows up to be a cop, he becomes a vigilante to exact his revenge. In *Deewaar*, his father's humiliation becomes his own, the tattoo a reminder; he carries that pain into adulthood, and we see it pour out in his confrontations with his brother Ravi. In Yash Chopra's *Trishul* (*Trident*, 1978)—not a gangster film—he sets out to financially destroy his industrialist biological father, who abandoned his mother when he was a child. The throughline from unhappy childhood to haunted adulthood is illustrated most succinctly in Ramesh Sippy's *Shakti* (*Strength*, 1982). Young Vijay hears his father, an upright cop played by the legendary Dilip Kumar, tell a gangster he wouldn't bend the law even if it meant his son's life. Distraught, he walks across the schoolyard, kicking a ball. In a single cut, we jump years into the future, with Bachchan as Vijay kicking a soda can down Marine Drive. It's a wonderful concise gesture, an unexpected cut that links the hurt boy and the unhappy man who will soon be at loggerheads with his father.

By the end of the '80s, Hindi cinema had started to turn out tougher, bleaker gangster films. They reflected the pessimism of a country that had just come out of the Emergency, the twenty-one-month period from 1975 to 1977 when Prime Minister Indira Gandhi suspended civil liberties and no elections took place. But some things remained the same. Two scenes in two films separated by thirteen years showed how Hindi gangster films had evolved, yet retained some essential beats. In Manmohan Desai's *Parvarish* (*Upbringing*, 1977), Shamsher Singh, deputy superintendent of police, raises Amit, the son of a *daaku* (bandit) he apprehended, along with his own son, Kishan. We see the boys playing cops and robbers. Amit, in khaki uniform, brandishes a toy gun and tells Kishan, the bandit, to surrender. There's a cut,

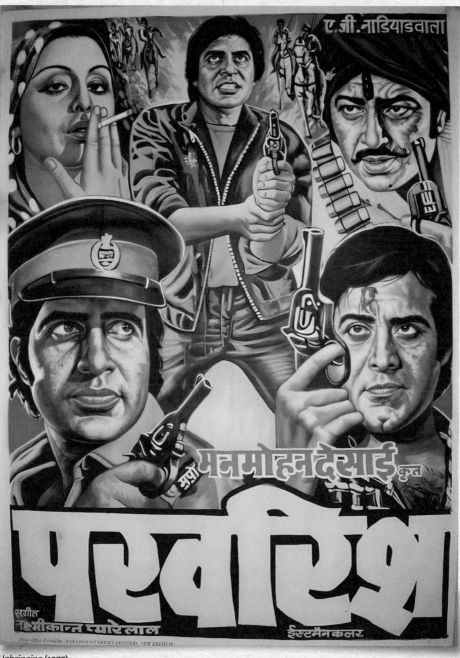

Upbringing (1977)

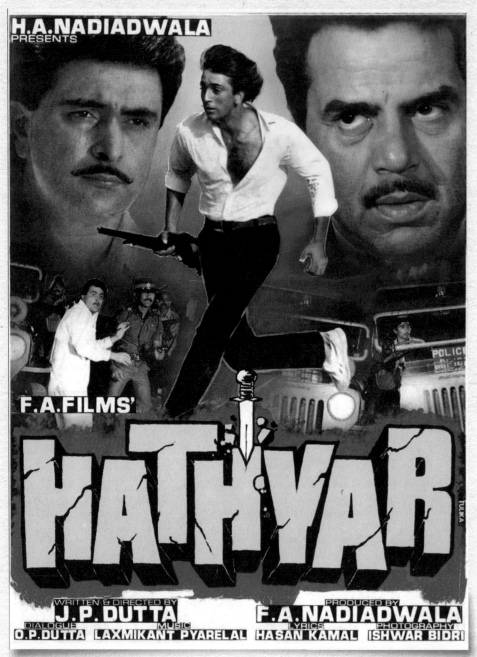

Weapon (1989)

and Amit, now grown up and played by Bachchan, is shooting at a gang of smugglers, which includes (though he doesn't know it yet) Kishan.

Jump to 1989, and another boy playing with a gun. J.P. Dutta's *Hathyar* (*Weapon*) opens with a family scene, where young Avinash rides a rocking horse, watched by his father and mother. His uncle walks up and, over the protests of his brother, hands the boy a toy rifle. Avi's father asks him to hand it over, but he says, "*hum khelenge*" (I'll play). Cut to the opening credits and a grown Avinash, played by Sanjay Dutt, points a rifle at the screen. He's aiming at a young deer; when it starts and bolts, his girlfriend enters the crosshairs. It's a bleak start to an impressively pessimistic film. Avinash grows up wild but on the right side of the law, until he kills a cop during a mugging gone wrong. He's forced to seek help from a local don, who hires him as a shooter. There's a scene after Avinash has settled into his job in which he tracks a rival gang member to a mudflat. As the man tries to get away, first on a makeshift skateboard, then on foot, Avinash readies his rifle. Taking his time, he settles on the target, then fires once. The man collapses in the distance. Avinash smiles. Ten years earlier, heroes killed in self-defense or for revenge. Avinash kills because it's his job. And though the film returns him to regret and trauma, in that moment on the mudflat he's enjoying himself. It's a significant step away from the reluctance shown in earlier films.

There was another Hindi gangster film released in 1989, more influential than *Hathyar*, and far better known today. Vidhu Vinod Chopra's *Parinda* (*Bird*) takes the well-worn template of two brothers, one innocent, the other a criminal, but makes it bleaker than it has ever been. Thirty minutes in, the younger brother, Karan (Anil Kapoor), loses his best friend, a cop, to a mob killing: it is an unforgettable sequence, with Karan left clutching the bullet-ridden body as startled pigeons—the *parindey* (birds) of the title—flap around them. Then, he nearly loses his older brother, Kishan (Jackie Shroff), who works as muscle for gangster Anna (Nana Patekar), to an assassination attempt at the Gateway of India monument. Karan, driven to breaking point, takes up the gun himself. It's a dark, dark film, with pyrophobic mob boss Anna adding a psychotic edge. The real tragic hero is Kishan, whose anguish at his brother's descent into darkness is only worsened by his guilt that he works for the man who ordered the killing. The narrative is punctuated by flashbacks that show Karan and Kishan as orphaned children on the streets of Mumbai, at that time still known as Bombay. On one fateful occasion, Kishan, egged on by Karan, runs off with a man's belongings, which starts him on a life of crime. "I ran that day, and I've been running ever since," an emotional Kishan tells his sibling. "It wasn't for myself ...," Karan protests, saying he

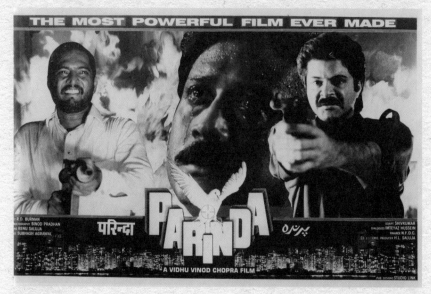

Bird (1989)

didn't want any of this. "Give it back then," Kishan says. "Give me my child-hood which was spent hungry on the streets, my youth which was spent in the dark of jail. Return my whole life to me." Jackie Shroff delivers a similar speech in the dramatic last scene of Priyadarshan's *Gardish* (*Adversity*, 1993). Having killed his rival, small-time hood Shiva holds onto an axe uncertainly as cops and onlookers stare at him. His father arrives, pleads with Shiva to give himself up. "I didn't want to be a criminal," Shiva yells in anguish. "My friends made me a criminal. My family made me a criminal. The law did. Everyone did."

In her book *Bombay Cinema*, Ranjini Mazumdar writes that the constant backward glances one sees in Hindi crime films of the '70s and '80s are an integral part of the revenge narrative: "When combined with revenge, anger allows one to create a temporality of past, present, and future through which the revenge plot reaches its climactic resolution. In the revenge narrative, the past is the site of traumatic memory to be settled in the future." The tragedy is that the past will never be truly settled, and revenge, even if attained, will come at too great a cost. Mani Ratnam's Tamil classic *Nayakan* (*Hero*, 1987) begins with a young boy being tricked by the police into leading them to his union leader father, who tries to flee and is shot. At the funeral, Velu stabs the policeman who killed his father and escapes to Bombay. As he emerges from Chhatrapati Shivaji Terminus, the plaintive "Thenpandi Cheemayile" is heard, Ilaiyaraaja's voice cracking as he sings, "O waxing moon, please don't wane / Don't sob your heart out / For your tears will break my heart." Velu Naicker (Kamal Haasan) grows up to become a Vito Corleone–like mob boss (modeled on real-life don Varadarajan Mudaliar). He dies, as his father did, from a bullet fired by someone in uniform, the shooter avenging, as he did himself, the death of *his* father. "Thenpandi Cheemayile" recurs at key moments in the film, including the very last scene, with Velu's daughter and grandson crouched over his dead body, all manner of tragic circularity achieved.

In the '90s, the rules finally changed. The city was transformed; Bombay was renamed Mumbai in 1995. The underworld was at its most visible in this decade, the power struggles of Dawood Ibrahim, Chhota Rajan, Chhota Shakeel, and others splashed across the front pages. Hindi crime films became tougher, more existential, drawn from reportage and the secondhand gang stories everyone seemed to have. Gangsters in films became less and less morally conflicted, even as they gained nuance. At the center of Shashilal K. Nair's *Angaar* (*Embers*, 1992) is a crime family: patriarch Jahangir (Kader Khan) and sons Farid (Mazhar Khan) and Majid (Nana Patekar). Jahangir is the most sympathetic of the three, but it's in Majid that we see the sort of complexity that Hindi film gangsters would soon be imbued with: soft-spoken, tender to his wife and special-needs child, yet also a ruthless businessman and an unrepentant killer.

There were fewer hard-luck stories, fewer sentimental links to childhood in these '90s films. It was also getting tougher to sentimentalize gangsters with the papers full of their bloody rivalries; the ending of *Angaar*, with high-rises blown up by Majid, had an eerie echo the following year in the Mumbai serial bombings said to be orchestrated by gangster Dawood Ibrahim. *Satya* (1998) was the first significant Hindi gangster film to imply that the past is irrelevant. As the opening credits end, the camera finds Satya (J.D. Chakravarthy) in the throng outside Chhatrapati Shivaji Terminus. We can guess he's from one of the southern states from his accent. We learn he's an orphan and an atheist. Other than this, we're offered no clues to his past or his motivations. No family, no god, no purpose—he's the existential foil to hotheaded, gregarious Bhiku Mhatre (Manoj Bajpayee), whose gang he joins. There is no reluctance in Bhiku or Satya or any of the other gangsters. Rather, the challenge is thrown at the audience—aren't these terrible, violent men fun to be around?

In its unassuming way, *Satya* rewrote the rules for gangster cinema. It was a reasonable commercial success for a mid-budget film, but its influence on Hindi cinema over the next two decades was profound. So many who kick-started their careers with this film—Bajpayee, writers Saurabh Shukla and Anurag Kashyap, actor Shefali Shah, composer-director Vishal Bhardwaj, editor-writer Apurva Asrani—went on to do crucial, industry-altering work. It encouraged other writers and directors to cast aside the strictures of Bollywood and make films they themselves would want to see. It ushered in the era of the "Hindie"—conservatively budgeted films with young directors, unknown actors, and an eye on the new multiplex-going audience.

Satya began a belated but glorious golden age of Hindi gangster cinema. The films came thick and fast—Ram Gopal Varma's kinetic, twisted *Company* (2002); Vishal Bhardwaj's *Macbeth* adaptation, *Maqbool* (2003); Rajkumar Hirani's screwball *Munna Bhai M.B.B.S.* (2003). There were comic gangsters and deadly serious gangsters and poetic gangsters (there'd always been singing and dancing gangsters). There were, increasingly, gangster stories set in cities other than Mumbai. There were new variations on the *daaku* or dacoit film, a genre adjacent to gangster film but with its own codes and rules, hugely popular from the 1950s till the end of the 1980s. Anurag Kashyap's *Gangs of Wasseypur* (2012) changed the game again. A five-hour film released in two parts after its premiere at the 2012 Cannes Film Festival, it finally ended Mumbai's stranglehold on the genre. There was also a crucial change in tone. Post-*Satya*, Hindi gangster films had largely given up on reluctance as a relic of a morally absolute cinema. The ghost of Warshow had been exorcised. The gangster hero was no longer tragic.

Uday Bhatia

OUTTAKE: THE REVOLUTIONARY MELODRAMA OF LINO BROCKA

Using the pretext created by the combination of a communist insurgency, a Muslim insurrection on the southern island of Mindanao, and mounting political unrest on university campuses, on September 23, 1971, President Ferdinand Marcos placed the Philippines under martial law. Backed by Washington, which supported his anticommunist politics and ignored his rampant corruption and human rights violations, Marcos ruled the Philippines for the next fourteen years. He used the army and unofficial paramilitary groups to target his opponents in the student movement, trade unions and other left organizations, and the media, resulting in widespread torture, imprisonment, and over three thousand extrajudicial killings. As the communist insurgency intensified, opposition to his rule grew in the cities, and the economy plunged into crisis, then American president Ronald Reagan encouraged Marcos and his entourage to seek asylum in the US. Under the cover of night on February 25, 1986, Marcos fled the Philippines, reportedly taking with him twenty-four suitcases of gold bricks and diamonds, part of the estimated 5 to 10 billion US dollars he ransacked during his rule.

One filmmaker who was deeply involved in what is referred to as the "People Power Revolution" that deposed Marcos was Catalino Ortiz Brocka. Lino—as he was commonly known—Brocka got his directorial start on the Filipino equivalent of anthology television shows such as *Kraft Theatre*. His first big screen film, *Wanted: Perfect Mother*, was released in 1970. He told one interviewer, "Since then, I have done over sixty or seventy films; I have lost count of how many." Much of his work is now impossible to screen for lack of decent prints. The bulk of Brocka's career, which was cut short by his death in a car accident in 1991, took place under martial law. A fervent Marcos opponent, Brocka was also openly gay in what was, and to some degree still is, a very conservative Catholic country. While Brocka's films do not boast overt revolutionary politics, he mobilized the melodrama and crime films popular with Filipinos to explore issues such as colonialism, rebellion, poverty, and resistance to corruption. His output under martial law was a direct critique of the Marcos dictatorship, albeit one that never fell into political didacticism.

French poster for *Manila in the Claws of Light* (1975)

Maynila sa mga kuko ng liwanang (*Manila in the Claws of Light*, 1975), Brocka's best-known film internationally, is a good example. A young fisherman, Julio (Bembol Roco), travels from his rural village to Manila to search for his missing girlfriend, Ligaya (Hilda Koronel). Robbed as soon as he arrives, he has no choice but to take a job laboring on the construction of a high-rise tower. The work is dirty and dangerous, and the foreman extorts a portion of the worker's wages and sacks anyone who complains. When Julio loses this employment, he ends up on the street, encountering criminal gangs and briefly contemplating sex work to survive. He discovers Ligaya working in a brothel. They reunite, but before they escape the city together, she is killed, most likely by one of her customers. A noir melodrama, *Manila in the Claws of Light* depicts the drabness, inertia, and lack of opportunities, especially for the poor, of life under authoritarian rule.

Insiang (1976)

Brocka followed this up with another film set in Manila's slums, *Insiang* (1976), about a young woman's relationship with her mentally unwell mother's abusive younger lover. *Bayan ko: Kapit sa patalim* (*This Is My Country*, 1984) focuses on a printer who must navigate a strike at the company he works for and is then forced to turn to crime to pay the bills of his hospitalized wife. *Macho Dancer*, made in 1988, four years after the end of martial law, tells of a young man, Noel (Daniel Fernando), who leaves his poor rural village for Manila and finds work as a "macho dancer" in a gay strip club catering to foreign sex tourists. He is befriended by another sex worker, Pol (Allan Paule), who is searching for his young sister, Pining (Princess Punzalan), who he fears has been trafficked into sex slavery. They eventually locate Pining working in a brothel protected by a brutal cop, Kid (Johnny Vicar), whom we have previously seen shaking down other sex workers. Noel and Pol rescue Pining, but Kid kills Pol in the process.

Both *Manila in the Claws of Light* and *Macho Dancer* feature young men politicized by their experience of inequality and injustice, and the

Lino Brocka shooting *Manila in the Claws of Light* (1975)

impunity enjoyed by the rich. Pushed to their limits, they exercise the only political agency they feel is available to them, lashing out in acts of violence. Julio murders the customer he holds responsible for Ligaya's death and is then hunted through the streets of the city by an angry crowd. Noel exacts revenge for Pol's death by killing Kid. That Noel gets away with this was one of the many aspects of *Macho Dancer* that alarmed Philippine censors.

Other influences, especially Italian neorealism, are apparent in Brocka's work. He filmed in real locations—small towns, slums, factories, and nightclubs in Manila's red light district—often mixing professional and nonprofessional actors and incorporating newsreel and documentary footage. Even at its grimmest, his work feels fresh and natural. As Noel Vera wrote in an online essay on Brocka for the Centre for Asian American Media in 2010, "You get the sense that he shot these pictures just outside the theatre and delivered them, still steaming, straight to the big screen."

Brocka not only had to work on the cheap but faced continual harassment from the authorities. It took a yearlong battle to get *Insiang* shown locally, as Brocka fought the censors and the Philippines' first lady Imelda Marcos, who wanted the film banned due to its depiction of poverty. *Macho Dancer* was also the subject of a fierce fight with censors who, in addition to objecting to the lead character's act of revenge, opposed the depiction of homosexuality, prostitution, and police corruption. Brocka often had to devise creative ways to smuggle prints of his movies out of the country to show at international film festivals.

Brocka was not the only radical filmmaker in the country working under martial law. *Sakada*, aka *The Tenants* (1976), is a social realist film directed by Behn Cervantes about seasonal sugarcane workers, called *sakadas*, on large hacienda-style plantations on the island of Negros. Investigating the ramifications when a sakada, also a union organizer, is killed by a security guard, the film enjoyed a brief theater run before copies were confiscated on the orders of Marcos. Female director Lupita Aquino-Kashiwahara's *Minsa'y isang gamu-gamo* (*Once a Moth*, 1976) is the story of a young nurse whose brother is killed by an American soldier stationed on a nearby US air force base, and Mike De Leon's *Sister Stella L.* (1984) portrays a nun radicalized during a labor strike.

Andrew Nette

TWO SIDES OF CINEMA NOVO

Glauber Rocha and José Mojica Marins

From March 31 to April 1, 1964, a military coup took place in Brazil, ousting center-left president João Goulart. Brazil had been a republic since 1889 when Pedro II, the country's last monarch, was overthrown, though its version of democracy wavered during these years. Still, the 1964 coup did depose a man who had been democratically elected, and it ushered in a period of military dictatorship. This lasted twenty-one years and was rife with repression and human rights abuses, including torture, forced disappearances, murder of political opponents, and censorship decrees affecting the arts, cinema among them. This essay will explore two strains of Brazilian cinema during the dictatorship and how each one dealt with the pressures bearing on them from various sides, from the government to the church to film critics to political idealogues. I'll focus on two filmmakers who approached cinema from opposite directions but whose work served, through different methods, as critiques of authority and the country's hierarchical structures: Glauber Rocha, a leading figure in the country's Cinema Novo movement, whose movies played the international art film circuit and garnered praise across the globe, and José Mojica Marins, aka Coffin Joe, the man who made Brazil's first horror movies and who worked on the fringes of Brazil's film industry for a long time.

On the surface, these two are cinematic polar opposites. But they shared important qualities as filmmakers. Each was single-minded in his pursuit of getting the vision he wanted on film, and each had a core disrespect for authority. Marins never formally belonged to the Cinema Novo, but like the filmmakers in that movement, he had a preoccupation with exposing hypocrisy and highlighting human beings living on the margins. Rocha's characters fight systems through political means; Marins's resist them by mocking and breaking social taboos. And both directors chart the territory where violence arising from a certain hunger and frustration in people becomes common and in its

José Mojica Marins as Zé do Caixão, aka Coffin Joe, in *At Midnight I'll Take Your Soul* (1964)

own ways political, even if not always overtly so. In Glauber Rocha's movies, this violence is presented through plots explicitly about political struggle between people of different economic classes and belief systems. Political violence is the subject of his films and is enacted on-screen. Marins's work shows a form of political violence through a horror film prism, the actions done by his Coffin Joe character serving as an audience-pleasing id to the superego of social conformity prescribed by the country's authorities. Rocha had critical respectability from the start of his career, and Marins didn't, but each contributed to the aesthetic and political rebellion that was going on in world cinema during the '60s and '70s.

Marins's career began first. Born in São Paolo in 1936 as an only child, he was an avid film watcher from a young age. His parents managed a movie theater for a time, and this allowed their son to devour films from all over the world. When he was ten, he asked his father for a movie camera for Christmas, and with the 8.5-millimeter camera he received, he began making short films. He acted in them himself and cast neighbors and friends. He bought an abandoned synagogue in 1953 and founded his own film company there, using the synagogue as his studio. He also used it as the place to teach acting and train technicians, and to raise the money that would fund his films. Marins directed, acted, and had a hand in writing everything from westerns to musicals. They were all low budget and independently financed. Around this time, in the early '60s, he had a nightmare that he found "awful" and "violent," and this dream inspired him to delve into a genre no Brazilian filmmaker had yet tried. "I was being taken to the cemetery to be buried, but I was still alive," Marins said of his bad dream. "I remember that I was wearing all black, so I started filming that way." Thus was born the character who would become his second self, Zé do Caixão, or as he is known in English, Coffin

At Midnight I'll Take Your Soul (1964)

Joe, the black-clad undertaker with long fingernails, in a film that Marins wrote, produced, starred in, and directed, *À meia-noite levarei sua alma* (*At Midnight I'll Take Your Soul*, 1964).

Coffin Joe is a monstrous figure. In the backwater Brazilian town where he lives and works, he terrorizes the local population. Unlike sometimes sympathetic monsters like Frankenstein or Dracula or the Wolf Man, he carries out his evil with unapologetic deliberateness. In addition to *At Midnight I'll Take Your Soul*, the official Coffin Joe trilogy comprises *Esta noite encarnarei no teu cadáver* (*This Night I'll Possess Your Corpse*, 1967) and *Encarnação do demônio* (*Embodiment of Evil*, 2008). Coffin Joe also appears in five other films Marins made, as a subsidiary character. But in the core trilogy, he is the protagonist, and in each of the three, Coffin Joe is obsessed with the continuation of his bloodline. He sees himself as superior to other human beings and wants to find the right person through which to pass this superiority along. Only the "perfect" woman can bear him the son (and it has to be a son) that he wants, the person who will be, in the Nietzschean sense, a superman. His ultimate goal is immortality, and he's convinced he will attain this through the birth of a son.

Coffin Joe is married when *At Midnight I'll Take Your Soul* starts. But when he discovers that his wife cannot procreate, he kills her. After that, finding the right woman for the task he envisions is difficult, because he has such stringent standards. He's not exactly a suave seducer either; he scares and tortures women to put them through his self-devised tests. He murders women he judges "imperfect." And anyone who impedes him— husbands of the women he's chosen, fathers, brothers, police—engenders his wrath. In the small town where the first two films of the trilogy are set, Coffin Joe regards virtually everyone he meets as an obstacle or enemy. He cuts a wide swath of violence and cruelty while trying to achieve his objective, but violence and cruelty in and of themselves are not unusual in the horror genre. It's the contradictions in Coffin Joe's character that are sui generis, and they contribute a great deal to what makes these movies fascinating.

Nothing in the Coffin Joe series is overtly radical. Coffin Joe is an utterly self-interested human being, a man determined to get what he wants to please himself, and he never voices the slightest interest in what is going on around him politically or socially. He has a narrowly focused will to power, and what goes on elsewhere and affects the conditions of others is no concern of his. Despite that, you could probably assume he sides with the patriarchal and repressive forces in Brazilian society. In how he demands subservience from women and views them as both exchangeable and disposable, he embodies sexism and patriarchy. He commits rape without compunction. His obsession with "the continuation of blood" sounds like something a Nazi would say. Even if it's not addressed within his films, he would seem to be an ally of the autocratic elements that took over in Brazil in 1964. But while he is intransigent and abusive, an apparent symbol of repression, he rejects many notions that the state upholds as essential. He has no respect for his neighbors or any of their customs and habits. An ardent rationalist, a denouncer of superstition, he looks down on those whose ideas he considers unscientific. He's an atheist, expressing over and over his contempt for Christianity, the Catholic Church—a key ally of the dictatorship—and anything associated with religion. Coffin Joe represents a threat to the establishment; he's like a character in a Marquis de Sade story, sexually disturbing but also an exponent of a personal freedom unhampered by religion, civic duty, morality, or the law. If you had a lot of characters like Coffin Joe running around and doing what they wanted, they would, without question, be a problem for the ruling class.

It's no surprise then that José Marins's films, despite their low budgets and occasional crudeness, found large audiences. Coffin Joe became at once an antihero and a hero. He was a villain for his actions but someone whose freedom could be seen as liberating, offering his viewers a feeling of catharsis. He became an outlet for audiences in the repressive climate of Brazil under the dictatorship, and the filmmaker quickly found himself at odds with Brazilian censors. First, he was putting images on film without precedent in Brazil, and second, the censors recognized a cinematic iconoclast when they saw one. Marins was not a blatantly political filmmaker or a person who often voiced opinions about the dictatorship, but in their scrutiny of social problems the authorities didn't want the public to dwell on, his films could be seen as a negative comment on the dictatorship. An accessible, if eccentric, filmmaker, he expressed his views about Brazilian society through genre, and his in-your-face use of this genre, horror, managed to offend his country's watchdogs.

A notable scene in *At Midnight I'll Take Your Soul* shows Coffin Joe, mocking and blasphemous, eating a leg of lamb while laughing at a Good Friday procession going past his house. In a seriously Catholic country like Brazil, this scene made an impact, though not necessarily one that audiences, thrilled at the shock and novelty, disliked. Coffin Joe gets punished at the end of the film, driven mad by the spirits of his victims and blinded, but he returns for the next film having recovered in a hospital. Absolved, somehow, for his crimes, he resumes his ruthless quest to find the perfect woman, cruel to all except children, who he deems untainted by the world's moral stains

Brazilian poster for *This Night I'll Possess Your Corpse* (1967)

Brazilian poster for *Awakening of the Beast* (1970)

and hypocrisies. In *This Night I'll Possess Your Corpse*, fed up with Joe and his evil, the villagers eventually surround and shoot him. He falls in a lake and drowns. This was the script's original ending, but the censors demanded cuts and changes. At their behest, Marins did more work on the film, and it reached theaters a year later. In its final form, at the story's conclusion, Coffin Joe does something remarkable, added by Marins to appease the censors. Approached by a priest while dying, Coffin Joe accedes to the priest's entreaty that he accept God so his soul can be saved. This is truly what you might call a fate worse than death for Joe, since his last words belie everything he has railed against for two films. It could have been his anger at this interference that prompted Marins, a few years later, to make *O despertar da besta*, also known as *O ritual dos sádicos* (*Awakening of the Beast*, 1970), a pseudo-documentary chock-full of social commentary. It's among the Coffin Joe films Marins made that are not part of the official trilogy, but as the filmmaker himself has said, he considers it his biggest achievement.

The film's genesis was simple. After seeing the arrest of a drug-using prostitute in São Paolo, Marins wondered why the police were cracking down on users and not drug dealers. This thought blossomed into a phantasmagorical exploration of drug use and the psychology of fear, in which a psychologist named Dr. Sergio shares his theories about the perversion and depravity that exists in all people. As part of his work, he tells stories illustrating his theories to a panel of so-called experts. These experts include José Marins himself, and one story recounts how Dr. Sergio had his experiment subjects watch *At Midnight I'll Take Your Soul*. While the subjects watched Marins's film, Dr. Sergio monitored their reactions. Dr. Sergio explains all this to the panel members, and they put down Marins and his films, calling them exploitative drivel. But Dr. Sergio explains to them how *At Midnight I'll Take Your Soul* affected the experiment subjects strongly. After exposure to the film, the subjects found Coffin Joe entering their fantasies.

Awakening of the Beast is an audacious fusing of social commentary and a meta-filmic defense of Marins's own work. As writer Sean Lindsay pointed out in 2005 a piece about the movie for the online journal *Offscreen*, "One of the triumphs of *Awakening of the Beast* is the parallel Marins draws between Dr. Sergio's analysis of drugs and criticism of Coffin Joe. It is Marins' intention to prove that Coffin Joe is a scapegoat for critics who are unable to acknowledge the real causes of social injustice. Coffin Joe, too, is merely an excuse for outrageous behavior. It is not Marins' fault if critics are naïve enough to think that misogyny, anger at the church, or violence are his creations."

During the filming of a scene in which characters smoke marijuana, bystanders called the police on Marins's film crew. The onlookers thought the counterfeit drugs being used were real. The police came prepared to arrest the culprits, but they recognized Marins as Coffin Joe and he persuaded them to help on the film. They wound up serving as consultants on the drug scenes, and Marins concluded that since they had no objections to what he was filming, neither would the government. He assumed he'd have no problems releasing the movie. But his assumption was wrong. After the film wrapped, the Brazilian censorship board started complaining, saying the film had subliminal political messages. The board didn't specify what these messages were, and Marins declared that he had no interest in politics, just in what he was seeing on the streets, but the censorship board said that cuts would be required. Marins's depiction of drug use in Brazil upset the board, and his protestations that he was trying to portray that social problem realistically didn't change the censors' minds.

Three months went by. At last, the censorship board said that they'd have to cut so much that nothing but the opening credits would be left. Marins tried everything he could to get the film shown, but the situation became, as he phrased it in an interview for the 2017 Synapse Films DVD release of the movie, "impossible." The government banned the film outright, and it wasn't released until 1986, a year after Brazil's return to civilian rule. The irony is, as Marins says in the same interview, that the film would have played as a comedy if the police had not helped him. As he realized when the police came on board, he knew nothing about drug use or how drugs affect people. It's likely that a comedy would have been regarded by the censors as inoffensive. Police input bolstered the film's realism, which in turn put off the censors and led to its suppression.

From 1970 to the mid-'80s, Marins had to contend with the censors and the power allotted them by the military dictatorship. He made numerous films on mini-mal budgets, high on horror and

Embodiment of Evil (2008)

sexual content, and even directed soft- and hardcore porn in the '70s and '80s; sexual content was apparently not heavily censored if devoid of social commentary. The Brazilian critics disdained him as a sleaze merchant, a low-grade filmmaker turning out junk. At the same time, though, he was a busy media presence in the country. He published Coffin Joe comic books and hosted horror-themed television programs. He kept prodding societal taboos without outright putting politics in his films, and this combination of populist, antiestablishment sentiments delivered without affiliation to a party or a movement or an ideology made him well-liked by the public but guar-anteed that he remained in the censors' sights. Because of this, he didn't get to make the planned third movie in the Coffin Joe trilogy until the late 2000s.

Embodiment of Evil takes place in São Paolo, in a world quite different from his earlier works. It's a film that sums up the adage "longevity is the best revenge," in this case both for the filmmaker and the character. After forty years in prison, Coffin Joe is released, and there is no sign of the religious conversion he supposedly made at the end of *This Night I'll Possess Your Corpse*. In *Embodiment of Evil*, he has gone back to his antireligious roots. Moreover, he is unrepentant in his desire to produce a superior offspring through the right woman. Except he's in a more secular world than decades ago, and in a flash, he finds acolytes, women who've heard about his past exploits and want to sire his offspring. He's like a serial killer who has groupies.

Freed from the censors' constraints, the military dictatorship gone, Marins unleashed his goriest and most graphically violent film yet, to acclaim. Even mainstream critics praised it. He'd outlasted the military regime and would go on to find himself revered by horror enthusiasts around the world.

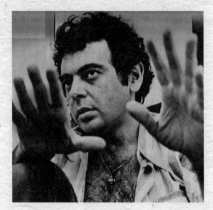

Brazilian director Glauber Rocha

One ally Marins had from early in his career was Glauber Rocha. In *Awakening of the Beast*, Marins incorporates a quote from Rocha describing Marins as "the leader of the New Brazilian Cinema." Rocha was known across the world as the leader of Cinema Novo, and this specific comment may be one Marins invented. But it is true that Rocha had been praising Marins since *At Midnight I'll Take Your Soul*, which Rocha described as a unique film. Rocha was a writer and film theorist as well as a director, and he admired Marins's films because of their fearlessness and experimentation. He saw how Marins's iconoclasm exemplified what Rocha called "the aesthetics of hunger," also the title of a 1965 essay he wrote that would become influential in the formation of Latin America's New Cinema movement. This essay, first published in Portuguese as "A estica de fome" in *Revista civilização brasileira* number 3, lays out Rocha's credo for Cinema Novo. He uses the word "hunger" to define pervasive misery in Latin America, an undernourishment both economic and philosophic. He says that "undeniably, Latin America remains a colony," and that "what distinguishes yesterday's colonialism from today's is merely the more refined forms employed by the contemporary colonizer." Because "hunger will not be assuaged by moderate government reforms" and what he labels "the cloak of Technicolor"—those forms of art that do no more than distract the hungry from their suffering—something more forceful is needed. Rocha comes right out and says that the most "noble manifestation of hunger is violence.... Cinema Novo reveals that violence is normal behavior for the starving."

With a polemical fervor that is very '60s, Rocha ends his essay by putting Cinema Novo in a global context, sounding a cry for solidarity among filmmakers: "Wherever there is a filmmaker prepared to film the truth and to oppose the hypocrisy and repression of intellectual censorship, there will be the living spirit of Cinema Novo. Wherever there is a filmmaker, of any age and background, ready to place his cinema and his profession at the service of the great causes of his time, there will be the living spirit of Cinema Novo. This is the correct definition which sets Cinema Novo apart from the commercial industry because the commitment of industrial cinema is to untruth and exploitation." Cinema Novo, to sum up, "is not a single film but an evolving complex of films that will ultimately make the public aware of its own misery."

Rocha had been artistic since his childhood in Bahia, a state in Brazil's northeast. He went to good schools and became politically

Black God, White Devil (1964)

active as a leftist early in life. By his twenties, he'd become a filmmaker. By 1962, at the age of twenty-three, he completed his first feature, *Barravento* (*The Turning Wind*), about a man who returns home to his fishing village and tries to free the people there of religious superstition and rid them of those exploiting the town's resources for profit. It contains the seeds of what Rocha would expand on in his subsequent films, *Deus e o diablo na terra do sol* (*Black God, White Devil*, 1964), *Terra em transe* (*Entranced Earth*, 1967), and *O dragão da maldade contra o santo guerreiro* (*Antonio das Mortes*, 1969). In these three works, Rocha showed the public with unflinching directness "their own misery."

What's dazzling about Rocha's films is how they convey political ideas and social themes through unorthodox techniques. His movies do have plots, generally pitting authoritarian forces backed by money and power against individuals and groups opposing that power, but plot is not what drives Rocha's films. They are emotionally charged yet fiercely intellectual, blending myth, dance, song, and speeches. He uses tropes from westerns, musicals, and historical dramas. Soundtrack music from Verdi to Heitor Villa-Lobos to Brazilian folk songs serve to comment on and structure action. The way characters comment on the stories they're in brings to mind Bertolt Brecht's distancing effects: Rocha doesn't want viewers to just lose themselves in a story, but to remember they are watching a constructed fiction about real-world problems. He wants his viewers to think critically and analytically about those problems. His films do not unfurl in a straightforward, linear manner, and this narrative complexity is perhaps one reason that they never took off with the public in Brazil. Though he was a driving force in Brazilian cinema for his entire adult life (he died in 1981, at age forty-two, of a lung infection), his movies garnered more acclaim in overseas film festivals such as Cannes and Locarno than from Brazilian audiences. Rocha fits right in to the experimental and adventurous cinema of that heady time, a filmmaker expanding the boundaries of cinematic language much like, for example, Jean-Luc Godard. He made films that portray how those in power use and manipulate the masses, but he never made conventional films designed to appeal to the masses.

Black God, White Devil was shot just before the 1964 military coup, during an interval of political openness in Brazil, when President João Goulart was calling for democracy and reform. The movie analyzes two types of rebellion historically significant in the country, religious messianism and social banditry, and Rocha sets the tale in the 1930s in the *sertão*, a barren, semi-arid interior region in northeast Brazil that had long seen the sort of violence he depicts. Throughout the film, Rocha makes two key references: to Antonio Conselheiro, a religious figure from the late 1800s who led impoverished villagers against the church, landowners, and the army in what became the brutal War of Canudos (1896–97), and to Lampiao, a charismatic bandit leader from the '20s and '30s who later became a Brazilian folk hero. Drawing on this history, the story follows ranch hand Manuel (Geraldo Del Ray) and his wife, Rosa (Yona Magalhaes), as they desperately try to improve their lives. They navigate between secular rebels and religious mystics all harboring class-based grievances. Violence is everywhere, perpetrated by the religious leader Sebastião (Lidio Silva) and by the bandits Corisco (Othon Bastos) and Dada (Sonia Dos Humildes). But as Rocha had said in "The Aesthetics of Hunger" and would say for years in interviews, this violence could be seen as the flip side of modern capitalistic violence, a symptom of colonialism. *Black God, White Devil* was released in Brazil without issues, despite its political content.

Rocha ran into trouble, however, with *Entranced Earth*. This contemporaneously set political allegory takes place in a fictional Latin American country called Eldorado. It directly addresses Brazil's political situation from 1960 to 1966, and especially targets Brazil's urban educated class, to which Rocha belonged. The movie dissects the intersection of politics, the media, and big business through a group of characters of varied ambitions and ideologies. Disenchantment pervades the film, and on its release, the

Geraldo Del Rey in *Black God, White Devil* (1964)

movie alienated both the right and the left in Brazil. Both sides come in for severe critique in the movie, and as usual, Rocha provides no simplistic answers. Brazil, even Latin America as a whole, is a mess, he posits, and the one legitimate recourse is to take up arms. But against whom exactly, and to what end, when the masses themselves seem so gullible, so exploitable? The Brazilian government was unhappy with *Entranced Earth* because they believed it hurt the country's image. The authorities forbade the movie from being shown domestically, and it took a protest from local and international filmmakers to make the government relent. It was allowed to debut at Cannes and to screen in Brazil, but it began a push and pull between Rocha and the military dictatorship.

Rocha returned to the *sertão* and a saga of landowners and the dispossessed with *Antonio das Mortes* (the literal translation from the Portuguese title is *The Dragon of Wickedness Against the Holy Warrior*), a film for which he brought back the character of Antonio (Maurício do Valle) from *Black God, White Devil*. In the earlier film, Antonio, a gun for hire, had been paid by landowners to kill rebels and bandits who were upending the established order of things. Now, older and adrift, he gets the call for a new job from a decrepit, blind cattle owner (Joffre Soares) and a district police chief (Hugo Carvana) to assassinate a young revolutionary leader (Lorival Pariz) who

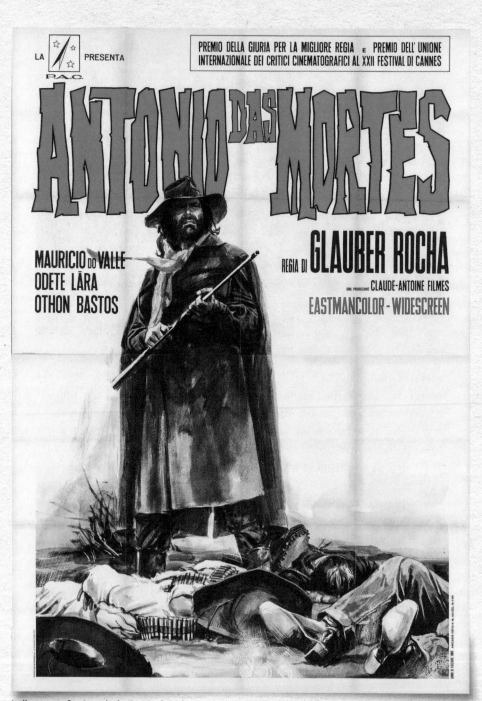

Italian poster for *Antonio das Mortes* (1969)

is gaining political support among the people. Antonio is working in the Brazilian tradition of the *jagunço*, an armed intimidator hired by plantation owners in the backlands to protect them and keep their peasants in line. Antonio arrives in town and kills his target, but after he has done so, something inside him shifts. He finds he has come to sympathize with the revolutionaries' ideals. He switches sides and aligns himself with the dispossessed, his skills and weapons now aimed at those in power. There are duels, showdowns, massacres, and it all occurs in a stark backlands village made up of huts and saloons. The film ends with an image of Antonio walking beside a road alone, in his long and dusty leather jacket, rifle in hand and hat on his head, facing an uncertain future but committed to a cause larger than himself. If this sounds like a western, that's because, in part, it is, though Rocha twists western tropes to his own ends. He does what Italian directors by then had been doing with Zapata westerns like Diamiano Damiani's *Quién sabe? (A Bullet for the General,* 1966), critiquing both the history and the political situation of any number of countries in the 1960s. The bulk of *Antonio das Mortes* unfolds in a town that seems to be in the past, but that final image of Antonio walking has him passing automobiles and a Shell Oil sign. In leaving town, he may have walked not just miles but decades. Yet has anything changed? Has the lot of the dispossessed improved? Who will he have to fight next?

Brazil's ministry of culture chose *Antonio das Mortes* to represent Brazil at the 42nd Academy Awards. It was not nominated for Best Foreign Language Film, but that the Brazilian authorities forwarded it for consideration at all is peculiar. It shows the ambivalent attitude they must have had toward Rocha's movies. The dictatorship seems to have recognized the value of his films and been proud of their stature worldwide, yet been leery of their content. Rocha remained outspoken in his articles and interviews, and by 1971, as the military dictatorship hardened and political repressions increased, he did not want to keep living in Brazil. He chose to go into exile. For the next several years, he lived abroad and shot films in Congo, Spain, and Italy. Not until 1981 would he return to Brazil, and by that time, he was ailing. He would die without seeing the end of the dictatorship, which occurred on March 15, 1985.

Glauber Rocha and José Mojica Marins are two extraordinarily distinctive filmmakers who had no choice but to work under the shadow of military rule, and, in their own distinctive ways, both reflected Brazilian political violence in their work. One can only speculate on what would have happened if these two had done a film together, which, as it so happens, they did discuss. Would the film have been a horror-western hybrid? And would it have been heavy or light on politics? Marins is on record in an interview as saying that "the meeting between Antonio das Mortes and Coffin Joe was Glauber Rocha's dream." A dream, if it had been realized, that would have promised a memorable film. It didn't happen because of Rocha's death, but it's a pairing to be imagined in that infinite space of alternative cinema history, a space where no censors, no governments, no cultural arbiters of any kind exist.

Scott Adlerberg

OUTTAKE: *YAWAR MALLKU (BLOOD OF THE CONDOR, 1969)*, JORGE SANJINÉS, BOLIVIA

Not many feature films can claim to have directly changed national government policy. One that can is Jorge Sanjinés's 1969 work *Yawar mallku* (*Blood of the Condor*), which was a major influence on the 1971 decision by the Bolivian government to expel the American Peace Corps from the country. Sanjinés was born into a middle-class family in Bolivia's capital, La Paz. He started making short films for the Ministry of Tourism in the early 1960s. In 1963, he was asked by the government to take over

Jorge Sanjinés (center)

the ailing Bolivian National Institute of Cinematography. Under its auspices, Sanjinés completed his first feature, *Ukamau* (1966), about the revenge extracted by a South American Indian villager on a *mestizo*—a Bolivian of mixed Indian and European descent—who rapes his wife. Dubbed into Spanish and Aymara, one of Bolivia's main Indian dialects, the film was initially widely shown. But the official mood toward the movie changed as a result of the labor strife in the crucial tin-mining industry and growing rural unrest that spread when Che Guevara entered the country illegally in 1966 to lead a guerrilla war against the military dictatorship, which had gained power two years earlier. The authorities seized all copies of *Ukamau*, destroyed them, and closed the institute. Along with several colleagues, Sanjinés formed the Grupo Ukamau film collective in 1969 and made *Blood of the Condor*.

Blood of the Condor opens with Ignacio (Marcelino Yanahuaya) and Paulina (Benedicta Mendoza), a couple who belong to the Quechua, one of Bolivia's two majority indigenous Indian populations, who are distraught about another failed pregnancy. Amid swirling rumors of a conspiracy, Ignacio and other village men are arrested by a corrupt police captain who

Blood of the Condor (1969)

Corrupt police execute protesting villagers in Jorge Sanjinés's *Blood of the Condor* (1969)

orders his officers to execute the prisoners en route to jail. Ignacio survives and, badly wounded, is taken to the city by Paulina. There they meet his brother, Sixto (Vincente Verneros Salinas), who is alienated by a grinding factory job and unsuccessful attempts to assimilate to urban life.

The film moves between Sixto's increasingly desperate attempts to find money for his brother's urgent medical treatment and flashbacks of the events leading to the arrest and murder of the villagers. The later sequence shows Ignacio discovering that many other women in his village have been unable to conceive children. He traces the problem to a nearby maternal health clinic set up by Americans working for the Progress Corps, a thinly veiled take on the Peace Corps, who he believes have been secretly sterilizing local women. The villagers storm the clinic and drive the foreigners out of the area.

Blood of the Condor has a stark, minimalist look and feel, no doubt because it was made with only basic equipment and a budget of less than $50,000. But while *Ukamau* generated controversy for its sympathetic portrayal of Bolivia's marginalized Indian population, *Blood of the Condor* was a much more overt assault on their poverty and the racist treatment they experienced. The film depicts the Quechua as having a rich collective culture in relative harmony with nature despite the hardships they endure, while foreigners and their mestizo allies are exploitative and materialistic. The film especially pours scorn on the Western aid workers, who are depicted as dishonest, manipulative hippies. Significantly, the corrupt police captain who later orders the murders of his prisoners first introduces members of the Progress Corps to the villagers and exhorts the women to go to the clinic for health checks. The final scene, a freeze-frame of the Indians upraising their rifles, is an explicit call for revolutionary action.

The Principal Enemy (1974)

Though the issue of foreign aid workers sterilizing Indian women without consent had been previously reported by the Bolivian media, *Blood of the Condor* blew it into a national debate. Sanjinés claimed his depiction was based on testimony he received from doctors and gynecologists who treated Quechua women. Whatever the exact situation, the activities of the Progress Corps are designed to serve as a foil for the wider exploitation of Bolivia's Indian people.

Grupo Ukamau had transported projection equipment and an electrical generator to show the film to remote Indian communities, who they discovered were critical of its complex flashback structure, borrowed from Western arthouse cinema. This led Sanjinés to the realization that while he had worked closely with local Indians, he was still imposing his own version of events and use of cinematic form on their community. In tandem with a similar trajectory undertaken by other members of Latin America's New Cinema movement, Grupo Ukamau started to develop a different approach. This is most evident in *Jatun auka* (*The Principal Enemy*, 1974). The film was shot in Peru, where Sanjinés had moved after being exiled by Bolivia's military government following his 1971 *El coraje del pueblo* (*The Courage of the People*), a documentary-style feature about the massacre of striking workers in 1967.

The Principal Enemy directly links the exploitation of the region's Indian population to foreign actors, principally American imperialism. It begins with an Indian villager confronting a landowner he believes has stolen and sold one of his cows. The landowner and his foreman murder the villager in the ensuing argument. Attempts by other villagers to secure justice for the killing using the official legal system fail, leaving them feeling hopeless, until a revolutionary guerrilla group arrives in their area. The precise political orientation of the guerrillas is not stated, although many of the group's members feature a remarkable resemblance to Guevara. The guerrillas are respectful of the Indians and their culture, gradually win their trust, and start educating them about the need to fight not just their direct oppressors but also the foreign imperialists backing them. Together with the villagers, the guerrillas arrest, try, and publicly execute the landowner and foreman. The remainder of the film depicts the brutal reprisals inflicted on the rebellious villagers by the military, overseen by US army advisers, and a pitched battle between the military and guerrillas in which the latter are victorious.

The Principal Enemy is far more dialogue heavy and much more politically didactic in content and tone than Blood of the Condor. It has a simpler, more linear plot and a completely nonprofessional cast. The film lauds pre-Columbian Inca heritage as a harmonious society in which everyone was fed and looked after, drawing a direct line between the "white exploiters" who destroyed the Inca Empire and the activities of foreign imperialists in Latin America at the time it was being made. The Principal Enemy also features an Indian amauta—a traditional Incan wise man responsible for passing along stories and preserving history from generation to generation—who appears at various points in the film to narrate the story and reinforce its political conclusion. "Learn the truth, brothers," he states at the end. "These men will never be on our side. They are our principal enemies."

Andrew Nette

OUTTAKE: ARGENTINA: NEW CINEMA AND DIRTY WAR

Argentina's parliamentary democracy was interrupted by military coups six times in the twentieth century. The final of these, the so-called Process of National Reorganization between 1976 and 1983, was the most brutal. Referred to as *la Guerra Sucia*, the "Dirty War," Argentina's military-led junta literally went to war against its own populace. It eradicated civil liberties, suspended parliament, and banned trade unions, political parties, and provincial governments. The official estimate of those accused of being left-wing subversives and disappeared stands at approximately nine thousand, though some estimates put the number as high as thirty thousand. These individuals were snatched by the army and paramilitary squads, kept in a giant network of clandestine prisons, and never heard from again. Political prisoners were thrown alive from planes and had their bodies dumped in mass graves. Pregnant prisoners, some of them raped in detention and killed after giving birth, had their children adopted by families of senior military figures and the rich. Declassified documents show that American secretary of state Henry Kissinger gave Argentina's military the green light to seize power and launch its campaign of state-sponsored terror. Argentina was also the operations center for Operation Condor, a US-organized anticommunist alliance between the then dictatorships of Argentina, Bolivia, Chile, Paraguay, and Uruguay. Created in 1975, Washington officially withdrew its support for Operation Condor under President Jimmy Carter, but there is evidence American military and intelligence assistance continued until into the early 1980s.

It is perhaps no coincidence that many of the countries that were the focus of Operation Condor were also centers of Latin America's "new cinema" movement of the 1960s and 1970s. Influenced by the Cuban revolution in 1959, this movement also took inspiration from the political upheaval sweeping much of the region and the world. But unlike the New Wave movement that emerged in Europe around the same time, Latin America's loose grouping of new cinema filmmakers sought to develop films that fused a new form of aesthetics with radical ideology and political practice. A central concern was the rejection of Hollywood, along with the exploration of cinema as a tool to help overthrow the region's neocolonial

mindset. These filmmakers
debated not just what to show
in their work, but how to show
it, including how their films were
distributed and screened. With one
of the largest and longest-running
film industries in Latin America,
Argentina played a vital role in the
movement. Especially influential
was the 1968 documentary *La*

Raymundo Gleyzer

hora de los hornos (*The Hour of the Furnaces*), codirected and cowritten
by Argentinian Fernando Solanas and Spanish-born Octavio Getino, who
migrated to Argentina in the 1950s. Shot guerrilla style, this four-hour film
sought to connect the upsurge in revolutionary activity globally in the late
1960s to Argentina and was mainly shown in underground venues.

Another Argentinian influenced by new cinema but who positioned
himself to its left was Raymundo Gleyzer. Primarily a documentary
filmmaker, his only feature film, *Los Traidores* (*The Traitors*, 1973), prefigures
the political violence that engulfed Argentina in the second half of the
1970s, especially the military's almost religious mission to eradicate what
it saw as subversive elements destroying the country. The key character,
Roberto Barrera (Víctor Proncet, who cowrote the screenplay), is a corrupt
right-wing trade union leader. The story begins in the early 1970s when
Barrera, facing defeat in an upcoming union election, hatches a plot to fake
his own kidnapping to generate sympathy among the rank and file and to
pin blame for it on the left-wing forces in his union trying to unseat him.
Flashbacks show Barrera as a radical trade union delegate in the late 1950s
and his rise to power in the 1960s, during which time he is co-opted by
management and actively works to hose down strike action. At the end of
the film, Barrera wins reelection but is assassinated by an unspecified leftist
guerrilla group at his victory party. Despite being under military rule, the
late 1960s and early 1970s in Argentina were a period of major left political
mobilization. Unions played a key role, leading what was virtually a popular
uprising in the city of Córdoba in May 1969. Barrera is shown collaborating
with the military to suppress this unrest. He also acts as a US asset in return
for funding from anticommunist American trade unions.

The Traitors illustrates a further complicating factor in postwar
Argentinian politics: the influence of Juan Perón. A former army general,
Perón was president from 1946 to his overthrow in 1955 and again from

1973 to his death in July 1974, when he was briefly succeeded by his widow until she was overthrown by the military. Revered by many as a modernizer who delivered substantial material gains to the working class, Perón was also a nationalist and fervent anticommunist, who continued to exert a powerful hold over Argentinian politics from his exile in Franco's Spain. During his absence, his support base split between right-wing anticommunists and radicals who organized their own guerrilla group, the Montoneros, and carried out bombings, shootings,

UN FILM DEL GRUPO CINE DE LA BASE MUSIDORA

LOS TRAIDORE$$

CGT

UN FILM SOBRE ELECCIONES SINDICALES, PODER, BUROCRACIA Y CORRUPCIÓN.

The Traitors (1973)

kidnappings, and bank robberies in the 1970s to early 1980s. *The Traitors* is Gleyzer's critique of the right-wing Perónism that came to dominate much of Argentina's labor movement in the early 1970s and his view that these people prevented a wider working-class mobilization. Gleyzer was a member of the People's Revolutionary Army (PRA), a guerrilla group positioned to the left of the Montoneros and whose politics took on an increasingly violent Maoist orientation. In 1973, Gleyzer cofounded the Cine de la Base collective, a sort of cinematic arm of the PRA. The collective focused on making left-wing films, distributing them outside mainstream distribution circuits, and organizing viewings in slums, unions halls, and factories, after which the audience was invited to participate in political discussion.

The Traitors makes extensive use of documentary footage of street demonstrations and labor unrest. While this imparts a vivid sense of the mounting political ferment in early 1970s Argentina, the film is hard to follow for anyone not familiar with the power that Perónism had on the nation's working class. Much screen time is spent watching Barrera and his cronies hash out tactics and his opponents debate political positions and ideology. Writing in a 2019 issue of *Cineaste*, Dennis West asserts that narrative clarity in *The Traitors* also suffered from the chaotic guerrilla style in which it was made: a shoestring budget and the imperative to evade official surveillance. Over a hundred actors took part, many nonprofessionals and volunteers, who for security reasons were never provided with a full script in advance. People came and went from the production, some without finishing all their scenes. Exposed film was smuggled out of the country for development in the US.

Two months after the junta took power on May 27, 1976, Gleyzer, then thirty-five, was abducted in broad daylight by the military. According to evidence given by Gleyzer's former partner, Juana Sapire, to an inquiry held many years after the fall of the dictatorship, a priest managed to access the secret military prison in which the director was being held. Gleyzer had been tortured, including having his eyes gouged out. That was the last time he was seen alive. After his disappearance, Cine de la Base rapidly dissolved.

The junta collapsed following Argentina's disastrous invasion of the Falkland Islands, economic crisis, and increased civil opposition. Filmmakers, heavily censored under military rule, were left to make sense of what had happened. The best known of the films in the 1980s that explored the Dirty War and the trauma arising from it is Luis Puenzo's 1985 drama *La historia oficial* (*The Official Story*). Set in 1983, the last year of the junta, it tells of a middle-class Buenos Aires couple who live happily with their adopted five-year-old daughter, Gaby. The wife, Alicia (Norma Aleandro), is jolted from her sheltered existence by the return of a friend from overseas, Ana (Chunchuna Villafañe), who confides she left after being arrested and tortured by the military due to a past relationship with a man labeled a subversive. Ana also says she witnessed pregnant detainees leave to give birth and return without babies, whom she asserts were sold to rich childless couples. Shocked by Ana's claims, Alicia investigates her daughter's background, which leads to the discovery that Gaby is the child of a disappeared female political prisoner. This forms part of Alicia's wider political awakening, which in turn drives a wedge between her and her husband, Roberto (Héctor Alterio), who organized the adoption through his military contacts but doesn't want to admit it. *The Official Story* depicts the mounting opposition to the junta and the sense of panic among the military and their allies, as their grip on power is slipping. While Alicia is economically privileged, she is gaslighted by nearly every man she encounters during her search: her husband and his friends, male doctors, and her Catholic priest.

Héctor Olivera's *La noche de los lápices* (*The Night of the Pencils*, 1986) is based on the abduction by security forces of a group of teenagers in

US poster for *The Official Story* (1985)

mid-September 1976 in the city of La Plata, south of Buenos Aires. The film shows six of the students, part of a group that had been agitating for lower bus fares, being violently seized from their homes in the middle of the night by masked men. A seventh, Pablo (Alejo García Pintos), is taken several days later. All are kept in an unofficial detention center, where they are tortured with electric shocks and subjected to mock firing squads, and the women are raped. Echoing *The Official Story*, tales circulate among the prisoners that pregnant inmates give birth and their children are taken away. Meanwhile, the

The Night of the Pencils (1986)

parents of one of the students, Claudia (Vita Escardó), search for their daughter, encountering brazen police denials she is being held prisoner and, contradicting these, accusations she has links to the Montoneros. Mirroring real life, Pablo is the only one to survive, because he is transferred to an official prison on subversion charges, where he serves four years before being released and eventually telling the story. The others remain among the 233 Argentinian adolescents who were still officially missing when the film was made in 1986.

The Night of the Pencils mixes hard-hitting social commentary with aspects of the thriller genre, typical of Olivera's more commercial style of work. His films included *La Patagonia rebelde* (*Rebellion in Patagonia*, 1974), a drama about the military's suppression of the anarchist-led union movement in the country's south in the 1920s. But he also made musicals and comedies, the latter including *No habrá más penas ni olvido* (*Funny Dirty Little War*, 1983), about the conflicts in the local government of a small rural town, a satire on the wider struggle between the Montoneros and right-wing Perónist forces. He spent the junta years working in Argentinian television and would go on to direct films coproduced by Roger Corman, including *Barbarian Queen*, *Wizards of the Lost Kingdom*, and *Cocaine Wars*, all of which appeared in 1985.

The Girlfriend (1988)

Other films that sought to both commemorate and make sense of the Dirty War are two works from Solanas, who spent military rule in exile in Paris: an Argentinian/French coproduction, *Tangos, el exilio de Gardel* (*Tangos, the Exile of Gardel*, 1986), about a group of Argentine political exiles in Paris who decide to stage a tango ballet in honor of singer and composer Carlos Gardel, and *Sur* (*The South*, 1988), the story of a political prisoner who only narrowly avoids being disappeared and on release is left to make sense of his life. Other films include: Alejandro Doria's tale of a love affair between a teenage boy and older woman who is being hunted by the authorities for being a political subversive, *Sofía* (1987); *Los días de junio* (*Days of June*, 1985), which follows an Argentinian actor who returns from exile in the dying days of the junta; and Argentinian-German director Jeanine Meerapfel's *La amiga* (*The Girlfriend*, 1988), about the friendship between a radical Jewish actress who is forced into exile by the junta and a working-class woman who refuses to abandon the search for her disappeared son.

Andrew Nette

OUTTAKE: *LATINO* (1985), HASKELL WEXLER, UNITED STATES

American filmmaker Haskell Wexler worked on sixty feature films and over one hundred documentaries and is commonly cited as one of the most innovative and influential cinematographers globally in the second half of the twentieth century. Wexler, who died in 2015, is also noteworthy for mixing major Hollywood fare such as *In the Heat of the Night* (1967) and *One Flew Over the Cuckoo's Nest* (1975), both of which he served as cinematographer for, with radical documentary and feature filmmaking. Wexler was a staunch antiwar activist, no doubt resulting from his World War II service in the merchant marines, during which his ship was torpedoed by a Nazi U-boat off the coast of Africa and he spent two weeks in a lifeboat until he was rescued.

According to an obituary in the *Guardian* by John Patterson, Wexler worked on Peter Watkins's *Punishment Park* (1971), a dystopian pseudo-documentary in which those deemed a risk to America's security are detained and given the choice of being sent to prison or a harsh stretch of desert called Punishment Park, and Ken Loach's *Bread and Roses* (2000), in which migrant office cleaners in Los Angeles fight for better conditions. He was involved in documentaries tackling civil rights (*The Bus*, 1965), the Vietnam War (*Interviews with My Lai Veterans*, 1971), the journey to Vietnam undertaken by actress Jane Fonda and her then husband and future California state senator Tom Hayden (*Introduction to the Enemy*, 1974), the Weather Underground (*Underground*, 1976), and the campaign against nuclear arms (*No Nukes*, 1980).

He also wrote and directed two feature films of his own. The first, *Medium Cool* (1969), continues to be critically lauded as a vital examination of the political upheaval and violence in the United States in 1968. John Cassellis (Robert Foster) is a cynical, dispassionate television news cameraman whose attitudes toward his craft slowly change due to his relationship with a single mother (Vera Bloom) and her young son, and the discovery that the network he is employed by has been passing his footage to the FBI and police. He takes a freelance assignment that plunges him into the "blue riot" in Chicago in 1968, when police brutally broke up antiwar demonstrators outside the National Democratic Convention. *Medium Cool*

Medium Cool (1969)

included cinema verité–style techniques, including dramatic footage shot during the protests by Wexler.

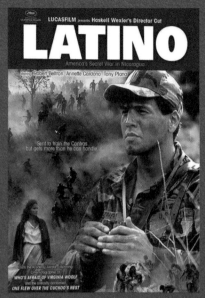

Latino (1985)

Wexler's second feature, *Latino* (1985), produced by Lucasfilm, was a political drama unambiguously supportive of the Sandinista National Liberation Front–led government established in Nicaragua after the overthrow of the corrupt dictator, Anastasio Somoza Debayle, in 1979. It was released at the peak of the Nicaraguan civil war—a conflict stoked by Washington's clandestine support for the right-wing contra rebels, led by elements of the former Somoza regime. Although praised at the Cannes Film Festival, *Latino* was quickly yanked from distribution in the US after performing poorly and, unlike *Medium Cool*, has been buried ever since.

Latino focuses on a Chicano Green Beret and Vietnam veteran called Eddie Guerrero (Robert Beltran), part of an American force deployed for maneuvers along the Honduran border with Nicaragua. In reality, he trains the contras and accompanies them on missions into Nicaragua, with the help of a friend and fellow Green Beret, Ruben (Tony Plana). Guerrero witnesses contras slaughtering livestock and targeting civilian infrastructure, indiscriminately killing and torturing civilians, and press-ganging others into joining the rebels. Wexler contrasts this with an almost bucolic depiction of life on a Sandinista collective sugar farm where Nicaraguan farmers struggle to protect their postrevolution gains, land, and sense of freedom from constant contra attacks.

Guerrero romances Marlene (Annette Charles), an agronomist and Nicaraguan émigré working in Honduras who begins to sympathize with the revolution after returning home for the funeral of her father, killed by contras. There's also a somewhat undercooked plotline about Guerrero's gradual crisis of conscience over what the contras are doing and the recognition that he is culpable in the death of other Latinos at the behest of an overwhelmingly white military structure. This doesn't stop him

US Special Forces soldier Eddie Guerrero (Robert Beltran) being captured by Sandinista farmers in *Latino* (1985)

from taking part in what is the film's climax: a major contra attack on the collective farm, where Marlene is now working, in which Guerrero secretly disobeys an order to remove his dog tags to ensure plausible deniability of official US involvement, should he fall into the hands of its Sandinista defenders.

Filmed in Honduras, *Latino* includes plenty of Wexler's trademark cinema verité flourishes. But it is a confused effort that can't quite decide on whether it wants to be a romantic melodrama or a hard-hitting exposé about the impact of Washington's policies in Latin America. The political depictions feel crude but maybe less so when viewed, as Wexler no doubt intended, as a political corrective to the widespread anti-Sandinista propaganda being peddled by the Republican administration and large sections of the mainstream media. And while the plot feels scrappy, it captures the chaos and confusion of shadowy proxy wars, in which it is never clear whether the person you encounter is going to be friendly or kill you.

Latino was among a raft of features set in Nicaragua in the '80s, when the country was a key Cold War battleground. *Alsino y el condor* (*Alsino and the Condor*, 1982) is a Nicaraguan/Mexican/Cuban coproduction directed by Chilean-born Miguel Littin, which examines a Nicaraguan boy's attempts to have a childhood as the area around him is engulfed by civil war. A mainstream but nonetheless surprisingly gritty and politically sharp effort is Roger Spottiswoode's *Under Fire* (1983), about three Western journalists working in Nicaragua during the revolution against the Somoza dictatorship. Nicaragua was also the setting for a range of exploitation movies: *Last Plane Out* (1983), in which an American journalist (Jan-Michael Vincent) struggles to get himself and other foreigners out of the country after Somoza's downfall; Enzo G. Castellari's *Striker* (1987), an English/American production riffing off *Missing in Action* (1984), in which a former soldier is hired to get an American journalist out of a Sandinista prison; and the somewhat similar *Delta Force Commando* (1987).

Andrew Nette

BREAD AND CIRCUSES

Peter Watkins and Hunting Humans On-Screen

Man is a dangerous animal. For decades, audiences have delighted in films in which human beings are hunted. From *The Most Dangerous Game* (1932) to *Hard Target* (1992) and *Surviving the Game* (1994) to *The Hunt* (2002), the list of "man hunting" movies continues to grow a title or two every year. Taking the predatory pursuit out of the jungle (urban or verdant), we find that mano a mano confrontations feel "safer" to audiences when placed in gladiatorial arenas of ancient Rome or in the distant future. Recreational bloodletting takes on a more political subtext, and the games find sponsorship with the state. While the filmic subgenre of "man hunting" movies may vary insofar as the sponsorship of the contest (whether it is a private weirdo, a cabal of venture capitalists, or state-sponsored entertainment), the early work of filmmaker Peter Watkins stands apart from the typical populist fare due to his keen political sensibilities. Watkins was a pioneer of the pseudo-documentary (also referred to as "mockumentary"), and while his films like *Gladiatorerna* (*The Gladiators*, 1969) and *Punishment Park* (1971) tread ground similar to other state-sponsored entertainment films, he does so with deadly seriousness rather than a wink and a grin. While I will be discussing "man hunting" films overall, I will be focusing specifically on Watkins's entries into the subgenre.

State-funded human-hunting contests stem from a desire to placate citizenry with cathartic violence. The attendees, or viewers, of these confrontations convey dronish complacency when not frothing at the mouth, chanting "Jonathan" while watching the latest *Rollerball* (1975) contest, or throwing themselves into the road for the love of Frankenstein in *Death Race*

2000 (1975). While the "people hunting people" subgenre owes much to Richard Connell's story "The Most Dangerous Game," from 1924, the science-fiction interpretations of gladiatorial contests as televised sports are indebted to Robert Sheckley's short story "The Seventh Victim," from 1953. Sheckley would go on to make a cottage industry out of this theme with stories and novels like 1958's *The Prize of Peril* (adapted as both *Das Millionenspiel* [1970] and *Le Prix du Danger* [1983] and heavily influential to *The Running Man* [1987]) and 1959's *Immortality Inc.* (adapted for the screen as *Freejack* in 1992).

The 10th Victim (1965)

In 1965, Sheckley's "The Seventh Victim" came to the silver screen via Elio Petri's Italian film *La decima vittima* (*The 10th Victim*). While containing the kernel of a good idea, *The 10th Victim* folds under the weight of its gynophobia. The film's protagonist, Marcello Poletti (Marcello Mastroianni sporting an unlikely head of flaxen hair), plays in a state-run contest wherein participants alternate roles from hunter to victim until they perish or retire after ten games. Poletti closes in on the end of his career, becoming the final prey to Caroline Meredith (Ursula Andress). *The 10th Victim* is the first of these sci-fi-tinged human-hunting films and introduces the framework, though it doesn't go as far with its political analysis as the films to follow; instead, the focus is on comedy and misogynistic tropes like the greedy wife.

Surprisingly absent in *The 10th Victim* is the concept of live broadcast. There are no television cameras in the film despite the growing power of the medium. It's one thing to hold a "man hunting" contest or competition, but it's quite another to broadcast the event, usually by despotic regimes, as entertainment masking a calculated effort to placate the population or cow them into submission. In 1964, Marshall McLuhan recognized that "the medium is the message" in his book *Understanding Media: The Extensions of Man.* By 1965, the Vietnam War was being broadcast to Western audiences on television. The style of reportage from Vietnam influenced filmmaker and provocateur Peter Watkins in his faux documentary *Culloden* (1964), which retold the 1745 Jacobite rebellion via an "on the spot reporter." The same year, Watkins presented his docudrama *The War Game* to the BBC, who had contracted him for their series *The Wednesday Play* (1964–70). On September 24, 1965, the film was screened for senior members of the Home Office. Six weeks later, the BBC announced that the film would not be screened due to it being "too horrific" for the medium of broadcasting.

While there is no "man hunting" in *The War Game*, it serves as an important stepping stone in Watkins's career. It's a feature-length pseudo-documentary based on the "what if" premise of a nuclear attack on the UK, which gives Watkins an opportunity to display just how useless the civil defense would be in the face of an actual nuclear emergency. The harrowing film starts off with a stentorian voice-over discussing British targets for bombs from the Soviet Union, before plunging into action with a news broadcast narration revealing the current state of emergency in the country. Through the use of the authoritative voices along with staged scenes of destruction, Watkins disarms the audience and makes one question the veracity of his work. It's all presented as real, making *The War Game* a terrifying experience.

Along with scenes of chaos on the streets, billeting evacuees, and vox populi interviews are moments of ironic levity, such as when a civil defense officer handing out a pamphlet about the dangers of radioactivity discusses how they didn't sell well at nine pence apiece. Additional irony comes from recreating actual statements from leaders of the day, like an Anglican bishop or civil defense minister, counterpointed by scenes of the destruction wrought by a nuclear bomb. Shot in black and white by Peter Bartlett (with an uncredited Peter Suschitzky, who would go on to work with Watkins again on *Privilege* [1967]), the film brilliantly mixes calm interview sequences with handheld scenes capturing the despair and destruction of the population of Kent. The nuclear threat remains a frequent topic in Watkins's work with films made in Sweden, like 1975's *Fällan* (*The Trap*) and 1987's *Resan* (*The Journey*). Despite being banned by the BBC, *The War Game* would go on to win an Oscar for Best Documentary at the 1967 Academy Awards. It would take until 1984 for the BBC to allow the airing of a similarly harrowing docudrama about nuclear war, Barry Hines's *Threads*.

Watkins's feature after *The War Game*, *Privilege*, would also employ the pseudo-documentary style in telling the story of Steven Shorter (Paul Jones), a messianic pop singer. Watkins was too ahead of his time in the portrayal of popular culture and the media commercializing the antiwar counterculture in order to render it ineffectual. Critics of the day condemned *Privilege* as misanthropic, unprofessional, and immoral. The film was denied distribution

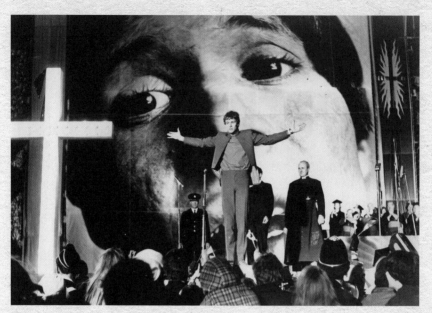

Paul Jones as pop singer Steven Shorter in *Privilege* (1967)

in the UK's national cinemas while Universal Pictures withdrew it from theaters after a few international screenings. After being censored by the BBC and attacked by critics for *Privilege*, Watkins went into exile from Britain. He was approached by the Sangers distribution company from Sweden, who offered to produce any film Watkins wanted to make, resulting in *The Gladiators*. Taking cues from the *Star Trek* episode "The Armageddon Game" (1967) and Michael Elliot's *The Year of the Sex Olympics* (1968), the narrator of *The Gladiators* informs the audience that "the peoples of the United Nations and the leading communist countries, determined to maintain international peace and internal security, to save succeeding generations from the scourge of yet another world war and to reaffirm faith in the dignity and worth of the human being, resolved the following: to organize international machinery from all races and creeds and political beliefs for the playing of a series of military games in special centers in the non-aligned countries, by which purpose it is hoped to divert the natural aggressions of mankind towards the true fundamentals of honorable sportsmanship and the spirit of the team."

Along with a handful of soldiers representing the aforementioned UN and "leading communist countries," there is a French university student provocateur who seems to have come straight from the May 1968 riots to disrupt the games. We follow the soldiers (who are often from UN countries) as they bicker their way through the gauntlet of challenges set up by Sweden.

SANDREWS

Peter Watkins
GLADIATORERNA

Foto Peter Suschitzky   FÄRG

Original Swedish poster for *The Gladiators* (1969)

All of this is being broadcast as real-ity TV and sponsored by a pasta company. The core idea of two men fighting out a global conflict fueled *The Gladiators,* as well as John Boorman's 1968 film *Hell in the Pacific.* It would also be used again in George McGowan's *The Challenge* (1970). Yet, despite the popularity of the idea, Watkins's film again faced a storm of controversy. Most critics found *The Gladiators* dreadfully boring, with the notable exception of Judith Crist of *New York* maga-zine, who called it Watkins's "finest film to date." However, Crist would find his next film, *Punishment Park,* to be "trashily hysterical anti-Amer-ican" rather than being the true jewel in the director's crown.

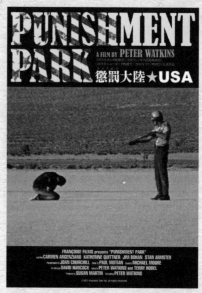

Japanese poster for *Punishment Park* (1971)

Watkins employed a set of stylistic conventions to give *Punishment Park* more weight. As with the lion's share of Watkins's oeuvre, he shot *Punishment Park* as a mockumentary (years before they were in vogue). The film begins with a prologue that explains its basis: "Under the provisions of Title 2 of the 1950 Internal Security Act, also known as the McCarran Act, the president of the United States of America is still authorized—without further approval by Congress—to determine an event of insurrection within the United States and to declare the existence of an 'Internal Security Emergency.' The pres-ident is then authorized to apprehend and detain each person as to whom there is reasonable ground to believe probably will engage in certain future acts of sabotage. Persons apprehended shall be given a hearing, without right of bail, without the necessity of evidence, and shall then be confined to places of detention." If this sounds familiar, that is probably because several of these tenets made their way into the Patriot Act, which the US Congress hastily passed after September 11, 2001. At the time of this writing, detention camps like the ones in *Punishment Park* don't openly reside on the US mainland but rather at Guantánamo Bay, Cuba.

As a "humane" and "fair" method of sentencing, those accused of insurgency have the option of either serving out their sentence in a federal penitentiary or taking their chances in Punishment Park. The "park" is a

Punishment Park (1971)

sun-baked, rocky landscape where participants have three days to complete a fifty-three-mile trek to a US flag. To add some "excitement" to the mix, the detainees must evade being captured by pursuing law enforcement officers. The officers have transportation, guns, and water. Supposedly shot for European television, *Punishment Park* follows the trial of a group of alleged dissidents. Having been held for two months without ever hearing the charges against them, they're given a chance to speak at this tribunal, but only to a certain extent. The kangaroo "courtroom" setting with the comments of those on trial and of their uptight, white, bourgeois jurors are intercut with scenes of the previous group of "troublemakers" making their arduous journey through Punishment Park.

Watkins doesn't skimp on ironic juxtapositions of action and sentiment between any of those involved. Yet Watkins spares viewers from ham-fisted theatrics or preachy sentimentalism common to other pseudo-documentaries. *Punishment Park* is thoroughly convincing. The "acting" never feels theatrical. Instead, the performances feel frighteningly real. Playing for a mere four days upon its US release (where it garnered violently negative reviews in the press), *Punishment Park* quickly disappeared from public view and remained largely unknown to younger cinephiles. Until 2002, the only version of *Punishment Park* available on video was a French-subtitled copy whose muddy picture quality only further emphasized the subversive subject matter

Turkish poster for *The Prize of Peril* (1983)

of the film. If *Punishment Park* feels so shocking and relevant today, this author wonders how disturbing it must have been for audiences in 1971, when the Vietnam War was still in high gear. Being "chosen" or "elected" to participate in one of the aforementioned "man hunting" contests would have brought to mind conscription via the draft. While showing barbarism in the distant past or sometime in the future provides some comfort to an audience, the real challenge comes when this kind of event takes place here and now—which likely explains the backlash against the film during its release.

The Game of Millions, aka *Chance for a Million* (1970)

After *Punishment Park*, Watkins continued his journey making docudramas and exploring politics. As the 1970s progressed, the influx of "people hunting people" movies would increase via the aforementioned German made-for-TV film *Das Millionenspiel* and French film *The Prize of Peril*. Additionally, films such as Paul Michael Glaser's *The Running Man* (1987), Boris Paval Conen's *Temmink: The Ultimate Fight* (1998), and Scott Wiper's *The Condemned* (2007) would continue the tradition of gladiatorial games broadcast for the masses. In 2000 and 2001, a pair of films would embrace the mantle of Watkins's controversial filmmaking with Kinji Fukasaku's Japanese cult classic *Batoru Rowaiaru* (*Battle Royale*) and Daniel Minahan's *Series 7: The Contenders*. Most of the aforementioned films end with either a lone survivor or a couple who work together to bring down the system that oppresses the people via the entertainment of gladiatorial combat. Yet in Watkins's films, these efforts are more often for naught, leaving the world in either the status quo or worse than before. *Punishment Park* and *The Gladiators* are audacious in scope and political commentary in the way they play off stylistic conventions and skewer the idea of appeasement of the masses with bread and circuses.

Mike White

OUTTAKE: REVOLUTION AS A CREATIVE ACT IN THE FILMS OF LINDSAY ANDERSON

One of the pillars of left-wing cinema in England, Lindsay Anderson helmed a series of confrontational films deeply critical of British society and the United Kingdom's legacy of imperialism. Anderson started out as a film critic and helped found the somewhat radical *Sequence* film magazine alongside like-minded future filmmakers such as Karel Reisz; he also wrote criticism for *Sight and Sound* and political journals like *New Statesman*. Anderson, Reisz, and several members of the *Sequence* group would shortly go on to launch the Free Cinema movement in the mid-'50s, with the shared determination to make unbiased documentaries not influenced by government propaganda or the need to appeal to mainstream audiences; this includes *Thursday's Children* (1954), about a school for deaf children. Anderson and his Free Cinema colleagues would progress to feature films by the late '50s and early '60s; this movement became known as the British New Wave and primarily focused on "kitchen sink" social realist cinema about working-class communities in England. Like the French New Wave, this younger generation of filmmakers were reacting against commercial cinema, which they saw as out of touch with British society. Anderson's *This Sporting Life* (1963) is a key example of the movement, with its exploration of how mounting social frustrations often lead to violence, especially for young men.

Anderson's outspoken politics deeply informed his work as a writer and director. Many of his films, particularly the loose "Mick Travis trilogy" he is best known for, are an expression of his feelings about the British Empire, its imperialism, and its waning legacy as a global power. His leftist views were likely shaped by his experiences growing up in South India as the son of a British Army officer, as well as Anderson's own service in the army during World War II, which included work as a cryptographer. In *Lindsay Anderson Revisited: Unknown Aspects of a Filmmaker* (2016), Isabelle Gourdin Sangouard writes, "Anderson repeatedly expressed a strong sense of national and cultural alienation, which shaped the identity of his work. He, for instance, liked to stress that he was a child of the Empire, thereby challenging the part in which his English upbringing and heritage had played in his work."

IF-1473-96

Christine Noonan in *If…* (1968)

In 1968, Anderson directed *If…*, perhaps his most celebrated work. It is certainly a film about alienated outsiders driven to violence by the oppressiveness of their social environment. Based on Anderson's own days in preparatory school, the film follows Mick Travis (Malcolm McDowell) and his few friends, all misfits in an esteemed boarding school. Slightly older boys who effectively run the school, known as "Whips," abuse their power at every turn, even sexually exploiting some of the younger students. Travis has increasingly surreal fantasies that are sexual and turn more and

If ... (1968)

more violent, coinciding with the boys' discussions of how it is possible to "change the world with a bullet in the right place," that "violence and revolution are the only pure acts," and that "war is the last possible creative act." When the Whips progress to outright torture as punishment, Travis and his friends finally snap. They uncover the school's supply of weapons (on hand as part of their military cadet program) and stage a bloody revolt against teachers, fellow students, and visiting parents in a nihilistic and rather fantastical display of violence.

Though *If* ... received critical acclaim throughout Europe—winning the Palme d'Or at the Cannes Film Festival the following year—it was controversial in England and received a doomed X certificate rating for its shocking violence and countercultural themes. Though *If* ... is essentially a satirical drama, it is no wonder it had too many parallels to the global events of 1968 for the British censors to be quite comfortable with. While Travis and his friends can't really be described as leftist guerrillas or student radicals, they are ostracized misfits reacting to years of abuse from the older, more powerful students, many of whom are clearly depicted as upper class.

Five years later, Anderson and McDowell returned to the character of Mick Travis with *O Lucky Man* (1973), though it is only tangentially connected to the first film. Here Travis is presented as a young, ambitious coffee salesman who travels through the UK and finds himself in increasingly fantastical, violent scenarios. In a blackly cynical reimagining of John Bunyan's influential spiritual allegory *The Pilgrim's Progress* (1678), Travis sets off on a journey in which he learns a series of ethical lessons, namely that if he wants to succeed in the world he must abandon his morals and principles. He winds up becoming the assistant to a corrupt businessman (Ralph Richardson), who is selling chemical weapons to an authoritarian, presumably Third World country, the fictional

O Lucky Man (1973)

Lindsay Anderson and Malcolm McDowell on the set of *O Lucky Man* (1973)

state of Zingara. Zingara is popular with wealthy tourists but is under siege by local rebels. The Zingaran dictator, Dr. Munda (Arthur Lowe), seeks to eradicate any opposition with the chemical weapons, and he and the businessman conspire to use Travis as a scapegoat; thus he becomes a victim of state violence himself.

Where *If . . .* uses the closed, authoritarian world of boarding school as a microcosm for postwar British society, *O Lucky Man* broadens this scope considerably as Travis journeys throughout England and Scotland and encounters leading industrialists and foreign governments. Anderson takes this to even further extremes with his follow-up film, *Britannia Hospital* (1982), which can best be described as a surreal, nihilistic black comedy skewering early Thatcherism through the lens of the British National Health Service. McDowell returns as Travis, this time in the role of an investigative reporter. He sneaks into a chaotic hospital—wracked by a series of strikes—to witness the horrifying medical experiments (a theme continued from *O Lucky Man*) of Professor Millar (Graham Crowden), about whom Travis is making a documentary. Travis has a more peripheral role in this film, and Anderson broadens the focus to include members of a hospital staff who will go to any lengths—including murder—to make

Britannia Hospital (1982)

sure a visit from Queen Elizabeth goes smoothly. The staff must also contend with demonstrators protesting that the hospital has a notorious African dictator as a patient. *Britannia Hospital* repeatedly shows hospital management and government officials enacting or enabling violence on working-class individuals to accommodate royalty and upper-class patients.

In its final act, *Britannia Hospital* takes an unexpected genre shift into sci-fi and even body horror; Professor Millar is revealed to be carrying out Dr. Frankenstein–like experiments and is even shown murdering patients. He ultimately kills Travis and attempts to use his head to reanimate a being composed of sewn-together body parts from different corpses. The film's conclusion suggests that an obsession with science, technology, and rationalism will only lead to violence, echoing what many twentieth-century philosophers, such as Theodor Adorno, have described as a key problem of the Enlightenment that led directly to World War II and twentieth-century genocide.

Britannia Hospital is even more openly critical of the British government under Margaret Thatcher, who became prime minister in 1979, and particularly her approach to foreign policy. In both *O Lucky Man* and *Britannia Hospital*, those in power are shown in close relationship with Third World authoritarian leaders. And with both films, Anderson explores the UK's attempts to move on from its imperialist past, which he views as essentially superficial. In these films, British economic and governmental powers are shown to be desperately holding on to their power by forging relationships with the dictators of countries suggested to be in the Third World, and they allow or at least enable the torture of and unethical medical experimentation on their own citizens. Notably, the release of *Britannia Hospital* coincided with the Falklands War between the UK and Argentina, a time when many British subjects were seemingly supportive of their government fighting to maintain their colonial interests abroad.

There was an extremely negative critical and popular reaction to *Britannia Hospital*, which nearly ruined Anderson's career. This is likely to do with the film's considerable tonal shift into slapstick comedy, nihilism, and body horror and its portrayal of British society as cruel and mean-spirited. Even the demonstrators and blue-collar strikers are knowingly blocking ambulances from entering the hospital, thus denying treatment to injured and dying patients. There is nothing quite like *Britannia Hospital*, though its use of absurdism, black comedy, and science fiction anticipates other British artists reacting to the growing wave of conservatism in

England: dystopian films like Michael Radford's *Nineteen Eighty-Four* (1984) and Terry Gilliam's *Brazil* (1985), or Alan Moore's graphic novel *V for Vendetta* (1982–85). Unlike Anderson's British New Wave colleagues from the '60s—such as Karel Reisz and Tony Richardson—he remained an outsider throughout his career, refusing to make more accessible mainstream cinema, always determined to highlight social injustice and governmental hypocrisy.

Samm Deighan

THE WHOLE WORLD IS WATCHING

Campus Revolt On-Screen

Riots and rock music. Long hair and love beads. Psychedelics and sex. The '60s youth rebellion is often described in colorful terms that conjure up images of adolescent hedonism, but underneath the evocative iconography, there were serious concerns. Cold War trauma, fear of the atomic bomb, rampant inequality, and systemic oppression gave birth to a New Left motivated by the desire to discard tradition and embrace revolution. During this period, student movements made up of mostly white and middle-class college-age youth united under banners such as Students for a Democratic Society and the Student Peace Movement to bring progressive changes to universities as well as the wider world, but these changes were hard won. The Kent State Massacre, the Orangeburg Massacre, and the Battle for People's Park are just three of many university protests that turned violent and left dead bodies in their wake, but bodily harm wasn't the only thing students had to worry about. Along with sending armed police and the National Guard onto campuses, the government was conducting psychological warfare on its citizens. State-sanctioned programs such as the CIA's COINTELPRO and the FBI's Operation CHAOS permitted the government to search residences without warrants, read mail, tap phones, infiltrate, agitate, suppress, threaten, and terrorize student activists as well as the Black Panthers, communist and socialist groups, antiwar organizations, and other New Left factions throughout the decade.

Hollywood also faced many forms of government repression. When the swinging '60s arrived, Tinseltown was in the final throes of the Red Scare, and the House of Un-American Activities Committee still loomed over the film industry. To quote director Stanley Kramer from a 1960 press interview: "The motion picture industry is the most frightened and the most easily intimidated of any major industry in the United States." Film artists who engaged in political activity at the time were stalked and harassed by the government. Kramer, a distinguished director who made classics like *Guess Who's Coming to Dinner* (1967) and the student revolt film *R.P.M.* (1970), was singled out as a "communist sympathizer" and had an extensive FBI file, as did many other filmmakers. Actors like Jean Seberg, Marlon Brando, and Jane Fonda were relentlessly hounded by the FBI, and many creatives found themselves on President Nixon's enemy list by the decade's end.

If filmmakers wanted to work in Hollywood, they were required to sign loyalty oaths before joining the Screen Directors Guild, a measure designed to root out communists and their leftist supporters. These oaths remained in place until 1966, when the Supreme Court finally ruled them unconstitutional. Loyalty oaths were also required by members of many other organizations, including the Screen Actors Guild, where they only became optional after members of the rock group the Grateful Dead refused to sign oaths while appearing in *Petulia* (1967). Additionally, filmmakers faced scrutiny by the Motion Picture Association of America, which had implemented the Motion Picture Production Code, known as the Hays Code. The code was finally replaced by a rating system in 1968, but both forms of creative control discouraged radical filmmaking and limited distribution. As media scholar Mark Shiel explains in "Hollywood, the New Left, and *FTA*" in *"Un-American" Hollywood: Politics and Film in the Blacklist Era* (2007), "A climate of fear kept a lid on the resurrection of coordinated leftist activism in Hollywood. That climate persisted in the 1960s, despite the tremendous social and political upheavals into which Hollywood and the United States were then thrown."

Filmmakers faced extreme difficulties trying to illuminate campus unrest, and critics were often quick to dismiss politically oriented films, habitually mocking their efforts to reach a younger audience and deriding attempts at artistic experimentation. That isn't surprising given the bourgeois nature of most film criticism before and after the Vietnam era. How else to explain the critical adulation heaped on an aggressively middlebrow film like *The Big Chill* (1983) that celebrated the defeat of '60s radicalism? But many in the New Left also rejected the student revolt films of the era. The reasons for this were complex and included the enormous popularity of revival movie houses showing an abundance of classic and foreign films, as well as the widespread availability of television. New films were also

MGM Presents A Michelangelo Antonioni Film
"ZABRISKIE POINT"
Panavision® and Metrocolor   70/58

Director Michelangelo Antonioni on the set of *Zabriskie Point* (1970)

competing with an explosion of cheap live music. Why spend two dollars on a movie ticket when a double bill of Phil Ochs and Joni Mitchell only cost three bucks? More importantly, why see a film about student protests when you could participate in one? And the broad swath of protests occurring on any given day included Berkeley students picketing local movie theaters to address inadequate wages and Yuppies boycotting screenings of *Woodstock* (1970) because they believed viewers shouldn't have to pay to see a documentary about a free concert. Along with the general unrest, Hollywood was contending with young people's growing distrust of corporate media and its commercial aims. University and underground newspapers frequently questioned filmmakers' motivations, and students exhibited a sophisticated media savvy. In one noteworthy example, student leaders at California State University, Long Beach, refused to allow MGM to use their campus as a backdrop for *Zabriskie Point* (1970) because the studio had produced films starring Ronald Reagan, the former actor who was the governor of California at the time.

During the '60s, divisions widened between producers who wanted to make money and filmmakers who wanted to make interesting art. The era's cinema was often thought-provoking, but the politics could be difficult to define. Forced to curtail leftist sympathies and antiwar sentiments, filmmakers used visual and auditory clues to let audiences know they were watching something transgressive. Posters of political figures such as Che Guevara and Bobby Kennedy and images of the execution of Viet Cong captain Nguyễn Văn Lém were employed as backdrops. Rebellious rock and folk music with social messages filled soundtracks. The best of the campus revolt films included footage of real protests, and despite frequent accusations of being "out of touch," they were often based on books or scripts written by actual student activists. The results were a hastily assembled kaleidoscope of shifting visions and rough-hewn ideologies that arrived in a flurry of publicity only to quickly disappear from theaters. Many of the films never aired on television and had limited distribution on videotape and DVD. But the years have been kind, and the passage of time has given these films an electric sting and profound potency due to what followed in their wake.

> It's very easy for an American to say to me, "You're an Italian; you don't know this country. How dare you talk about it!" . . . But in some ways a foreigner's judgment may be . . . not better, necessarily, but more objective. Illuminating precisely because it is a little different.
> —Michelangelo Antonioni, *New York Times*, 1970

No campus revolt film received more publicity or government interference than Michelangelo Antonioni's *Zabriskie Point* (1970), which opens with Pink Floyd's "Heart Beat, Pig Meat" (1969). The song functions like a rhythmic call to war, and as the camera shifts in and out of focus, we catch glimpses of attentive young faces gathered at a student meeting. But they aren't just any faces. They're the faces of real activists, including Black Panther members Kathleen Cleaver and Landon Williams, Oakland Seven members Frank Bardacke and Bob Mandel, Bill Garaway of the draft resistance movement, and Jeff Zinn, son of author and radical historian Howard Zinn. A condensed copy of the collected works of Karl Marx and Friedrich Engels can be seen resting on a table. The group argues about protest tactics and their aims. They debated the struggles that were occurring within the student movement at the time. Angry voices rise and dissipate as they discuss how committed they are to revolution. Mark (Mark Frechette), the film's male lead, is visibly annoyed by all the talking and disrupts the conversation to say he's "willing to die too and not out of boredom," before angrily leaving the meeting. Off-screen, a black voice can be heard responding, "Start teaching him out of the Red Book or something. Teach him the first page that teaches about how if there's going to be a revolution there must be a

Kathleen Cleaver, then communications secretary of the Black Panther Party, on the set of the 1970 film *Zabriskie Point*. She appears at the film's beginning chairing a student meeting.

revolutionary party. That bourgeois individualism that he's indulging in is going to get him killed."

This prophetic observation is the key to understanding Antonioni's film, which follows Mark's evolution from student radical to armed fugitive. After participating in a college protest that turns deadly, Mark steals a small plane from the Los Angeles airport. He soon finds himself in California's majestic Death Valley, where he meets a young woman, Daria (Daria Halpin). After smoking a joint, the two make love in the desert, surrounded by a mirage of naked, entwined couples, before parting ways. Mark flies back to LA, where he's killed by police, while Daria finds herself at a midcentury manor belonging to her boss (Rod Taylor). When Mark's murder is announced on the radio, it provokes Daria to envision blowing the house to smithereens in a slow-motion montage of exploding debris.

> In a sense, there is a violent revolution taking place too, one that is caused by things, objects which are supposed to be helping people. They do help some people, of course, but they also assault and disrupt. That is why a refrigerator behind a shop window in Watts becomes a revolutionary object. In *Zabriskie Point*, I suggest that the material wealth of America, which we see in advertisements and on billboards along the roads, is itself a violent influence,

Spanish lobby card for *Zabriskie Point* (1970)

> perhaps even the root of violence. Not because wealth is bad, but because it is being used not to solve the problems of society, but instead to try and hide these problems from society.
>
> —Michelangelo Antonioni, *New York Times*, 1970

Before making *Zabriskie Point*, Antonioni spent a year crisscrossing America interviewing student activists and witnessed some of the decade's most impactful protests firsthand. He was in Chicago during the 1968 Democratic National Convention and shot film in Berkeley during the 1969 People's Park protest as it erupted in violence. Antonioni's coscreenwriters included playwright Sam Shepard, but it was journalist and antiwar organizer Fred Gardner who helped shape the film's final form. Gardner also introduced the director to many of the activists who appear in the film, which faced incredible obstacles before finding its way to the screen.

Conservative MGM employees were vicious to Antonioni. They referred to the director as "the wop" and "pinko pornographer." Before filming even began, they complained about having to work on a "hippie picture" and grew angrier after realizing the studio had given the director unlimited resources and creative control over his film. During production, scripts went missing and an espresso machine was deliberately destroyed. But these minor inconveniences pale in comparison to the government's interference. The FBI tracked and harassed the cast, as well as some crew members. Phones

ZABRISKIE POINT

MICHELANGELO ANTONIONI

METRO-GOLDWYN-MAYER présente une PRODUCTION CARLO PONTI "Zabriskie Point"
UN FILM DE **MICHELANGELO ANTONIONI** AVEC **MARK FRECHETTE DARIA HALPRIN** ROD TAYLOR
SCÉNARIO MICHELANGELO ANTONIONI FRED GARDNER SAM SHEPARD TONINO GUERRA CLARE PEPLOE
MUSIQUE ORIGINALE **PINK FLOYD ROLLING STONES** JERRY GARCIA THE GRATEFUL DEAD THE YOUGBLOODS
DIRECTEUR PHOTO ALFIO CONTINI PRODUCTEUR DÉLÉGUÉ HARRISSON STARR
UNE DISTRIBUTION MISSION LICENCE HOLLYWOOD CLASSICS LIMITED

Zabriskie Point (1970)

were tapped and mail was read. Anonymous calls threatened businesses participating in location shoots. Authorities accused the filmmakers of desecrating the American flag and paying the Black Panthers to attend the People's Park protest, which was a lie, although Antonioni did pay the Panthers to participate in his film. These allegations were followed by the Department of Justice accusing Antonioni of violating the Mann Act, which prohibited taking women across state lines for immoral purposes. Prosecutors foolishly assumed that the fictional orgy scene performed by an experimental dance group in the film was real, but the case was eventually dismissed. In one final humiliation, Antonioni was arrested for cannabis possession on his flight back to London following *Zabriskie Point*'s premiere in New York and forced to spend a night in jail. This film angered people in power, so it's not surprising that critics also went on the attack.

Antonioni's outsider status and Marxist sympathies made him a target of the American media, who didn't appreciate an Italian leftist criticizing their country. The ambiguous script, the unaffected acting of the film's stars, and the director's perceived anti-Americanism were the main complaints, but the contradictory consensus seemed to be that *Zabriskie Point* was both impenetrable and superficial. The truth is that Antonioni, better than any American director at the time, understood that capitalism and imperialism were linked hand in hand. *Zabriskie Point* is a modern masterpiece that still resonates today because the problems the film illuminates—political apathy, police violence, easy access to guns, disregard for human life, rampant consumerism, and our inability to form a more perfect union—are still with us today. America hasn't changed much in fifty years. In fact, its problems have only gotten worse. But its supreme beauty, so magnificently captured by Antonioni's picturesque landscapes and in the striking faces of his young cast, also remains.

> Young people know exactly what is going on in this world. They see it clearly, and they don't like a lot of it. They must react. Some tune out, as in *Easy Rider*. Some tune in, as in *The Strawberry Statement*. The latter, while certainly more constructive, can be deadly for the participant.
>
> —Stuart Hagmann, *San Francisco Examiner*, 1970

Stuart Hagmann was just twenty-eight years old when MGM tapped him to direct *The Strawberry Statement* (1970). The former drama teacher from the University of Southern California had previously worked in television, but *The Strawberry Statement* was his first feature film. With his shaggy hair and large glasses, Hagmann looked almost identical to his film's young star, Bruce Davison, who plays an apolitical college jock motivated to join the student movement after developing a crush on one of its female members (Kim Darby). As a result, Davison's character becomes more radicalized and begins participating in protests with his roommate (Bud Cort). This leads to a violent confrontation with police in the school's flag-draped auditorium during the film's climax. The script was written by playwright Israel Horovitz (father of Beastie Boys member Adam Horovitz) and based on James Simon Kunen's

East German poster for *The Strawberry Statement* (1970)

autobiographical novel describing his experiences at Columbia University during the 1968 protests. Students at Columbia demanded that the college end its partnership with the US military and stop the construction of a segregated gym. The unusual title comes from an interview with Columbia's dean of Graduate Faculties, wherein he stated: "Whether students vote 'yes' or 'no' on a given issue means as much to me as if they were to tell me they like strawberries." The film adaptation deviates from Kunen's original text to appeal to the general public, but its sympathies are with the students and its politics are undeniably progressive.

Kunen worried about the film's commercial aims and gave a large percentage of his royalties to the Black Panthers. Still, he participated in the production and even appeared in the film as one of the protesters. This may explain why *The Strawberry Statement* looks and feels more authentic than many of its contemporaries. Despite moving the location from the East Coast to the West Coast due to Columbia University's refusal to participate, the inclusion of real news footage and radio snippets grounds the film in the political pandemonium of the times. Hagmann's innovative direction took advantage of low angles, cross-cutting techniques, rack focus, and zoom lenses, while the film's creative montages of student encounters and unrest contribute to its temporal ambiance. And the exceptional soundtrack featuring songs by Joni Mitchell, Thunderclap Newman, and Crosby, Stills, Nash

Kim Darby is roughed up by police as they break up the student sit-in.

MGM Presents
A Robert Chartoff-Irwin Winkler Production "THE STRAWBERRY STATEMENT" Metrocolor

The Strawberry Statement (1970)

& Young, along with John Lennon's "Give Peace a Chance" (sung by the cast), cement its status as one of the more sincere campus revolt films of the period.

Like Antonioni, Hagmann had to deal with a hostile MGM crew that accused the director of making "commie propaganda." Posters of Che Guevara were damaged on set, and rolls of film were destroyed or went missing. While shooting an actual antiwar rally in San Francisco that appears in the film, Hagmann delivered a supportive speech to the crowd. Afterward, four crew members quit. *The Strawberry Statement* survived the on-set drama and debuted at the 1970 Cannes Film Festival just days after the Kent State Massacre. Whether the film's reception benefited or was hurt by these horrific real-life events is debatable, but it received an enthusiastic ovation and took home a coveted Jury Prize. The foreign press praised the film, with one French critic calling it "the fairest, the most poetic and the most honest picture given so far on the subject of the American student consternation." But American critics weren't so kind, and *The Strawberry Statement* was primarily met with nitpicking disapproval while the youth audience it hoped to attract largely stayed away. Its inability to find an audience was typical of all the campus revolt films. Student activists criticized the films for being too commercial and trivializing the movement's political aims, while the general public didn't seem particularly interested in watching films that dramatized the daily news headlines.

A heated critical debate unfolded in the *New York Times* when one of Kunen's Columbia classmates, Dotson Rader, wrote a scathing review of the film, claiming it was "a cheap attempt at the commercial co-option and exploitation of the anguish of a generation." Screenwriter Israel Horovitz countered with his own editorial, stating, "Of course the film seems, in terms of radical politics, 'naive.' Damn it all, I didn't write it for radicals! I wrote it for that 15-year-old girl.... She's got to take her first step. If she

Getting Straight (1970)

doesn't, we will suffocate with her. She is America: frightened, always thinking and believing that 'Things could be worse.'" Amid the debate, the book's author mounted an evenhanded defense of the film in *New York* magazine, describing its use of real police and students as extras while suggesting it might encourage activism: "Hollywood is well aware that revolution makes good theatre. What the movement should bear in mind is that theatre makes good revolution. When a lot of people get together to act, what you have is an action. If a radical plays the role of someone throwing a rock through a window, he may be aware on one level that he is not in reality a rock-thrower, but the window breaks all the same."

Columbia Pictures released two lesser films about student unrest that focus on the difficulties encountered by teachers trying to navigate the student movement. The first was Richard Rush's *Getting Straight* (1970), based on a novel by Ken Kolb that dramatizes his time as a student at an unnamed university in California. Robert Kaufman wrote the amusing script about a thirtysomething graduate student named Harry Bailey (Elliott Gould) attempting to get his master's degree to become a full-time teacher. When he's not romancing female classmates, Harry is clashing with fellow student radicals or battling the reactionary administration. As tensions grow on campus, he's forced to decide between a teaching career or participating in the student revolution. He chooses the latter. The film suffers from a stiff formality, but it's creatively shot by Rush and cameraman László Kovács, who make great use of the campus setting while Gould is at his manic best as the wise-ass womanizing Bailey. Bailey is not particularly likable, but Gould gives him nuance and depth. Gould's costars include Candice Bergen as his confused girlfriend, who can't decide if she wants to embrace the swinging '60s ideals or settle for a more conventional life, and Max Julien as an earnest campus radical leading student protests.

Getting Straight was a minor box office success largely due to the appeal of its star, who appeared in Robert Altman's Academy Award–winning *M.A.S.H.* (1970) that same year, but it received some of the harshest reviews. Critics repeatedly referred to the film, which included interracial relationships and many sexual innuendos, as "immoral," and like all the campus revolt films, it was criticized for trying to cash in on student rebellion. Judith Crist of *New York* magazine singled it out as the "worst of the youth-exploitation pictures, and one with Elliott Gould at his most fresh and salable to give it respectability and box office appeal, ... an amoral, venal work that managed to degrade both student revolutionaries and the university establishment right along with the audience." Gould responded to the criticism in a lengthy interview with *Playboy* magazine in which he stated, "It amazes me that so many people attack *Getting Straight*.... To criticize the motives of the film as purely commercial makes me wonder if those people really know what the fuck is going on in this country."

Stanley Kramer brought his usual gravitas to *R.P.M.* (1970), a glossy Hollywood production starring Anthony Quinn as Perez, a liberal Hispanic professor asked to negotiate a truce between a conservative college administration and student radicals who have taken over the campus. The film's sympathies are with Quinn as he attempts to navigate a sticky situation, and his frustration and confusion reflect the director's own uncertainty about the times. Like previous campus revolt films, the student protest eventually turns violent, and Quinn's character is forced to resign, but he doesn't just lose his job. He also loses the respect of the students who initially cheered his arrival. Kramer is a capable director, but *R.P.M.* fails to capture the zeitgeist. In later interviews, Kramer called it "about the most unsuccessful film I ever made." He further explains, "It didn't ring true, and it didn't because it was attempting to join in the confusion of the times, rather than take a step ahead and speculate on the reason for that confusion." Quinn and Ann-Margaret, as his unlikely love interest, are both good actors but ill-cast here, and Erich Segal's original script is leaden. But there are interesting moments between Black and white student leaders (Paul Winfield

R.P.M. (1970)

and Gary Lockwood) that speak to the ongoing racial tension within the student movement at the time.

Other interesting films that emerged during this period include *The Activist* (1969), *Changes* (1969), *Captain Milkshake* (1970), and *Up in the Cellar* (1970), but by 1971 the genre had become outmoded. The New Left and the student movement that it spawned had splintered. Members began focusing on singular issues such as civil rights, women's rights, and gay liberation, while others concentrated on ecological concerns and escaped big cities, often in communal groups, to participate in the back-to-the-land movement. The Students for a Democratic Society held their last contentious convention in the summer of 1969, and the Weather Underground emerged from the rubble. The times they were a-changin', and while many filmmakers struggled to find their footing during this transitory period, some expressed their frustrations.

> I know people are trying to do good things, but I don't see a lot of success in all the attempts. The revolutionaries have created a voice, but I don't see anyone listening to the voice.
>
> —Jack Nicholson, *Ramparts*, 1971

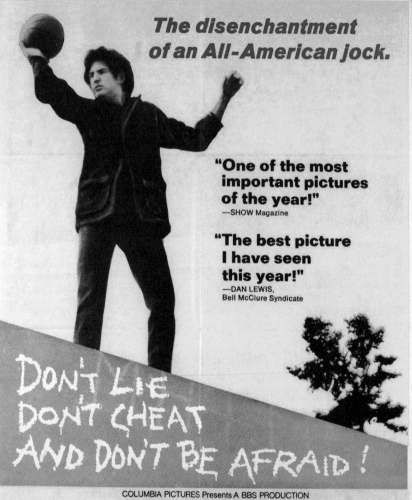

Drive, He Said (1971)

Like Stuart Hagmann a year earlier, Jack Nicholson hoped to impress critics when he brought his directorial debut to the Cannes Film Festival in 1971. Produced by BBS Productions and released by Columbia, *Drive, He Said* (1971) was based on an award-winning novel by author and antiwar activist Jeremy Larner that tells the story of a college basketball star (William Tepper) and his radical roommate (Michael Margotta) trying to navigate the political and sexual revolutions taking place on campus. Nicholson's direction was innovative, edgy, and bold, much like his acclaimed screen performances, but critics weren't ready to see that same creative zeal manifest in the actor's directing efforts. Instead of praise and applause, *Drive, He Said* met with loud jeers and boos at Cannes while fistfights reportedly broke out in the auditorium. The film's ambiguous characters, plentiful nudity, adult language, and political nihilism were an affront to the festival audience that had welcomed *The Strawberry Statement* with applause a year earlier.

Drive, He Said and *The Strawberry Statement* share much in common. Both films are based on popular books written by student radicals. Both feature apolitical jock protagonists more interested in sex than revolution. Both use competitive sports as metaphors for American aggression at home and on the world stage, and both show students engaged in campus protests inside a school auditorium. Despite the similarities, the two films couldn't be more different in their outlook. The jock in Nicholson's film doesn't have a political awakening. Instead, he finds empty satisfaction in continuing to play ball by the rules enforced by his coach (Bruce Dern). Furthermore, the student revolutionary's attempts at antiwar activism fall flat. When Margotta's character stages an impressive guerrilla-theater-style protest during a basketball game, it's met with indifference by his classmates. And instead of ending the film with students uniting in a violent uprising that implies change is needed or inevitable, Nicholson's film concludes with the solitary revolutionary having a mental breakdown and being hauled off to a madhouse while his classmates listlessly look on.

Nicholson's film is a panoramic, pessimistic statement about the end of an era, typically made decades after its participants have had time to absorb and analyze their contributions, which might explain why the negative response was so vitriolic. Many weren't ready to give up the promise of a contemporary American revolution. Certainly not the student protesters who fought so hard to bring much-needed change to a country that responded with violent opposition. And the foreign press at Cannes was probably holding out hope that America might drop its imperial grandstanding, face up to its war crimes in Vietnam, and start practicing that thing called democracy that the country's leaders so often crowed about. *Drive, He Said* was a giant middle finger to all that from an artist who had helped shape the counterculture in films such as *Easy Rider* (1969) just a few years earlier. And the angry response it received in 1971 suggests more than just prudish opposition to the film's sex scenes. The aspirations of the student movement that appeared so promising and imminent when the '60s began now seemed like a mad fever dream. A dream that was violently and systematically dismantled and placed in a red, white, and blue straitjacket.

A year after the release of *Getting Straight*, Elliott Gould would produce and star in *Little Murders* (1971), based on the award-winning off-Broadway production by acclaimed playwright and cartoonist Jules Feiffer. Feiffer also wrote the film's script, which was a darkly humorous and profoundly political look at life in America at a time when crime was on the rise and apathy was becoming endemic. Feiffer was radicalized in 1951 after being drafted during the Korean War and returned from his military experience with a temperate desire, as he put it in a 2018 interview, to "overthrow the government." He transferred that rage into his work and, in the process, became one of the first cartoonists critical of the Vietnam War. *Little Murders* was an extension of Feiffer's revolutionary aims and reinforced Gould's role as an American counterculture figure. The film can be appreciated as an unofficial sequel to *Getting Straight* in which Gould's character—now called Alfred Chamberlain—has cast off his college ambitions and is living in New York as a photographer who takes photos of feces for a living. His laissez-faire approach to the political issues of the day has given way to an all-consuming existential crisis, but his life begins to change when he meets a committed woman named Patsy (Marcia Rodd) and they marry. Not long after their wedding, Gould delivers a haunting monologue to his new wife while trying to explain the source of his inertia that recalls his days as a campus radical: "In college, the government couldn't decide whether I was a security risk or not. I used to protest a little then. So they decided to put a mail check on me. Every day the mail would come later and later. Corners torn. Never sealed correctly. I was more of an activist then.... It's very dangerous. It's dangerous to challenge a system unless you're completely at peace with the thought that you're not going to miss it when it collapses."

After Alfred concludes his apt description of how many in the New Left felt by 1971, he embraces his wife, who is abruptly killed by an unknown sniper. Was this a random act of gun violence or something more sinister? Was the killer's target actually Alfred, the onetime activist hounded by the government? The film refuses to provide a clear-cut answer, but the

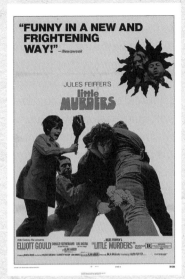

Little Murders (1971)   Elliott Gould in *Little Murders* (1971)

warranted paranoia it exposes is palpable. Feiffer wrote *Little Murders*, a title that evokes the death-by-a-thousand-cuts strategy employed by the government against the New Left, in response to assassinations of progressive leaders in the '60s. The inability of Americans to address, much less offer solutions, to the nation's trauma is represented by the deranged detective (played by Alan Arkin, who also directed the film) in charge of finding out who killed Alfred's wife. Arkin delivers an unhinged diatribe reminiscent of the right-wing rhetoric that helped suppress and finally put an end to the student movement: "We are involved here in a far-reaching conspiracy to undermine our most basic beliefs and sacred institutions. Who's behind this conspiracy? ... Their names would astound you. People in low places. Concealing their activities beneath the cloak of poverty. People in all walks of life, left-wing and right-wing, Black and white, students and scholars.... We need the army! We need a giant fence around every block in the city. An electronically charged fence! And anyone who wants to leave the block has to get a pass and a haircut and can't talk with a filthy mouth.... And if they catch you doing anything funny to yourself or anyone, they break the door down and beat the shit out of you!"

The film concludes with Gould buying a gun and going on a shooting spree. One of his victims is the detective suggesting violence may be the only sane response to the madness of the moment. The bleak finale evokes the "Bring the War Home" strategy employed by hard-left militant groups like the

Weather Underground and Symbionese Liberation Army that fragmented the student movement and eventually led to its decline. In a 1971 interview with *Newsday*, screenwriter Feiffer makes it clear that he wanted to shake up the status quo with *Little Murders*: "We are living in a country that can very easily absorb the atrocities of My Lai and maybe think of it as a less interesting version of the Manson trial. There's absolutely no horror committed by us that we cannot absorb and yet still retain our vision of ourselves as the good guys. I think some work has got to be done on the illusion of us as the good guys. Look, so far, the prescriptions have all been optimistic. They haven't worked. So let's try some destructive ones. I think that until you're willing to admit how bad things are, you can't possibly be ready to move in other directions."

Response to this extraordinary 20th Century Fox release was surprisingly positive. Critics, for the most part, praised *Little Murders*, even hailing it as "this decade's *Dr. Strangelove*," but the public wasn't all that interested in wrestling with the uncomfortable truths alluded to in this dark satire. The film quickly departed from theaters, and fifty years later, it plays like a bitter postscript to the campus revolt films that came before it. In the '80s, filmmaking took a hard right turn after Ronald Reagan rose from his role as the governor of California, where he spent his days throttling student protesters, to become president of the United States. Youth-oriented films abandoned politics entirely, and to this day, American cinema characteristically remains free of any leftist ideology. Modern audiences may be bombarded by relatively safe liberal polemics emphasizing the evils of racism, sexism, and classism, but few films examine the underlying systems in place that cause social division. And with rare exception, films addressing the destructive impact of American imperialism at home and abroad are conveniently missing from our cinema altogether. Today, the '60s campus revolt films are solemn reminders that the issues so many student activists fought and died for remain unresolved.

Kimberly Lindbergs

OUTTAKE: *ICE* (1970), ROBERT KRAMER, UNITED STATES

New York–born filmmaker Robert Kramer remains largely unknown in the US, despite a body of work that comprised nineteen feature films and over twenty documentaries between 1965 and his death in 1999. The reaction to his films was very different in Europe, particularly France, where he relocated for several years in 1979 and where, according to film academic David Fresko, his work was often spoken about on the same level as Jean-Luc Godard's.

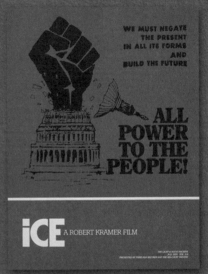

Ice (1970)

The main reason for Kramer's obscurity was his relentlessly political style of filmmaking. According to Fresko in an essay for the Metrograph site, Kramer's "unwavering commitment to anti-imperialism, anti-capitalism, and anti-racism and antipathy for Hollywood (and corporate media more generally) dashed any hopes for his commercial integration into the culture industries." As Kramer put it in a 1968 *Film Quarterly* interview: "You want to make films that unnerve, that shake assumptions, that threaten, that do not soft sell, but hopefully (an impossible ideal) explode like grenades in people's faces, or open minds like a good can opener."

One film that embodies Kramer's conception of filmmaking is *Ice* (1970). Set in New York in the near future, *Ice* depicts an underground group of mainly white revolutionaries plotting armed insurrection against an authoritarian American government involved in a largely secret war in Mexico—an obvious stand-in for Vietnam. It starts with a series of slides—what emerges as a film-within-a-film being made by the revolutionaries' documentary wing—with text announcing the intention to open a second front of combat in solidarity with Mexicans fighting US aggression. The

French poster for *Ice* (1970)

The time has come

for open

insurrectionary activity

Ice (1970)

American revolutionaries are led by Kramer, played by Robert Kramer, who in addition to directing also wrote the script, and who is one of the only people specifically named in what appears to have been an almost completely amateur cast.

The plot implies that the revolutionaries are part of a wider alliance called the National Committee for Independent Revolutionary Organizations. There are references to like-minded groups across the country and to a Black Revolutionary Army, but none of these other actors are seen. Halfway through *Ice*, the revolutionaries mount guerrilla-style attacks throughout New York: shooting an unidentified man, sabotaging a power station, breaking into a prison to release the inmates, and executing one who is reported to be a police informer. In a series of nonconsecutive scenes, the revolutionaries conduct a floor-to-floor sweep of an apartment building, gathering the tenants and attempting to politically indoctrinate them. Although the government remains largely hidden, we do see it retaliate. Kramer is assassinated and there are scenes involving anonymous men who appear to be trying to infiltrate the revolutionary movement but whose exact motivations are unclear, heightening the general mood of uncertainty and paranoia.

The bulk of the film, however, is focused on the mechanics of organizing and alliance-building. The revolutionaries debate how to

Robert Kramer in *Ice* (1970)

gain the support of Black and Chicano groups, and whether the timing is right to launch an offensive in New York, the first stage in what they hope will be a national uprising (and here we might note that while they generally praised his work, the critics around French film magazine *Cahiers du cinéma* reportedly criticized *Ice* for its "political adventurism"). The revolutionaries discuss logistics, how best to communicate, how to acquire and transport weapons, and where to secure reliable medical care and safe beds for their wounded. Kramer also depicts the more mundane day-to-day minutiae of political organizing, scenes that will be familiar to anyone who has spent time in a political movement: managing group dynamics, including political differences and sexism; dealing with dysfunctional activists; and the ever-present need to find more people and resources.

Ice is inconclusive as to whether the uprising is succeeding or the revolutionaries are deluding themselves. This is one of the most interesting aspects of the film and Kramer's work generally: while unashamedly partisan, he did not shy away from depicting the left's problems and failures. *Ice* contains a series of moments, some quite intimate, in which the revolutionaries admit their confusion about what is happening and their fears of getting wounded, captured, or killed by the authorities. It is Kramer's studied approach to the mechanics of political organizing and the reality of life in radical groups that differentiates *Ice* from the wave of American films in the late '60s and early '70s that depict radical and revolutionary youth taking to the streets to seize power.

Ice evinces a wealth of cinematic influences. While it can be viewed as a thriller, the depiction of a simultaneously run-down and modern New York, governed by a largely unseen but powerful surveillance state, gives it a science-fiction tone and aesthetic. This has led some to compare it to Godard's *Alphaville* (1965). Godard's influence, especially *La Chinoise* (1967), can also be seen when the revolutionaries read aloud from their program. There are nods to cinema verité and the inclusion of slogans on the screen such as "Now is the time for people to take up arms against the state." The final scene, in which mechanical toys depict imperialism attacking the Third World, feels reminiscent of Sergei Eisenstein and Grigori Aleksandrov's 1928 work *October (Ten Days That Shook the World)*.

Kramer was a founding member of Newsreel, a radical documentary group which positioned itself as the propaganda arm of the New Left. Newsreel reported on the activities of radical movements and distributed films from Vietnam and Cuba in the US. As part of Newsreel, Kramer also made documentaries overseas, including *The People's War* (1970), which was shot in North Vietnam and apparently incurred Hanoi's ire for not be sufficiently laudatory of the regime, and *Scenes from the Class Struggle in Portugal* (1977), about that country's 1974 "Carnation Revolution." *Ice* was one of three feature films Kramer made under Newsreel's auspices. The others are *In the Country* (1967), which explored a young American revolutionary's sense of alienation from the struggle around him, and *The Edge* (1968), about an activist's plan to assassinate the US president to stop the war in Vietnam. Kramer's other notable feature films include *Milestones* (1975), which explores the lives of several New Left members following the decline of the antiwar movement in the '70s, and *Guns* (1980), made in France, in which a former radical journalist investigates a vaguely defined gunrunning ring. Unfortunately, all the films mentioned here and Kramer's wider filmography remain incredibly hard to access and view.

Andrew Nette

LOUDER THAN A BOMB

On *The Spook Who Sat by the Door*

Located on 145th and 7th Avenue in New York City, the Roosevelt Theater was once a sparkling jewel of a movie house in Harlem, but by the 1970s it was run down and had become primarily a showcase for spaghetti westerns, horror flicks, and Black-casted—and sometimes directed and produced—films known as Blaxploitation. The genre moniker was created in 1972 by the then president of the Beverly Hills branch of the Hollywood National Association for the Advancement of Colored People, Junius Griffin, but regular folks didn't use the word until later. *Blaxploitation* wasn't a term intended to be complimentary, and though many of the genre's stars rejected its usage, it soon became the blanket term for the Black films of the 1970s that began with the release of *Cotton Comes to Harlem* (1970), *Sweet Sweetback's Baadasssss Song* (1971), *Shaft* (1971), and *Super Fly* (1972). Decades later, those films would inspire rappers, visual artists, writers, and other filmmakers, namely Spike Lee and Quentin Tarantino, but at the time of release, those low-budget movies were pushed to the back of the New Hollywood bus.

Directed by Ivan Dixon, *The Spook Who Sat by the Door* (1973) was categorized as Blaxploitation, but it was actually more political than most of the releases during that era. Starring new-to-the-screen Lawrence Cook, who'd appeared in Dixon's previous feature, *Trouble Man* (1972), the militant movie was based on the debut novel by Sam Greenlee, a Chicago native. Published in 1969, the same year as fellow Black revolt novels *Siege* by Edwin Corley and *Afro-6* by Hank Lopez, Greenlee's book is the only one to be adapted into a film and the only one that remains in print. When the movie opened

COMING ATTRACTIONS at the
Moncada Library
FILM PROGRAM

SUNDAY, MARCH 28

THE SPOOK WHO SAT
BY THE DOOR

THE SPOOK WHO SAT BY THE DOOR is a Hollywood movie from the early 1970s that never received wide distribution because of its revolutionary theme. It is a fictional -- yet believable -- story of a Black man who joins the CIA to gain information and training to put to the service of the Black liberation struggle. He leads a double life --assigned by the CIA to attempt to control and contain Black urban rebellions -- he uses these contacts and intelligence to in fact build a highly sophisticated Black armed underground movement to wage war against amerikkka for the liberation of Black people. At this time of heightening u.s. government counterinsurgency against the Black Nation and the advance of the Black Liberation Army this great, and previously hard-to-find film must be seen. $3 / 7:30 p.m.

SUNDAY, APRIL 25

POTEMKIN

The Bolshevik Revolution of 1917 changed forever the balance of power in the world and the course of history by creating the first socialist state, the Soviet Union, run by and in the interests of the working class. POTEMKIN, by master filmmaker, Sergei Eisenstein, is one of the classic films of that revolution, as powerful today as it was 65 years ago. It is the story of how the sailors of the battleship Potemkin took over their ship, at one of the critical moments of the revolution, transforming it from a weapon of the state -- to a tool of the revolution. $3 / 7:30p.m.

SERIES TICKETS: $10
(Young People: $1/film)
CHILDCARE AVAILABLE

Moncada Library
434 Fifth Avenue, between 8 & 9 St., 2nd fl., Brooklyn
Hours: Tuesday & Thursday 3-7, Saturday 1-5. 499-2767

Flyer for a public screening of *The Spook Who Sat by the Door* and Sergei Eisenstein's 1925 film *Battleship Potemkin*, organized by the anti-imperialist Brooklyn-based Moncada Library sometime in the 1970s (Image courtesy of the Freedom Archives)

in September 1973, I was a ten-year-old kid sitting in the middle row of the Roosevelt next to my mom, slouched down in a crimson velveteen seat and completely absorbed by the strange drama on-screen.

Unlike most of the early 1970s Black films, *The Spook Who Sat by the Door* didn't open with a shoot-out, a car chase, a naked woman, or a street or bar brawl, but inside a white senator's sterile office in Washington, DC. The senator (Joseph Mascolo), his wife (Elaine Aiken), and his Black secretary (Beverly Gill) try to figure out how to get the senator's poll numbers up "with the Negroes." After pondering the question for a few minutes, his wife suggests that they make public that the CIA didn't have any minorities on staff, forcing them to hire a Black agent. "Whoever they select will be known as the best spy since 007," the secretary says. Raised on a steady diet of James Bond flicks, I assumed this was where the action was to begin, but I was mistaken.

Instead of tricky gadgets and explosives, the film showed "Negro" CIA trainees at Quantico, located in Virginia thirty-five miles from Washington, DC. The men shoot guns on the range, swim laps, learn martial arts, and participate in the bone-breaking preparation and instruction it takes to be the perfect "spook." That word in the film's title serves as a double entendre, with *spook* being slang for spies as well as a derogatory slur to describe Black folks. Nearly ten minutes into the film, the audience is finally introduced to protagonist Dan Freeman (dig that last name, played by Lawrence Cook), a laid-back dude who was at the top of his class but still managed to stay under the radar, even in the presence of his own people.

Cook plays the character with intense restraint, but it soon becomes clear that he is a man on a mission. Freeman comes from the slums of the South Side of Chicago, but he never saw the ghetto as an obstacle. The other Black men in the CIA training program are from a different socioeconomic background, children of the Black bourgeoisie with their class consciousness, exclusive clubs, and fraternities. "We the first spooks to be spooks for the CIA," jokes one guy. Still, it's obvious from their cliquish ways the others aren't feeling Freeman's standoffish attitude and superior intellect. When he is accused of not being part of the team, Freeman snickers, "I'm not playing games."

The majority of the eligible men seem to be thinking primarily of the upward mobility they imagine a good government job would afford them, while Freeman, with his studious face and serious demeanor, absorbs all he can in the hopes of leading a "revolution" in the name of freedom, as is later revealed. Although I was young, only in fifth grade, I was a television junkie who had already heard several Black radicals and intellectuals using the word *revolution* on the news, as well as on various Black-themed television programs such as *Black Journal*, *Like It Is*, and *Soul*. Still, it is difficult to comprehend how the revolutions taught in school related to the hood and other Black communities throughout America. Was that explosive word on the tongue of Malcolm X, Huey Newton, Angela Davis, Stokely Carmichael, and countless others supposed to be a metaphor, or was it literal?

For Freeman, it was the latter, but the brother man was in no rush. In the words of confidence men throughout the land, Freeman goes for the long con, one that drags on for years as he gains the knowledge and trust of his white bosses, policeman buddies, and social worker girlfriend. After months of training, where he is literally the last man standing, Freeman is basically given a job Xeroxing top secret reports and is never assigned to work outside of the building. Though smart and well trained, he is still believed to be inferior. A couple of years later, he is "promoted" and starts working in his bosses' office, usually assigned as tour guide to visiting VIPs. The only women in Freeman's life include a Washington, DC, hooker he calls Dahomey Queen (Paula Kelly) and a longtime girlfriend, Joy (Janet League), whom he has dated since college. The female characters are literally whore and Madonna, though it's the former who is shown to be true to the cause and Freeman. Joy breaks up with him, believing that Freeman isn't serious enough about their future. When Joy tells him of her decision to wed, Freeman asks, "The lawyer or the doctor?" Quickly, she answers, "The doctor."

Five years into Freeman's career, he suddenly quits and returns to Chicago, where he goes to work for a social service program supposed to help control the gang situation that has taken over the Black community. In real life, Windy City gangs known as the Blackstone Rangers and Vice Lords ruled the ghetto streets in 1960s Chicago. In *The Spook Who Sat by the Door*, the fictional gang Freeman once belonged to was called the Cobras, and it was those bad boys hanging out in the pool hall with a picture of Malcolm X on the wall that he aimed to recruit to take his plan for Black Revolution to the next level. When one gang member named Pretty Willie (David Lemieux) asks Freeman what exactly they are fighting for, Freeman simply answers, "I want to be free."

Many Black radical writers, artists, and filmmakers have come out of Chicago, including Richard Wright, Lorraine Hansberry, Archibald Motley, Margaret Walker, and Melvin Van Peebles. Chicago was also the home of author Sam Greenlee, who was born on the South Side in 1930 and raised in the Washington Park and Woodlawn neighborhoods. As a youngster, he attended George Washington Carver Elementary School with *Sweet Sweetback's Baadasssss Song* (1971) auteur Van Peebles, and Englewood High School with future playwright Hansberry, author of *A Raisin in the Sun* (1959). "His mother was a dancer, singer, and actress," Andrew Peart reported in a 2018 *UChicago* magazine story, "and his father worked on the Santa Fe Railroad and was later maître d' at the Cliff Dwellers Club." Greenlee's neighborhood around 63rd Street and St. Lawrence Avenue was a strivers' community. "It was understood that I would get an education," Greenlee told Peart. His family couldn't afford to send him to college, but, as he said, "it was taken for granted that I would figure out some way to do it on my own." Attending the University of Wisconsin–Madison on a partial track and cross-country scholarship, he graduated with a degree in political science in 1952. Encouraged by a University of Chicago coach to go to graduate school there and run track, Greenlee, according to Peart, "studied international relations in the Social Sciences Division from 1954 to 1957." "I went to two white, brainwashing institutions," Greenlee told the *Chicago Reader* in 1994. "But I'm the black dog that didn't fall for Pavlov's scam."

Later, Greenlee was recruited to a junior officer training program that led him to the US Information Agency. After graduating, he was stationed in Iraq, Pakistan, Indonesia, and Greece, but he was aware of the civil rights struggles happening in America. The movement's primary leaders, Martin Luther King and Malcolm X, were polar opposites. King's pacifist ways of boycotting, sit-ins, and marching was met with fire hoses, German shepherds, and death. This resulted in some rights granted and political advances made, but at the cost of much anger and sorrow. Malcolm X's view that "the so-called Negro" literally fights gunfire with gunfire was, in his belief, the only way life was going to change for "colored folks" in America. On August 11, 1965, six months after Malcolm X's murder, Greenlee was on leave and back in Chicago watching news reports about the maddening Watts Riots that erupted in Los Angeles after an alleged drunk driver and his family were beaten and arrested. This wasn't an isolated incident, as the LAPD was well known for their constant mistreatment of Blacks and Mexicans. Contrary to the kind Los Angeles police image depicted on television programs like *Dragnet* and *Adam-12*, the truth was closer to the angry abusers captured in the novels of James Ellroy and on the infamous Rodney King videotape. The Watts Riots raged for six days, and the National Guard was called in in hopes of bringing peace, but instead escalated the violence.

Riveted by the uprising, Greenlee soon returned to the Greek island of Mykonos, where he was stationed. Processing all he'd seen in the States, he used the violence he'd witnessed on television, as well as his own experiences with racism, to begin writing his novel. Combining current events, speculative beliefs, and wishful thinking, a year later *The Spook Who Sat by the Door* was complete. It took two years and many submissions before Greenlee finally found a publisher, the British company Allison & Busby, willing to take a chance on such a volatile new voice. The company's co-owner, Black Englishwoman Margaret Busby, was introduced to Greenlee through poet Alexis Lykiard. In a June 2014 obituary for Greenlee in

Uptight (1968)

the *Guardian*, Busby writes, "I borrowed £50 to serve as down-payment on the publishing contract for what became one of A&B's first titles in March 1969. I designed the book jacket myself, including endorsements cajoled from Dick Gregory, Len Deighton, and Stephen Vizinczey, and a blurb that began: 'The CIA needs a Negro: there have been accusations of racial discrimination. So black Dan Freeman begins his lone career in an all-white world. Dan Freeman: tame, conspicuous, harmless. But behind this mask he coolly develops his subversive expertise in judo, guns, women, strategy.'" Months later, the book was reprinted in America by Richard W. Baron Publishing Company. Baron had previously worked at Dial Press, where he'd published politically charged writers James Baldwin and Norman Mailer. Though the cover blurb untruthfully declared *The Spook Who Sat by the Door* as "the first black nationalist novel," it also stated it was "a chiller in the tradition of *1984*." Walking a fine line between literary and genre fiction, the book appealed to people who liked either. "I don't write for Black bourgeois intellectuals," Greenlee said in 2004. "I write for people on the block where I live."

Although the Black film movement hadn't begun to flourish yet, Greenlee was already thinking about his literary creation's cinematic potential. Greenlee teamed up with Melvin Clay to write the screenplay. Though Greenlee has never mentioned the film *Uptight* (cowritten by the stars Julian Mayfield and Ruby Dee) as an influence, it was released in 1968 and also speculates on the rise of Black revolutionaries in the Midwest, who were ready to riot days after Martin Luther King was killed in Memphis, Tennessee. *Uptight* was directed by formerly blacklisted filmmaker Jules Dassin, a Brooklyn native known for film noir classics *Brute Force* (1947) and *The Naked City* (1948). He moved to Europe in 1953 after friend and fellow director Edward Dmytryk named him in the House Un-American Activities hearings and the US government labeled him a communist. Seventeen years later, *Uptight* was Dassin's first post-blacklist production. Though the film spent considerable time with Black Panther–esque rebels who called themselves the Committee, we never see the actual uprising. Still, that didn't stop the film, which was produced by Paramount Pictures, from being labeled un-American in the fear it might encourage violence. Even during the film's production, the FBI dug into its content and the patriotism of the cast and crew. In an FBI report to then governor of California Ronald Reagan, it was written that the film "can be expected to further racial discord and disorders in this country." One crew member "had disassociated himself with the production of this movie as he felt it would prove to be a disservice to the United States." Furthermore, "other persons who had been associated with this production have voluntarily contacted the Bureau warning of the effects this film will have on the racial situation in the United States and advising that it would certainly damage the image of the United States abroad, where it is scheduled to be released in the near future." Five years later, *The Spook Who Sat by the Door* wouldn't pull any punches when it came to violent unrest and action. It was one of the most political films to come out of Blaxploitation, and though some viewed it as a fantasy or satire, others (again, supposedly, the FBI) believed it to be serious as a hand grenade that might cause Black America to erupt. Years later, the same language would be used to try to discredit Spike Lee's masterwork, *Do the Right Thing* (1989), but those barbs came from film critics as opposed to a government agency.

Blaxploitation was the Black side of the New Hollywood era, when major studios were bankrupt creatively and needed guidance from creative hippies, artists, protesters, and Vietnam vets. Thinking back to those many Saturday or Sunday afternoons in the 1970s when I went to the movies with friends, no one ever referred to them as "Blaxploitation." That industry label was added to my vocabulary years after I'd first seen *Shaft*, *Super Fly*, and *The Mack* (1973). While I have no problem with the term, I don't believe that every Black film made in the '70s should be labeled under that banner. For me, the "Blaxploitation" description should be reserved for the more action-packed shoot-'em-ups that include the three titles mentioned above, as well as films like *Gordon's War* (1973) and *Come Back, Charleston Blue* (1972), which

Japanese poster for *Shaft* (1971)

weren't political and usually revolved around Black antiheroes who were gangsters (*Across 110th Street* [1972] and *Black Caesar* [1973]), dope dealers (*Super Fly*), pimps (*The Mack* and *Willie Dynamite* [1974]), or badass super women (*Cleopatra Jones* [1973] and *Friday Foster* [1975]). A few other political examples like *The Final Comedown* (1972, starring Billy Dee Williams) and the underrated Richard Pryor vehicle *Which Way Is Up* (1977) snuck through, but mostly these were more about action and adventure than a message.

However, *Sweet Sweetback's Baadasssss Song* (1971), the film that most Blaxploitation aficionados cite as the flick that launched the movement, was actually a hybrid of politics and action. It was hailed by the Black Panthers and gathered fans city by city, with the film's director, writer, and producer Melvin Van Peebles having created a template for others who wanted to deliver a militant message but also sell tickets. In addition, for Black film-makers who needed to raise funds outside of the traditional studio system, Van Peebles also showed that there was no shame in hustling for their own budgets by any means necessary, shooting guerrilla style on the streets, dodging unions, and handling their own distribution.

That wheeling and dealing Hollywood world was new to Sam Greenlee, but thankfully he partnered with a thirty-nine-year-old Black Hollywood vet willing to show him the way and make his celluloid dreams into a reality. Director Ivan Dixon met Greenlee in California in 1970, when Greenlee had gone to Los Angeles in search of funding. In an interview published in *The 50 Most Influential Black Films: A Celebration of African-American Talent, Determination, and Creativity* (2001), the usually press-shy Dixon explains, "Either they turned him down, or he turned them down. I found him, had a talk with him and he sold me the rights.... I read it [*The Spook Who Sat by the Door*] in 1968 or '69, and it took me until 1972 to put it together." Dixon paid out of his own pocket, but he and Greenlee were full partners.

Originally from Harlem, Dixon grew up in the Sugar Hill section in a brownstone on 150th Street, but as a teen still managed to get into trouble. After being busted for running with a neighborhood gang, the judge gave his parents the option of sending Dixon out of state or shipping him to a reform school. His parents sent him to Lincoln Academy, an African American boarding school in Bessemer City, North Carolina. The school straightened him out, and a few years later, Dixon went to college at North Carolina Central University in Durham. He thought about studying law, but instead got a degree in political science and history. In college he became interested in acting while working in school productions. A teacher at Central helped him obtain a scholarship to Case Western Reserve University in Cleveland, where

"NOTHING BUT A MAN"

starring IVAN DIXON / ABBEY LINCOLN with Gloria Foster & Julius Harris / Produced by Robert Young-Michael Roemer-Robert Rubin
Directed by Michael Roemer / Written by Michael Roemer and Robert Young / A Roemer-Young Du-Art Production / A Cinema V Presentation.

The Spook Who Sat by the Door director Ivan Dixon in the 1964 film *Nothing but a Man*

he also got involved with the famed Ohio cultural center Karamu House. The theater had been an early training ground for Harlem Renaissance writer Langston Hughes, who presented a few plays there, and future *Super Fly* star Ron O'Neal. Dixon left Case Western before earning his degree, returning to New York. He studied at American Theater Wing alongside James Earl Jones, while also appearing in off-Broadway and Broadway productions. Working with Sidney Poitier and Diana Sands, he costarred in the Broadway and film productions of *A Raisin in the Sun* (1961), playing African exchange student Joseph Asagai.

I first saw Dixon in a *Twilight Zone* episode called "The Big Tall Wish," which originally aired in April 1960. Dixon played an aging boxer named Bolie, whose loser's luck is turned around after his neighbor's son wishes him to be a winner. Four years later, Dixon starred in the underrated *Nothing but a Man* (1964), a moving drama that documented a young Black man living down South, trying to navigate life as a railroad worker, union organizer, new husband, and tortured son. Directed by Michael Roemer, the low-budget, arty film was groundbreaking, one that took Black lives seriously and didn't just present them as racist fodder to provide laughs or a quick tap dance for white audiences. Although it did well at the New York Film Festival, in the rest of the country it was a failure. Over the years, it has been shown at many college campuses, repertory theaters, and film festivals, but it wasn't until *Nothing but a Man* was reissued decades later that it began to receive the acclaim it deserves. Though barely recognized when released, *Nothing but a Man* was later viewed as "remarkable" by Roger Ebert and "a minor masterpiece" by former *Los Angeles Times* critic Kevin Thomas.

Dixon didn't quite become the next Sidney Poitier, but that same year he launched Negro Actors for Action, an organization designed to help Black actors get roles that would destroy the Mammy/Uncle Tom images they'd been slotted into for decades. "What we need to see is the Negro in normal, everyday life," Dixon told the *New York Post*, "the Negro as folk hero. What we need as a people [are] heroes we can identify as our own." While working for that organization, he attended a workshop for Black screenwriters, where veteran writer Richard Powell taught. He and Dixon became cool. Powell was writing the pilot for *Hogan's Heroes* (1965–71) and was instrumental in getting Dixon the role as radio operator Sgt. James Kinchloe on the bizarre prisoner-of-war comedy series in 1965. In a YouTube video interview Dixon granted to ReelBlack owner Michael J. Dennis in 2006, Dixon explained that he had wanted to direct for a while, but being married with four kids prevented him from going back to school, so he learned what he could on various sets by asking questions of cameramen and directors.

According to film historian Spencer Moon, "*Hogan's Heroes* became his graduate school in directing. He was on the set every day for five seasons.... He talked with the editor and got to edit some film. He talked with the cameraman Gordon Avil, who gave him his personal time on the weekends when he found out that Dixon really wanted to learn about directing." Dixon stayed on *Hogan's Heroes* until 1970. That year, his friend Bill Cosby was given his first solo sitcom, and he allowed Dixon to hang out on set before Dixon earned the star's confidence to finally direct. Decades before Cosby was exposed as a serial sex offender, he was a mentor to many; that same year, he loaned Melvin Van Peebles $50,000 to complete *Sweet Sweetback's Baadasssss Song*. In 1971, Dixon was hired to direct *The Bill Cosby Special, Or?* However, Dixon longed to direct a feature and was offered the film *Trouble Man* (1972), a neo-noir/Blaxploitation flick written by John D.F. Black, who was coscreenwriter of *Shaft*. Attempting to cash in on that previous hit, Black simply used *Shaft* as a template and changed the names and location. 20th Century Fox produced the film and hired Dixon, who had no real passion for the project. Dixon's sole motivation was to prove to prospective backers of *The Spook Who*

The front page of the *Black Panther*, June 19, 1971, featuring the film of the same year *Sweet Sweetback's Baadasssss Song* (Image courtesy of the Freedom Archives)

Sat By the Door, which was in development, that he could make a feature. As with many artists working in a commercial medium, Dixon was willing to compromise in order to later "do a film that I really want to do."

The Spook Who Sat by the Door was that film, but raising money to make it wasn't easy. Thankfully, he and Greenlee found creative collaborators, including soundtrack supplier Herbie Hancock, to work cheaply. Considering that having a funky soundtrack by an established name musician was essential in the world of Blaxploitation, they were blessed. During the filming of *The Spook Who Sat by the Door*, there was still a question of who was going to supply the music. In the January 11, 1973, issue of *Jet*, Greenlee told a reporter that they were "trying to get either Freddie Hubbard [trumpeter] or Herbie Hancock [keyboardist] to score the movie." Hancock, himself a Chicago native as well as a friend of Dixon's buddy Bill Cosby, was chosen. In *Herbie Hancock: Possibilities*, his 2014 autobiography, he writes, "I got a call about a movie. Ever since doing [the Michelangelo Antonioni film] *Blow-Up* in 1966, I had wanted to write more soundtracks, but the only film I'd gotten since then was the TV movie *Hey, Hey, Hey, It's Fat Albert* [produced and created by Bill Cosby in 1969]. So, I got real excited when a producer got in touch ... the producers didn't have much money, but I didn't care—I really wanted to do the music for this film." During that period, Hancock called himself Mwandishi, which was also the name of his group, a sextet consisting of saxophonist Bennie Maupin, trumpeter Eddie Henderson, trombonist Julian Priester, bassist Buster Williams, and drummer Billy Hart. Mwandishi played on the soundtrack, though Hancock used tons of electronics as well. He writes, "I wrote songs that were heavy on electric instruments and synthesizers which excited me." Coming at a time when most people weren't using synths on film work, Hancock's score was as innovative as Wendy Carlos's 1971 work on *A Clockwork Orange* (1971) or Tangerine Dream's brilliant *Sorcerer* (1977).

Ivan Dixon and Sam Greenlee approached big-money Black folks in Chicago, including *Ebony/Negro Digest* publisher John H. Johnson and George E. Johnson Sr., founder of Johnson Products Company, but they refused to contribute. Instead, the duo began raising money among non-moguls who simply believed in the necessity of the project. "A Black woman in real estate put up $50,000 while a mortgage broker gave me another $50,000," Dixon told ReelBlack. Altogether they raised $600,000, which wasn't enough, but they started shooting anyway. Mayor Richard J. Daley refused the production permits to shoot in Chicago, but they still "stole" some shoots around the city, using handheld cameras. Daley was afraid of the themes of racial unrest, but the first Black mayor of Gary, Indiana, Richard G. Hatcher, allowed them to

The Spook Who Sat by the Door (1973)

shoot in his city. However, three and a half weeks later they ran out of money and had to suspend production. Luckily, Dixon approached United Artists executive David V. Picker, showed him footage of shoot-outs, and made the company believe it was regular Blaxploitation fare. "It looked good, the action was good, camera work was good," Dixon told Torriano Berry. Picker gave them $325,000 to finish the film. As a company cofounded by D.W. Griffith, director of the racist *The Birth of a Nation* (1915), it's ironic that they were involved in *The Spook Who Sat by the Door*, a decision they'd soon regret. Months later, the film was screened for forty United Artists staffers who were expecting the next *Shaft* and instead had an urban *Battle of Algiers* (1966), complete with political rhetoric, raging riots, and police, military, and politicians being overpowered, embarrassed, and slain. "It was totally different from what David Picker surmised it to be," Dixon said. "At the end of the screening, no one said anything. There was absolute silence. They just kind of looked at each other."

From the beginning of the film, when confronted with the arrogance and superiority of the white instructors and other agents who are trying to sabotage the Black trainees, we see the racial tension that then builds throughout the film. Indeed, even when Freeman proves to be better at various assignments than his teachers, he is given minimal responsibilities

The Spook Who Sat by the Door (1973)

in the agency. Considering the book was written in the 1960s, we should assume that Freeman had been coping with American racism and Jim Crow segregation for years, and for him, the dream of freedom means revolution. Upon returning to Chicago, Freeman sees that nothing has changed for Black people in the ghetto: the community is still depressed, and the people are constantly repressed. The revolution finally begins when small-time drug dealer Shorty Duncan (Pemon Rami) is killed fleeing police custody. Earlier, Freeman had warned Shorty that the cops were gunning for him, because he hadn't paid them off, but it is still shocking to see two cops shoot an unarmed man in the back. From that moment, Freeman's trained street gang is transformed into a troop of freedom fighters. The fighting intensifies when the police release German shepherds on the crowd and call in the National Guard. Like a bomb, the Chicago ghetto explodes, but the boom is soon felt throughout the city.

The studio wanted Dixon to recut the movie and assigned him an editor. Though he shortened some of the scenes, he refused to make it less political: "I instructed them that the ending could not be changed and that was our deal. They also asked that I remove some of their names from the credits. I did that." United Artists, according to Dixon, fired David Picker, but the studio was contractually obligated to release *The Spook Who Sat by the Door* in thirty-five cities. On Friday, September 21, 1973, the movie opened at the Roosevelt Theater, where two days later ten-year-old me sat in the dark beside my apolitical mother and watched as that fiery movie flickered onto the screen. While I was young, I was already a film aficionado who'd been watching non-age-appropriate films for years. I didn't yet have the language to express what I'd seen, but I knew it was different from any other film experience. Years later, I compared the intense riot to the neorealism of Roberto Rossellini's outstanding *Roma città aperta* (*Rome, Open City*, 1945), and the handheld camera shots of the Chicago streets and subway to John Cassavetes's Times Square/Museum of Modern Art sculpture garden scenes in *Shadows* (1959), and the overall intensity to *The Battle of Algiers*.

Many of the roles were played by nonprofessional actors, including gang members from the Cobras, the crew Freeman transformed from wild street kids to a street-fighting military unit. Star Lawrence Cook was a New York City stage actor at the time of filming, and, while he could be intense, his performance was understated and gave Freeman a quiet intensity that tilted between soothing and scary. Dixon would later go on record saying he thought of the film as "a fantasy," while others called it a satire, but it was neither to author Sam Greenlee. "I wanted people to look at that movie and come out of there thinking," Greenlee says in a special-feature video commentary from 2004.

Two weeks after its release, it was pulled from theaters, and it wouldn't be released on video until nineteen years later. Actor/producer Tim Reid, best known as Venus Flytrap on the 1970s sitcom *WKRP in Cincinnati*, reissued it on DVD through his production company. Greenlee claimed the FBI was behind the plot to bring the movie down, confiscating prints and threatening theater owners. In his 2020 *New York Times* essay "The Spy Movie That Upset the American Dream," respected film critic J. Hoberman writes, "*Spook* opened in September 1973 in the midst of televised Watergate hearings, several years after the FBI's secret Counterintelligence Program (COINTELPRO) disabled the Black Panthers. Paranoia was high. The year's other independent features included the white vigilante tale *Walking Tall* and the John F. Kennedy conspiracy docudrama *Executive Action*. An anticipatory article in *The Chicago Defender*, the nation's preeminent African-American weekly, wondered if 'Greenlee's masterpiece' might 'touch off race warfare.'"

The film's most serious flaw, which can be traced to the book, was the lack of women involved with the Cobras and the revolutionary movement. In the real Black Panther/Black Power era, there were celebrated writers and radicals like Elaine Brown, Kathleen Cleaver, Assata Shakur, Angela Davis, and others, as well as the thousands of rank-and-file women who ran the various Black Panther public assistance programs and kept the machinery moving smoothly. In *The Spook Who Sat by the Door*, the only women seen are wives, girlfriends, mothers, and secretaries.

For Sam Greenlee and Ivan Dixon, *The Spook Who Sat by the Door* would be their last feature film. Dixon moved on to a prolific television directing career that included episodes of *The Waltons*, *The Rockford Files*, and *Magnum, P.I.* Greenlee continued to write novels (*Baghdad Blues*, 1976), poetry, and short fiction. A wonderful piece he wrote about a junkie former-pimp wannabe jazz musician, "Blues for Little Prez," was published in *Black World*, formerly *Negro Digest*, in 1973. Greenlee hoped to adapt the story into a movie, but it never happened. Greenlee was named poet laureate of Chicago in 1990.

The Spook Who sat By the Door (1973)

The film's leading man, Lawrence Cook, though an excellent actor, only worked sporadically in sitcoms and soaps after *The Spook Who Sat by the Door*. His last major film was the 1993 Black western *Posse*, directed by Mario Van Peebles, whose father made *Sweet Sweetback's Baadasssss Song*. As Ivan Dixon points out in his 2006 ReelBlack interview, while there was no proof that their work on the film was held against them by the (white) Hollywood establishment, it wouldn't be unreasonable to believe that was an issue.

The Spook Who Sat by the Door wasn't a box-office hit or a Caucasian critical darling in 1973, but it still made a lasting impression on the psyche of generations. "There are only a couple of things of over thirty-five years in this business that I am sincerely proud of," Ivan Dixon said. "*Nothing But a Man* as an actor and *The Spook Who Sat by the Door* as a director." Thankfully in their lifetimes, the creative forces witnessed the film being reevaluated by critics. It also became a cultural touchstone for countless artists, including Public Enemy, Darius James, Kara Walker, and Ava DuVernay. In the 1990s, many young rappers began referencing the title in their songs, including Naughty By Nature ("1, 2, 3"), Dilated Peoples ("Triple Optics"), and WC and the MAAD Circle ("Get Up on That Funk"). Others (Dead Prez, Quasimoto, Masta Killa) simply sampled the movie itself. In 2012, *The Spook Who Sat by the Door* was added to the National Film Registry, which annually chooses twenty-five films that are "culturally, historically or aesthetically significant." Famed producer/director Lee Daniels (*Precious* [2009], *The Butler* [2013]) reportedly bought the rights to create a television series remake. Greenlee died in 2014 and, four years later, was inducted into the Chicago Literary Hall of Fame alongside Upton Sinclair, Nelson Algren, and Saul Bellow. "Sam represented a voice of consistency," said actor Pemon Rami, who remained friends with Greenlee after costarring as Shorty in the film. "He was consistent in his message: consistent in his message to the city, consistent in his revolutionary fervor, consistent in his criticism of things affecting the community. People loved him for that."

Michael A. Gonzales

OUTTAKE: OCCUPATION "URBAN GUERRILLA": THE CINEMA OF PATTY HEARST

The February 1974 kidnapping of Patricia Hearst by the self-proclaimed Symbionese Liberation Army (SLA) ignited a popular-culture feeding frenzy. Front and center of this was Hearst's transformation from innocent nineteen-year-old granddaughter of newspaper publisher William Randolph Hearst to "Tania," a gun-toting, bank-robbing militant revolutionary. But the story also plugged into the fascination with celebrity culture, the ongoing collapse of the '60s radical project, and sex, particularly the unspoken allure of miscegenation, a staple of pulp fiction and exploitation cinema.

A tiny far-left urban guerrilla group whose politics were a mishmash of Third Worldism, Maoism, and the ideas of the French philosopher and Marxist revolutionary Régis Debray, the SLA only existed from 1973 to 1975. Most of its members, including its leader and only Black participant, ex-convict Donald DeFreeze—or Field Marshal General Cinque, as he referred to himself—died in a shootout when police raided their Los Angeles headquarters in May 1974. But Hearst and two other SLA members continued to elude the authorities until September 1975, when they were arrested in San Francisco. When she was booked into jail, Hearst listed her occupation as "urban guerrilla."

The court case that followed focused on Hearst's culpability for her actions: whether she was brainwashed, willingly joined the SLA, or did so only to avoid death. Hearst, who compared her state of mind while she was with the SLA to that of a traumatized prisoner of war, told the court she was threatened with execution unless she joined. She also said she was raped by male SLA members, including DeFreeze. She was convicted of bank robbery and using a firearm during the commission of a felony and given the maximum sentence possible of thirty-five years' imprisonment, although this was later commuted by President Jimmy Carter.

A *New York Times* article in July 1974, while Hearst was still a fugitive, noted that there was a wave of books about the kidnapping out or pending publication. But the most bizarre book to tap into public interest in the case, *Black Abductor*, was actually published two years earlier by a short-lived outfit called Regency and republished to take advantage of the

Abduction (1985)

Still from Paul Schrader's *Patty Hearst* (1988); Natasha Richardson as Hearst is second from the left, top row

case's prominence by Dell as *Abduction: Fiction Before Fact*, coincidentally only a month before Hearst was arrested. *Black Abductor* describes a plot by a small radical group to kidnap the daughter, also called Patricia, of a prominent conservative politician. She is subjected to sexual abuse at the hands of her captors before adopting the group's views and taking part in their activities. The author of *Black Abductor*, Harrison James, was pseudonymous, and the identity of whoever actually penned the novel remains unclear. It has been most often linked to a little-known science fiction writer called James Rusk Jr. But some online sources have speculated it was the work of CIA spook turned pulp writer E. Howard Hunt. Hunt helped mastermind the overthrow of Guatemala's elected government in 1954, played a role in organizing the Bay of Pigs in April 1961, and possibly had a hand in the 1967 murder of Che Guevara. He went on to become one of the so-called "plumbers," undertaking clandestine activities for the Nixon administration. Briefly jailed for his role in the Watergate scandal, he wrote seventy-three books under his own name and pseudonyms. *Black Abductor* does not appear in his official bibliography.

The similarities between the plot of *Black Abductor* and the SLA's kidnapping of Hearst are indeed uncanny. And one can only speculate as to whether this is mere coincidence, whether the book influenced the SLA to snatch Hearst, or whether the book's author went on to become involved in the actual kidnapping. One person *Black Abductor* did influence was then-twenty-nine-year-old wannabe director Joseph Zito. Zito, who would go on to make the Chuck Norris films *Missing in Action* (1984) and *Invasion U.S.A.* (1985), had just completed his first feature, a sexology film called *Citizen Blue*, in 1971. He saw the potential of *Black Abductor* as a way to riff off the Hearst kidnapping without incurring legal action from the Hearst family. Thus, in the middle of the heiress's 1975 trial, his film *Abduction* was released.

Opening with the highly disingenuous statement that "any similarity to persons living or dead is purely coincidental," *Abduction* shows Patricia Prescott (Judith-Marie Bergan), the daughter of a shady real estate developer (Leif Erickson), snatched from her campus apartment mid-lovemaking by a radical left-wing group. Prescott is kept tied up and blindfolded in the gang's apartment while they deliberate about what to do with her. She is forced to record a statement that she is a political prisoner, and in return for her release the group demands the destruction of her father's new luxury apartment complex, built with funds earmarked for low-cost housing. In real life, the SLA had its origins in outreach work done by University of California student activists to an education group in Vacaville Prison, which included DeFreeze among its members. Prescott's ordeal is intercut with a subplot in which FBI agents, led by classic film-noir tough guy Lawrence Tierney, brutally interrogate a campus radical who has been peripherally linked to one of the kidnappers via illegal wiretaps of his home phone, an obvious reference to the FBI's infamous COINTELPRO operation.

The politics of *Abduction*'s kidnapper are kept vague in favor of the film's key focus: sex. Prescott is raped by the gang's leader and only Black member, Dorian (David Pendleton), an act assisted and filmed by the women members. Videotapes of the act are sent to her father, who is shown watching them. Prescott is also filmed having sex with one of the gang's female members, a videotape of which is also dispatched to her father. The film intimates that Dorian's virility is enough not only to make Prescott his willing lover, but to convince her to join the gang and agree with his argument that violence is "the only way to change society."

Abduction's sensational content and aesthetic mirror that of the teen-in-danger movies that were a staple of midday television viewing in the '70s and '80s. There's a procession of breathless news announcers lamenting the growth of domestic terrorism that the Prescott kidnapping represents, alongside lots of explicit sex and female nudity. Perhaps this sleazy film's only saving grace is the ending. The group temporarily splits up to travel to a new city. Dorian and Prescott are about to leave when they are caught by two cops. Prescott acts relieved to be rescued. The police lower their guard with her, at which point she murders them with a shotgun, the ultimate act of submission to her new lover.

Based on Hearst's 1982 autobiographical account, *Every Secret Thing*, Paul Schrader's little-seen *Patty Hearst* (1988) is a more sober—especially by the director's standards—and sophisticated examination of the kidnapping and what followed. A young, naive

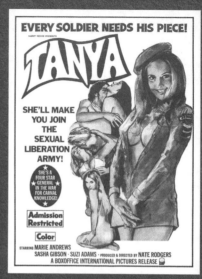

Tanya (1976)

Hearst (Natasha Richardson) is blindfolded, tied up, and kept in a cupboard, where she is first raped by the group's messianic Black leader, Cinque (Ving Rhames). Her captors remain in shadow and out of focus until thirty minutes into the film, when Hearst agrees to join the SLA. Schrader implies her decision has as much to do with the brutality of her captivity and how it broke down her capacity for independent thought as it does the need for her to ape the SLA's radical politics to survive. Her voice-overs in the film recount her suicidal thoughts, physical deterioration, and diminishing mental state.

Patty Hearst depicts the SLA as a small sect of politically deluded, middle-class white people mouthing jargon laden with anticapitalist, antiracist, and antisexist sentiments, at the same time as they are riven with petty jealousies and sexual dysfunction. They also condone rape in the guise of free love. The last part of the film details Hearst's trial and the legal wrangling over why she joined the SLA. She is shown to be so mentally damaged by her ordeal that even she can't really explain or understand her actions. What she does realize, however, is that the public and law enforcement resentment directed against her comes from the fact she survived, and there would have been far more sympathy for her plight had she not emerged alive. Linked to this is a clear understanding she is a victim of a sexual double standard. As she puts it: "I was forced to have sex by my captors so they [the public] think I am a whore."

THEY IMPRISONED HER BODY,
BUT FREED HER MIND.

VIRGIN FILMS and WORLD...VISUAL ENTERTAINMENT plc
in association with LES PRODUCTIONS BELLES RIVES present
A DON BOYD PRODUCTION
CAPTIVE
STARRING IRINA BROOK · OLIVER REED
XAVIER DELUC
CORINNE DACLA · HI...ARAI
MUSIC COMPOSED BY
THE EDGE AND MICHAEL...
EXECUTIVE
PRODUCERS AL CLARK AND STA......OP...
PRODUCED BY   BY
DON BOYD · PAUL M......RSBERG

Captive (1986)

Sidney Lumet's 1975 satire *Network* features a hard-charging female network programming director (Faye Dunaway) who cuts a deal with a small left-wing group called the Ecumenical Liberation Army (ELA) to make a reality television show called *The Mao Tse-Tung Hour*. At one point, the negotiations between the network and the ELA are disrupted by an unmistakably Hearst-like character, a young, white, gun-toting, beret-wearing woman, who protests because the ELA is selling out. The Hearst kidnapping would feature more directly in numerous other films throughout the '70s and '80s: *Patty* (1976), a mockumentary where various experts discuss the kidnapping case; a sexploitation parody, *Tanya* (1976); a made-for-television film directed by Paul Wendkos, *The Ordeal of Patty Hearst* (1979), told from the perspective of the FBI agent in charge of the search for the heiress; the 1989 docudrama *Citizen Tanya* (1989), directed by artist Raymond Pettibon and David Markey and starring Pat Smear, lead guitarist for the LA punk band the Germs and sometime member of Nirvana and Foo Fighters, as Cinque; and *Captive* (1986), an Anglo-French film loosely based on Hearst's experiences, which starred Irina Brook as the Hearst character and Oliver Reed as her tycoon father.

Andrew Nette

AMERICA THE BEAUTIFUL, AMERICA THE VIOLENT

Documenting America's Decline in the Mondo Film

On August 1, 1966, Charles Joseph Whitman, an engineering student at the University of Texas at Austin, climbed a clock tower on campus and shot thirteen people over the span of two hours. This event is not significant because of the violence alone. America has known violence since the country was first forged in the heat of gunfire and cannon blasts. What made this event so unusual is the level of fame afforded to Whitman in the wake of the murders. Since 1966, countless pieces of media, ranging from songs by artists like Harry Chapin and Kinky Friedman to documentaries and television programs, have been devoted to eulogizing Charles Whitman. Although Whitman himself did not appear to be making a political statement with his actions, the media has embraced him as a political figure—the patron saint of mass murder. *Do unto others as you would have them do unto you.*

The embrace of figures like Whitman highlights the political dimension to media depictions of violence. Violence in America is a kind of entertainment, a modern gladiatorial competition for the attention of a horrified but enraptured public, intended to further atomize and isolate. This battle pits the destitute, the aggrieved, and the criminally insane against innocent bystanders, American against American, in pursuit of the American Dream. Fame.

Images of violence have dominated American media from the beginning of modern history, influencing how Americans perceive and engage in violent acts. Some of the earliest blockbusters of American cinema, such as *Birth of a Nation* (1915), depicted vigilante violence, helping to revive membership in fascist political organizations like the Ku Klux Klan, and later media coverage of real-life vigilantes like Curtis Sliwa and his Guardian Angels alternated between horror and admiration, allowing for these figures to become media stars and political leaders. This is in part because depictions of American violence are inescapable. If you turn on the news, you will see yet another mass shooting, but if you try to escape to a movie theater, you are just as likely to see one on the big screen. One is left wondering why America is so violent—is it the culture, the politics, the media? And what is its purpose? Are we trying to scare ourselves to death? In a country where the quickest path to stardom (or notoriety) is shooting your neighbor, the answer is complex.

Early propaganda reels like the Frank Capra series *Why We Fight* (1942–45) depicted the actions of brave American men fighting the good fight, so to speak, in a semi-documentary format. In contrast to modern-day "reality" television, where violence is no less political but often handled in ways where it seems divorced of any political context, this kind of violence always served a purpose and taught a moral lesson, with Capra using World War II to highlight a heroic American violence that could purge the world of its evils. Director John Ford, working first as the head of the photographic unit for the Office of Strategic Services and later as an officer in the United States Naval Reserve, directed documentaries like *The Battle of Midway* (1942) and *This Is Korea!* (1953) in an attempt to depict American violence as a liberating force.

The earliest images of reality, such as we know them today through film and television, came not from Americans attempting to use violence as an instructional tool but from jaded foreigners in search of the world's most extreme experiences, in the form of the mondo film. Made primarily by Italian filmmakers, at least early on, mondo films sought to exploit the local customs and practices of foreign countries, to offer Western audiences a voyeuristic experience into cultures they would never see on their own, whether for a lack of financial means or intellectual curiosity.

What distinguished mondo films from the documentary format of that particular period, beyond sometimes less-than-honest production techniques and advertising campaigns, was a universal nihilism. If an American documentary like *This Is Korea!* sought to contribute to the war effort by depicting violence in a very narrow (and mostly positive) light, a mondo film like *Mondo Cane* (1962) offered the exact opposite. Violence as pure entertainment. Never might this be clearer than in the film's opening narration, where an unnamed figure intones: "All the scenes you are about to see are real and were shot as they were taking place. If sometimes they seem cruel, it is only because cruelty abounds on this planet. And anyway, the duty of a reporter is not to make the truth seem sweeter, but to show things as they really are."

All The Scenes You Will See In This Film Are True And Taken Only From Life. If Often They Are Shocking It Is Because There Are Many Astounding And Even Unbelievable Things In This World.

MONDO CANE

Produced by Gualtiero Jacopetti   TECHNICOLOR   A TIMES FILM RELEASE

Mondo Cane (1962)

Released in 1962 by Italian filmmakers Gualtiero Jacopetti, Paolo Cavara, and Franco Prosperi, *Mondo Cane* might best be described as a travelogue made by the Marquis de Sade. While not technically the first mondo film (the Jacopetti-penned *Europe by Night* and *World by Night* preceded it in 1959 and 1960 respectively), *Mondo Cane* was among the first to document the more outré aspects of the human experience, with the filmmakers flying across the globe to spy on everything from nude women enjoying the French Riviera to the practices of a cannibal community in New Guinea. But America specifically was an unusual target for *Mondo Cane*'s filmmakers, given that prior to the emergence of mondo films, documentaries rarely criticized the superpower. In *Mondo Cane*, however, we find the idolatry of America's then-burgeoning celebrity culture, the excesses of its appetites and extreme wealth, and the aftermath of its most depraved act of violence toward another nation (in stark contrast to the rah-rahing of Ford's war documentaries).

In hindsight, we might now regard *Mondo Cane*'s compulsion for chronicling extremity and perversion as more uniquely American than anything presented by American filmmakers of the era precisely because many of its vignettes blurred the line between fact and fiction. In what would later become a staple of American reality television and even some American news programs, the *Mondo Cane* team cuts between authentic images and staged reenactments. (Jacopetti would only ever admit to staging one scene,

Gualtiero Jacopetti and Franco Prosperi in 1962

in *Mondo Cane*'s sequel, of a self-immolation inspired by Vietnamese monk Thích Quảng Đức.) The purpose of the trick was to exaggerate the eccentricities and embellish the traits that American filmmakers might otherwise obscure. *Mondo Cane*'s filmmakers sought to achieve a higher state of being, a more perfect union of film and subject, through deceit, because at the heart of the mondo film is exploitation. Filmmakers exploit distinctions between real and fake in the documentary genre, or those things that happen of their own occurrence and are documented in something resembling real time versus those things staged by the filmmakers to appear as if they were naturally occurring. This also means exploiting fears in audiences of a world nearing cataclysm with documentary images of what film critic Nick Pinkerton referred to in his mondo film monograph *Neither/Nor: Mondo Cinema and Beyond, 1960s–1980* (2016) as "nuclear paranoia, religious fervor, ecological catastrophe, and pandemic violence." These real images are placed alongside out-of-context stock footage, deceptive editing tricks, and mundane observations on the nature of human cruelty, making it impossible to discern which is real and which is not.

Yet it would be too easy to dismiss mondo films as only a collection of shocking images and sound bites. While it is true many mondo films approach their subjects with a shock-for-shock's-sake tendency, the best examples use that perspective to offer a political critique of violence as endemic to societies

US poster for *Africa Addio*, aka *Africa: Blood and Guts* (1966)

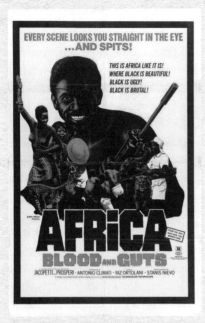

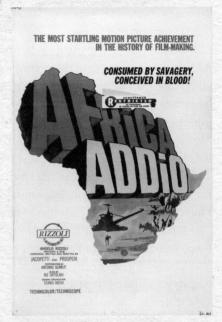

US poster for *Africa Addio*, aka *Africa: Blood and Guts* (1966)

Italian poster for *Africa Addio*, aka *Africa: Blood and Guts* (1966)

in decline. The exploitation that takes place in the production mirrors that found in everyday life. So, while mondo filmmakers of the past might have fixated on the violence found in colonial conquests in places like Africa, a frequent subject of Italian directors Jacopetti and Prosperi, some were just as likely to focus their lenses on bloodshed found among colonial powers. The difference is in degrees. Violence in films like *Africa: Blood and Guts* (1966), a Jacopetti and Prosperi production, results from the history of colonialism, the film covering civil wars in countries Western nations exploited for resources.

Compounding this distinction is the separation between filmmaker and subject in the mondo film. In a strange bit of irony, the illusory nature of the mondo genre would work against Jacopetti and Prosperi, as the two were accused of participating in war crimes for filming *Africa: Blood and Guts*. The filmmakers traveled to Kenya, Zanzibar, and Congo in the early to mid-1960s to film scenes of revolutions, but in the process captured images of executions and other examples of political violence. After an Italian newspaper accused the two of collaborating on an execution for the film, Jacopetti was tried for and acquitted of murder. The filmmaker-as-murderer distinction is not new, going back to at least French writer Guillaume Apollinaire's short story "Un beau film" (1907), about a group of filmmakers who force a man to murder a couple for the camera, but the mondo film often took it to unusual and uncomfortable places.

Maybe this is why the mondo film and Jacopetti in particular were the perfect vehicles to begin the process of documenting America's obsession with violence, because violence in mondo films about America has always been about a sickness hidden deep at the core of that country, one that emerges only as the country falls into moments of decline and despair. *Mondo Cane*, the first such example to observe this, makes a dramatic statement with its depiction of the testing of the atomic bomb at Bikini Atoll. The filmmakers capture the aftermath of the tests in footage of sea turtles rendered sterile by the nuclear fallout tending to eggs that will never hatch. Violence is a path that leads in one direction: death.

Following the success of *Mondo Cane*, violence became a distinct feature of the American experience in mondo cinema. Among the first of the America-obsessed films was *Mondo Hollywood* (1967), a pseudo-documentary created by an American expat who had previously made the polemic *Committee on UnAmerican Activities* (1962) on the red-baiting committee in America. *Mondo Hollywood* probes the extremes of America's City of Dreams, Los Angeles, or, as its director, Robert Carl Cohen, later described it in *Mondo Hollywood: The Interview* (2007), America's "center of illusion." Cohen has stated he did not intend to make *Mondo Hollywood* as a normal mondo film, but viewed years later it is more representative of the apocalyptic currents present in that genre than other documentaries of the period.

Mondo Hollywood introduces the viewer to a cast of typically and atypically Hollywoodian figures, from hippies and sex workers to activists and cult members, in a kaleidoscopic view of an American counterculture both under and on the attack. Cohen presents each individual as beyond judgment, so members of the Christian Anti-Communism Crusade, a far-right lobbying group endorsed by stars from John Wayne to Ronald Reagan, and antiwar protesters, mostly college students and young leftists opposed to the Vietnam War, are given equal time to air their grievances. This is no endorsement, however; if Cohen is saying these two groups are equal in any sense, it is that they are both equally products of a paranoid and delusional culture driven by violence—one side promoting war with expensive dinners, the other one fighting it through song and dance.

This apocalyptic paranoia—the notion that no American is ever truly safe—is clearest in brief segments covering Hollywood hairdresser Jay Sebring and musician Bobby Beausoleil. Two years after *Mondo Hollywood*'s release, associates of Beausoleil in the Manson Family would murder Sebring;

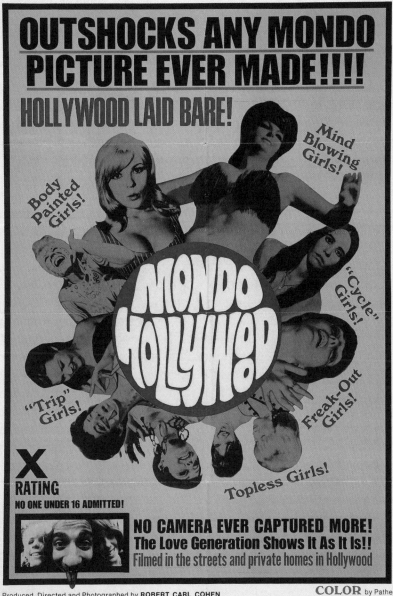

Mondo Hollywood (1967)

at the time of the murder, Beausoleil himself was in prison for a separate murder. Although the two men are not connected in the film, the presence of a victim and his aggressor presents an unusual insight into American culture. Hiding beneath its surface is a pervasive brutality that strikes at random. Hollywood, America's center of illusion, is a place where dreams are made and ended.

Another example of this fervor is the *This Is America* trilogy: *Jabberwalk* (1977), *This Is America Part 2* (1980), and *America Exposed* (1991). Across the three films, violence is a subject that moves from the periphery to the foreground, displayed initially in brief yet comedic snippets until it becomes the main focus of the series. What is so fascinating about this process is that it happens in tandem with a shift from the faux documentary style of early mondo films, found in parts one and two, to full dramatic reenactments, as shown in the final film. The process is not dissimilar to that of the mainstreaming of mondo-style media on American television networks in the late '80s, where reality programming like *Unsolved Mysteries* (1987) and *America's Most Wanted* (1988) began using dramatic re-creations of real events.

Jabberwalk and *This Is America Part 2* portray an American violence that is almost uniformly comedic, a byproduct of eccentrics focused on other, more prurient obsessions. America, in the tradition of more raucous mondo films like *Mondo Nudo* (1963) and the Russ Meyer–produced *Mondo Topless* (1966), is a place of endless (and sometimes unusual) sexual desires. Occasionally, this overlaps with violence, shown briefly in an S&M sequence toward the end of *Jabberwalk*, but most depictions range from kung fu–fighting nuns to rowdy bar fights. This changes at the end of *Part 2* in an abrupt tonal shift that foreshadows the final film, when director Romano Vanderbes stages an execution—possibly an unintentional reference to the Jacopetti Affair in Africa—as part of an extended sequence on capital punishment. The segment ends abruptly, as if arguing life in America is short, tumultuous, and cruel—then you die.

The last film in the series, *America Exposed*, is by far the most violent and certainly the most offensive. It begins at a Soldier of Fortune convention in Las Vegas, tag-teaming mercenaries and porn stars on a gun range, then travels through small towns where Santa Claus is burned in effigy and impoverished residents resort to bank robberies. The film's centerpiece, involving contrasting images of Black and white racial violence, can be ranked among the vilest of images committed to the screen, an ignominious distinction to be sure. Near the end of the film, Vanderbes re-creates a Ku Klux Klan summer camp where children are indoctrinated into white supremacy, up to and including sequences depicting burning crosses and small arms training. This is placed alongside scenes of inner-city gang violence. The point of this within the context of the three-film arc, strange as it may seem, is to illustrate that violence, rather than a comedic byproduct of American eccentricity, is a pervasive evil that lingers in every corner and crevice of the country—a kind of sickness that infects everything it touches.

The notion of violence-as-sickness permeates every frame of *The Killing of America* (1982), the apotheosis of the mondo cycle and one of the most damning indict-

Advertisement for the opening in Melbourne, Australia, of *The Killing of America*, *The Sun*, July 14, 1983

ments of America ever made. The violence seen in the film is unusual by the standards of the mondo film, in that there is no dramatic re-creation; everything on-screen is real, culled from archival footage, interviews, and news broadcasts. Where the *This Is America* series dramatizes the worst aspects of American culture to parody and satirize, *The Killing of America* captures many of those same images in graphic, unblinking detail to make a political statement about the nature of American violence and the media's role in perpetuating it.

The Killing of America begins with a warning: "All of the film you are about to see is real. Nothing has been staged." While a similar tactic may have been employed by Jacopetti et al. in *Mondo Cane*, this is no sleight of hand. After a brief journey through the grimy streets of then-decaying American cities, the viewer is inundated with what *New York Times* critic Janet Maslin described as "a compendium of everyone's favorite real-life death scenes." The film never goes more than a few minutes without a shooting, a dead body, or some other grim reminder of American carnage.

Assembled from a combination of archival footage and interviews shot by codirector Sheldon Renan, *The Killing of America* is, in many ways, the polar opposite of *Mondo Cane*. *Mondo Cane* details the excesses of American material culture in a grotesque circus of sideshow bits and geek shows. Where it does offer depictions of violence, as in the sequence at Bikini Atoll, it views its subject from a distance. You could even argue that *Mondo Cane* maintains a level of reverence and awe for its subject, allowing Jacopetti, Cavara, and Prosperi to inject humor to undercut the film's darker moments. For example, although the sequence on the dropping of the atomic bomb at Bikini Atoll acknowledges that nuclear fallout has rendered the turtles sterile, the scene begins on a lark, with a joke about a species of fish that can survive out of water thanks to the radiation.

A still from the "Zapruder film," the only film of President John F. Kennedy's assassination in Dallas, Texas, on November 22, 1963

The Killing of America, on the other hand, is a product of its culture, created by filmmakers intimately familiar with its evils. Renan and fellow codirector Leonard Schrader devote their attention to an epidemic of violence afflicting American cities in something more akin to a soliloquy read by a man slowly losing his mind. There is no humor to be found here. We do, however, get an extended sequence that graphically portrays the JFK assassination, sourced from the Zapruder film, the only known footage of the shooting, with a close-up of the final shot showing Kennedy's head exploding like a watermelon. Reflecting on the event, the film's narrator states solemnly, "A few weeks after the assassination of President Kennedy, the murder rate exploded upward, tripled in just ten years. And continues to the present day."

The assassination is a pivotal moment in *The Killing of America* because it is where the viewer is first introduced to the violence-as-sickness motif. The present day at the time of *The Killing of America*'s release would have been 1982, a year in which there were over twenty-two thousand murders recorded in the United States. The Kennedy assassination, just shy of its twenty-year anniversary by that point, lingered as a scar on the country's psyche. This moment, per the film, is where that sickness was first revealed. "The way we structured it," Renan recalled to an American critic in 2016, was "going from the wilds to more civilized America, then to the sense of corruption or hidden violence at the core of that, including a historical throwback to gunfights and things like that." In this sense, the Kennedy assassination is like Pandora's box, or a moment from which all sorts of evils emerge. Soon after Kennedy's death, America is set upon by snipers and mass shooters, cult leaders and their followers, child murderers and serial killers.

It is this last group, and one serial killer in particular, that make up the most substantial portion of *The Killing of America*. The film was produced by Towa Productions, a Japanese company. According to Renan in an interview with *The Quietus*, an American mondo film called *Faces of Death* (1978) had been a hit in Japan, and the producers wanted to re-create its success but with an explicit focus on American violence. To that end, Schrader and Renan were encouraged to pursue the most lurid subjects they could find. Thus, they sought out Edmund Emil Kemper III, or more popularly, Ed Kemper, the Co-ed Killer. Between

Kidnapper Anthony Kiritsis holding mortgage broker Richard Hall hostage with a shotgun; photograph by John H. Blair, originally distributed by United Press International on February 11, 1977, winner of the 1978 Pulitzer Prize for Spot News Photography

May 1972 and April 1973, Kemper murdered and dismembered ten women, including his own mother.

Kemper, like many of the men who would go on to become known as serial killers, had complicated motives. Which is to say he could never explain why he did it. Depending on whom he talked to, he was either a "demented person," as he told one true-crime magazine, or he was out to make a "social statement," per his words at a parole hearing. Speaking directly to Renan, Kemper is more pointed. "I am an American, and I killed Americans," Kemper states, his massive, cherubic face framed in uncomfortable close-up. "I am a human being, and I killed human beings. And I did it in my society."

Schrader and Renan position Kemper and the other subjects of the film as grotesque media sensations—objects of intense revulsion, but also idols of equal and enduring devotion. In assembling *The Killing of America* entirely out of archival footage and shooting only minimal interviews, instead of relying on dramatic reenactments or staged events as in the mondo tradition, the directors make a compelling case for American media's obsession with violence. These images, repurposed from ostensibly apolitical sources such as evening news broadcasts and police footage, take on a political dimension as the filmmakers turn the camera lens back on a media in search of its next victim.

Beginning with the Zapruder film, Renan and Schrader argue that the camera itself is a weapon not unlike the guns that appear so prominently in nearly every scene. Men like Ed Kemper, or Charles Whitman for that matter, do not know why they kill until the media grants them a voice, at which time their murders become statements and their images godlike. The Zapruder

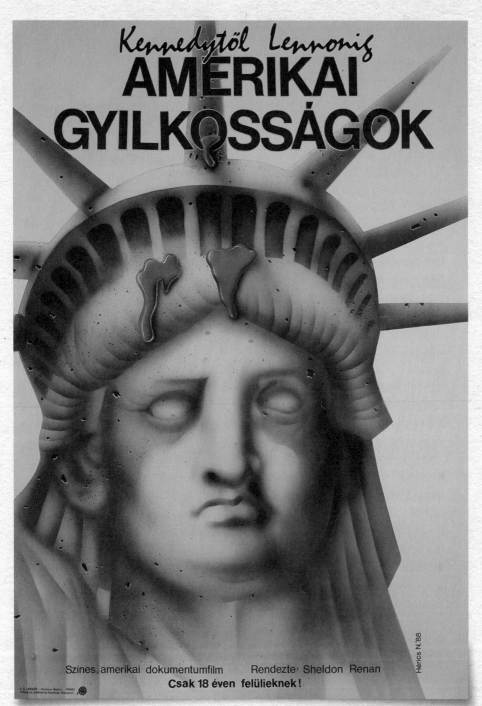

Hungarian poster for *The Killing of America* (1977)

film, rather than a document of one moment in history, is a blueprint—a Bible, of sorts. That Schrader and Renan could find so much material to work with is a testament to the endless feedback loop that is American violence: violent acts begetting violent images begetting violent acts begetting violent images, and so on. What makes *The Killing of America* so powerful is that it explicates this process, where like a sickness, the moving image passes violence on from one host to another.

Despite the film's graphic nature, *The Killing of America* wants the viewer to understand that violence is never content-neutral. The violence displayed in American media is a unique hybrid of entertainment and politics—a kind of terrorism rearranged as spectacle and transmitted to the viewer to entertain and threaten, amuse and oppress. Early mondo films like *Mondo Cane* predicted this merger, and later examples like *Jabberwalk* parodied it, suggesting that the mondo film, far from an aberration in time, a cinematic mistake, presaged something that Americans are still enthralled with to this day.

But *The Killing of America* subverts the viewer's expectation of mondo traditions, or at least its more lurid tendencies, by politicizing violent images that mondo viewers might take for granted. While Renan and Schrader might carry on the tradition in some sense—an air of exploitation is always present because of the subject matter—they reveal American media as a loaded gun aimed directly at the head of the viewer. Because in America, the violence never ends, for while bodies may expire, the image never fades, and Americans achieve immortality when the media redeems their violent acts through the process of preservation. No American will be forgotten if their neighbors can watch their shooting sprees on television, film, and the internet.

This point might have been best expressed by Robert Benjamin Smith— one of the many subjects of *The Killing of America*—on November 12, 1966, just three months after the Whitman clock tower shooting. That day, Smith, a perennial loser and social misfit at his Arizona high school, felt a kinship for Charles Whitman, so he walked into the Rose-Mar College of Beauty in Mesa, Arizona, and shot seven people. When asked why he did it, he said he wanted to be famous. "I wanted to kill about forty people so I could make a name for myself," he told a police officer. "I wanted people to know who I was."

Robert Skvarla

THRILL-SEEKING FEMALES

The *SCUM Manifesto* Ideology of the "Girl Gang" Rape-Revenge Film

> Life in this society being, at best, an utter bore and no aspect of soci-
> ety being at all relevant to women, there remains to civic-minded,
> responsible, thrill-seeking females only to overthrow the govern-
> ment, eliminate the money system, institute complete automation
> and destroy the male sex.
> —Opening Lines of the *SCUM Manifesto*, Valerie Solanas (1967)

In her book *Against Our Will* (1975), Susan Brownmiller named the phenomenon of rape as a method of misogynist possession and control, positing that "concepts of hierarchy, slavery and private property flowed from, and could only be predicated upon, the initial subjugation of women." The antirape movement had been brewing since as early as the 1830s, with abolitionist groups helmed by white women naming the rape of enslaved women of African descent as one of the significant human rights violations of the transatlantic slave trade. Second-wave feminist consciousness officially began in the 1950s alongside the civil rights movement, but it wasn't until the 1970s that the antirape movement gained traction. Within conscious-ness-raising circles, rape was being named as physical, psychological, and institutional brutality. In 1970, groups like Chicago Women Against Rape formed organizing coalitions. In January 1971, the New York Radical Feminists held a "speak-out" on rape at St. Clement's Church in New York City. Within patriarchy, rape is understood as the most painful taboo and the ultimate

SCUM (Society for Cutting Up Men) Manifesto, Olympia Press (1968)

mark of shame for women. The act of sharing these stories marked a dramatic shift in American women's understanding of sexual violence.

But in the late 1960s in New York City, some years before the "official" beginning of the antirape movement, there was an outsider artist disseminating radical sentiments concerning the subjugation of women. Often remembered as the woman who shot Andy Warhol, Valerie Solanas published her transgressive, rageful *SCUM Manifesto* (1968) almost five years prior to the events that are typically heralded as the beginnings of the movement. SCUM stands for "Society for Cutting Up Men," and in her manifesto, Solanas outlines the various deficiencies of a male-dominated society, as well as her vision for a future run by women. The *SCUM Manifesto* is almost never discussed in conjunction with the American feminist movement, unacknowledged as a subversive, revolutionary text even within leftist circles. Solanas's manifesto is dismissed as the ramblings of an insane, disenfranchised woman. While there is no denying an element of unhinged abandon at the core of the text, it seems counterintuitive to ignore the words of those most affected, the women who are driven to madness by being discarded within the patriarchal state. *SCUM* is an insane war cry, often wrongheaded, vulgar, hilarious, and revolutionary in equal measure.

Though it is typically dismissed as an outlier, women at the time of *SCUM*'s publication and the attempted Warhol assassination were definitely listening to Solanas's call to action. In her chapter "The 'Sweet Assassin' and the Performative Politics of the *SCUM Manifesto*" for the essay collection *The Queer Sixties* (1999), Patricia Juliana Smith names the treatise as "an important shift in social style and consciousness centered around the reworking of the status quo." She posits that the shooting of Andy Warhol was a deliberate performance carried out to incite revolution. Women organized in support of Solanas, with a group in Greenwich Village distributing a broadside that read "PLASTIC MAN VS. THE SWEET ASSASSIN . . . NON-MAN SHOT BY THE REALITY OF HIS DREAM . . . A TOUGH CHICK WITH A COP CAP AND A .38 . . . VALERIE IS OURS." Roxanne Dunbar-Ortiz, a revolutionary then living in Mexico, canceled her move to Cuba after reading the news report of the Warhol shooting and immediately returned to the United States, convinced that a women's revolution had begun. Dunbar-Ortiz then formed a Boston-based women's group called Cell 16 whose first order of business was reading *SCUM*. Back in New York, Ti-Grace Atkinson, the president of the National Organization of Women, declared that Solanas would go down in history as the "first outstanding champion of women's rights." What began as a fringe political stance was brought to the media main stage through an act of violence. In

THRILL-SEEKING FEMALES   313

the text of *SCUM* itself, Solanas advocates for the murder of men who do not comply with SCUM's mission.

The sentiments expressed by Solanas lend themselves to the extremity of horror/exploitation cinema. Although she was generally considered an outlier, there is ample evidence that the "solutions" of female supremacy and violent revolution that she proffered were floating about in the ether of the political zeitgeist. Given the growing cultural consciousness in the United States around sexual violence and the thriving women's liberation movement, it is unsurprising that American exploitation cinema would explore this topic to its most titillating conclusion via the rape-revenge film cycle. Additionally, with the publication of Abbie Hoffman's anarchist texts, there was a general pro-violence revolutionary sentiment in leftist circles of the time; the pacifism of the hippie movement was giving way to disillusionment, leading to a burgeoning faction of left-wing extremists. The failures of the flower children were a particularly popular topic in grindhouse cinema made after the Tate-LaBianca murders carried out by the Manson Family in 1969. Films like *I Drink Your Blood* (1970) and the rape-revenge classic *The Last House on the Left* (1972) exemplify what Alexandra Heller-Nicholas has described in her critical study of rape-revenge films as "the looming reality of the death of progressive ideals of the 1960s" that demonstrates the end of the hippie dream, giving way to cinema that depicts "a nihilistic world where there is little place for romantic idealism."

Although viewers generally think of exploitation films when the topic of rape revenge is mentioned, Heller-Nicholas has also demonstrated in two editions of her study that it is an expansive cycle that encompasses a wide range of cross-genre films. For the purposes of this essay, I will focus on films that fall into the exploitation genre and production conditions. Exploitation rape-revenge films often follow the same plot: an unsuspecting woman (usually a career gal) who is horrifically raped in a drawn-out, graphic scene decides to take revenge on her attacker, or men in general, in the form of a murderous rampage. The most famous example is Meir Zarchi's *I Spit on Your Grave* (1978), which garners controversy in feminist film circles to this day over the supposed eroticization of the arduous rape scene. Within the subgenre are a small number of films that capitulate around a group of victimized women who form a "girl gang" to carry out their revenge plots, and it is to those films that I turn my attention.

I will use Valerie Solanas's *SCUM Manifesto* as a framework through which to analyze the "girl gang" rape-revenge film and how the films relate to the general philosophy and action points articulated in the manifesto. I seek to position these contemporaneous texts in frictive conversation with one another. I will argue that Solanas's manifesto, though an entirely different medium and set of production conditions, is in communion with the extremity of exploitation/grindhouse cinema through its use of shocking rhetoric and ideologies. What follows is an analysis of three "girl gang" rape-revenge films: *Act of Vengeance* (aka *Rape Squad*, 1974), *The Black Alley Cats* (1973), and *The Ladies Club* (1986), and how they reflect the ideology of *SCUM*. I am using the structure of the *SCUM Manifesto* to frame my study and further marry the films to Solanas's text, though I will omit certain headings from the original manifesto in service of clarity. I have chosen and combined some of Solanas's headlined sections of the manifesto that best support my thesis. For the sake of consistency, I use bio-essentialist language such as *male* and *female*, as those are the terms Solanas uses in *SCUM*.

"War"

Solanas opens *SCUM* with an indictment against war. She proposes that men as a gender have "no compassion or ability to empathize or identify" and therefore must validate their own existences through mass destruction and violence. This act is positioned as an extended suicide, as the man knows his own life is "worthless, he would rather go out in a blaze of glory than to plod grimly on for fifty more years." This is a typical outdated feminist talking point, the idea that men are responsible for all wars and that if women ran the world there would be none. Of course, given that many women across history have been more than happy to lend their murderous hands to the patriarchy in the form of the war machine, it is a naive proposition that mass death would cease to exist were the "fairer sex" in charge. But to dismiss Solanas's indictment as naivete is to ignore the inherent irony of her position: in the same breath with which she condemns war, she advocates for guerrilla warfare and mass death conducted by the women of SCUM.

The irony of Solanas's antiwar position is present in the girl-gang rape-revenge film. While the graphic nature of these films seems to condemn violence, the revenge act carried out by guerrilla girl gangs is celebrated diegetically (occurring linearly within the narrative) and is meant to be cathartic for the viewer (nondiegetically). For example, in *Act of Vengeance*, the "rape squad" formed by the female characters, who all share the same experience with the same rapist, enjoys a quite comical arc in the middle of the film. In one scene, the gang sends member Linda (Jo Ann Harris) to a disco to seduce a would-be rapist. She follows a man back to his apartment, where he attempts to assault her. When Linda yells in protest, the squad bursts in and subdues the man

LET THE
REVENGE
FIT THE
CRIME!

They all had
one thing
in common.
They
had been
violated
in the
same
savage
way...

...NOW
THEY'RE
OUT TO GET
EVEN!

RAPE SQUAD ®

JO ANN HARRIS · PETER BROWN · JENNIFER LEE · LISA MOORE · CONNIE STRICKLAND · PATRICIA ESTRIN · LADA EDMUND JR. & TONY YOUNG

Australian lobby card for *Rape Squad*, aka *Act of Vengeance* (1974)

and trashes his apartment. They handcuff him to the bed and dangle a vial of blue substance menacingly over his exposed penis, tauntingly telling him that it is sulfuric acid. There is a moment of tension as the smiling women pour the vial onto the screaming man's genitals, only for him to soon realize there is no burning sensation. The gang explains that what they actually dropped on his penis was a blue dye that will mark him as a rapist to any unfortunate woman he encounters. This scene is played as comedy, and it is quite funny. There is a stark contrast between the framing of the dye scene and the rape scenes with multiple women that preceded it: the former is playful and funny, the latter bleak and reprehensible. The film holds space for the terror of mass violence as well as the humor inherent in "turning the tables."

The Black Alley Cats demonstrates similar contrasts. The film opens with a group of young women walking together at night, harassed en masse by a large gang of men loitering on the darkened street. The men attack the group in a scene that recalls classical depictions of the Rape of the Sabine Women, chasing the girls into an abandoned, condemned house and gang-raping them in a warlike attack. Echoes of rape as warfare permeate the chaotic scene, which is in direct contrast to the following humorous scenes of the Black Alley Cat gang, now donning black panties and blindfolds and robbing businessmen and rich partygoers. In both films, patriarchal warfare is positioned as inherently evil, the male perpetrators apelike and contemptible, while the girl gang's revenge act is radical and celebratory.

"Niceness, Politeness, and 'Dignity'"

At various points in the manifesto, Solanas attacks ideas of social propriety and politeness. In this section, she describes men as knowing deep down they are "worthless pieces of shit" who cloak their inadequacy in polite language around sex like "copulate" or "have relations with." To Solanas, this is "the suit on the chimp." To counteract

Rape Squad, aka *Act of Vengeance* (1974)

the stilted manners enforced by male supremacy, Solanas uses crass language throughout the manifesto, freely cursing and making crude sexual jokes, qualities that are typically seen as inherently "mannish."

The reclamation of vulgar, "mannish" speech patterns throughout the manifesto reinforces Solanas's thesis, which is that men have convinced women that women are men and men are women. In other words, the qualities typically associated with men, such as "emotional strength and independence, forcefulness, dynamism, decisiveness, coolness, objectivity, assertiveness, courage, integrity, vitality, intensity, depth of character, grooviness, etc.," are actually female traits. Therefore, undesirable qualities associated with women, such as "vanity, frivolity, triviality, and weakness," are actually male traits. Within the Valerie Solanas school of thought, the logic would then follow that because crassness is associated with men, it is actually a female trait. Solanas reifies this by utilizing lewd language and humor throughout the manifesto.

The girl-gang rape-revenge film demonstrates the SCUM refutation of niceness, politeness, and "dignity" through various diegetic and nondiegetic elements. First, the film titles function in a similar manner to the title of the *SCUM Manifesto* itself. Smith expands on and articulates the power of linguistic upheaval:

Take its name, for example: the term "SCUM" shifts from signifying the rejects of society to naming a vanguard class, but can "SCUM" really come to mean hip revolutionaries who will save the world? The SCUM manifesto parodies the performance of the patriarchal social order it refuses. It claims universal authority to run the world based on a seamless "we" of SCUM women, but by the appropriation of universalizing discourse, the manifesto reveals how the universe is not universal at all. . . . In principle, the bourgeois public sphere offers a utopian universality where individuals' embodied specificities (backgrounds, status, gender) are bracketed so that all citizens may participate equally and objectively, but in practice, only white, male, literate, and propertied citizens can transcend their bodies and status by representing themselves as abstract, objective, and universal.

The title of *SCUM* functions on multiple levels. It is a humorous and confrontational acronym (Society for Cutting Up Men) and is in line with the Jonathan Swift–esque parody of the text. Its use is ironic, as it calls attention to the repulsive uselessness of the male-dominated society, reducing it to scatological grotesque refuse, as noted by Avital Ronell in her introduction to the 2015 reissue. But as demonstrated by Smith, it is also a reclamation of a term that signifies the garbage dregs of society, a position that Solanas occupied as an impoverished, mentally ill, traumatized, queer sex worker.

Exploitation film titles function on a similar linguistic, nondiegetic level. Often named by studios or producers seeking to make the most money from the most shocking presentation, exploitation titles function to mark the film as lowbrow "trash." The titles themselves function to cash in on the scandalous push and pull between societal rejection and viewer titillation; the audience gets to delight in feeling like bad little boys and girls for watching trashy, taboo movies. At the same time, the titles brazenly mock the bourgeois sensibility that would render such art as "low culture" in the first place. The shocking titles (and poster art) call attention to the friction between the viewer's reticence and judgment and their desire to engage with graphic media.

The alternate title for *Act of Vengeance* is *Rape Squad*, a reference to the girl gang at the center of the film as well as to the violent act the group coalesces around. As mentioned previously, the act and experience of rape are shrouded in secrecy and silence. Up until recently with the rise of the #metoo movement, it has historically been considered "uncouth" to openly discuss the matter of sexual violence. Of course, the idea that rape should not be spoken about openly serves to protect perpetrators and enablers by instilling shame in the victim so that they do not dare seek justice, for fear of being exposed as "damaged goods." The idea that it is impolite to speak of these injustices is inherent within the text of the *SCUM Manifesto*, which deliberately aligns shock-factor outspokenness with revolutionary women. Silence

Rape Squad, aka *Act of Vengeance* (1974)

and shame reify the bourgeois order of predators at the top of the food chain, with victims at the bottom stepped on and discarded. While titillating, shocking, and, yes, "exploitative," the name *Rape Squad* is also a powerful refutation of the historical silence invoked by rape culture that protects predators.

The function of the title of *The Black Alley Cats* is titillation and reclamation. The name (also the name of the gang in the film) is a clear reference to the terms "back alley" and "alley cat." The collocation "back alley" connotes seediness, illegality, and taboo acts committed in secrecy, while "alley cat" refers to feral felines and is often used to describe women of ill repute. That "back" is replaced by "black" in the title refers to the primarily Black female cast and the titillation of the "taboo" interracial sexual relationships on display in the film. The suggestive title exploits the eroticism of the miscegenation taboo and marks the pornographic film as a piece of low culture, something only fit to be viewed in a "back alley." It reifies the idea of racialized sexual relations not belonging to the realm of polite society. However, it also mocks the conceit entirely by daring to brazenly address it. Similar to the utilization of the title *Rape Squad*, *The Black Alley Cats* renders on display what is traditionally unspeakable, even illegal.

The Ladies Club is another title that invokes prejudiced degradation, referencing the denigrating, sexist habit of referring to women patronizingly as "ladies," or diminishing the power of women's groups by calling them "clubs." That the "club" is a calculating coalition of castrators taking revenge on the men who raped them is an ironic twist on the sexist referentiality of the title. Additionally, it functions as a warning: don't dismiss these chicks, you may find yourself with your balls cut off. The title is a mockery of the misogyny of the gendered terms being invoked. Furthermore, *The Ladies Club* is a rare rape-revenge film directed by a woman, Janet Greek, making the invocation all the more powerful and familiar to a female viewer. As a female genre director, Greek is in the minority and is surely familiar with the sexist tropes of many exploitation films that position violence against women as titillating. She subverts the tropes by spotlighting and filling in the gaps left by shallow narratives with deeper complexities and plot points.

The Black Alley Cats (1973)

In fact, Greek has spent her career advocating for women's resistance; in 2006, Greek published a book titled *The Divorce Planner: Self-Defense for Women When They Need It Most*, which she wrote after going through two divorces.

While the titles reinforce the SCUM concept nondiegetically, the characters in the films themselves eschew concepts of niceness, politeness, and "dignity" on a diegetic level. They scream in anger, swear freely, wear skimpy outfits, and enact violence on men who dare cross them. The entire proposition posed by the plot points of women taking revenge on men who rape them is one of rejecting the norms of a polite, patriarchal, white supremacist society that insists women be "good girls"—always quiet and complacent and never making a fuss. In *Act of Vengeance*, Linda lives out the fantasy of many women by making a veritable scene at the police station while reporting her rape. The realism of this scene might be surprising coming from director Bob Kelljan, an exploitation "hack" most known for his Count Yorga films. Directors like Kelljan have historically been derided by feminist critics who posit that they enforce misogynist stereotyping and exploitation in their crass works. If anything, *Act of Vengeance* demonstrates the nuance of this issue. While it can't be denied there is some element of misogyny at play, as we live in a patriarchal world, human beings are far more complicated, our implicit biases and revolutionary spirits often colliding in a frictive embrace. Genre cinema has historically been a welcome arena for radical, subversive thought; challenged by moralistic censorship brigades, exploitation/horror directors of the 1970s saw themselves as bucking against antisex puritanism by boldly showing the human body and sex acts. By engaging in both voyeurism and transgressive feminism, *Act of Vengeance* is a perfect example of how one director's work cannot be categorized into "good" and "bad" representation or praxis.

The *Black Alley Cats* is another example of this friction. In one scene, the women enjoy a messy shower fight, which showcases their "bad girl" attitudes, as well as the voyeuristic pitfalls of the male gaze. The film is directed by white Danish director Henning Schellerup, who largely worked in exploitation. Schellerup filters the unique cruelty of American racism through his own European lens, engaging in the taboo of it as well as spotlighting its horrors. While the women are debased on every level, they are also bombastic, sharp, and cunning. These are not films that value quiet, meek, polite femininity. They are the SCUM ideal of "dominant, secure, self-confident, nasty, violent, selfish, independent, proud, thrill-seeking, free-wheeling, arrogant females."

Japanese poster for *The Black Alley Cats* (1973)

"Suppression of Individuality and Conformity"

While the women in these films do share the same goal, through their various characterizations, they are separated as individuals, often having conflict with one another about the proper way to reach their goal. For Heller-Nicholas, "the fascinating thing about many of these films are the fractures that occur among the women as they negotiate their ethics in the face of a preliminarily shared goal, or how they struggle to get other survivors on their side and join them." The strongest example is from one of the more powerful scenes in *The Ladies Club*. In a very 1980s nod to the women's consciousness-raising groups of the previous decade, such as the Chicago Women Against Rape, Joan (Karen Austin) and Constance (Christine Belford) contact and recruit other women to help them take justice into their own hands after being dismissed by the authorities. The women hold a meeting at Constance's house (another nod to grassroots organizing), during which they passionately argue over the ethics of revenge and how best to serve it. They are a group coalesced around a singular goal that honors the individuality of its members.

Act of Vengeance contains similar nods to grassroots feminist groups like Chicago Women Against Rape and Sisters of Color Ending Sexual Assault. Linda shows her fellow victims an article about women forming "rape squads"

RAPE SQUAD

74/156

A lobby card for *Rape Squad*, aka *Act of Vengeance* (1974)

after they meet at the police lineup to identify their assailant, the "Jingle Bells Rapist" (he makes his victims sing the carol while he attacks them as a way to show his dominance). Inspired, they decide to form a hotline where other women can call in and ask to join their squad, posting flyers that read "SISTERS! STOP! RAPE! NOW!" This kind of organizing rhetoric was used by second-wave feminist groups like the Feminist Alliance Against Rape.

While united in their goal, the gang is shown to be made of individual women with differing approaches. Linda is the leader, an outspoken feminist, and more of an upper-middle-class "career woman." Karen (Lisa Moore), a reserved seamstress, is the most mature and the sole Black woman in the squad, who is obviously working-class and living within lower means. Her rape is racialized, something she points out to the other members. Tiny (Lada St. Edmund) is the group's muscle with a black belt in karate, bucking traditional gender norms. Teresa (Connie Strickland) is the angriest, spitting vitriol at the lazy police officers during the lineup scene. In a later scene, she fires back at two men who sexually harass her, her unfiltered trauma and rage cowing them completely. During a training scene where Tiny tells the women to take their rage out on a punching bag labeled "RAPIST," she breaks down and is comforted by Angie. It is alluded to that she may have a

Men who attack women
have two big problems.

The Ladies Club

is about to
remove them both.

NICK J. MILETI Presents "THE LADIES CLUB"
Starring KAREN AUSTIN • DIANA SCARWID • CHRISTINE BELFORD • SHERA DANESE • BEVERLY TODD • MARILYN KAGAN
KIT McDONOUGH and BRUCE DAVISON • Based on the novel "SISTERHOOD" by BETTY BLACK and CASEY BISHOP
Screenplay by PAUL MASON and FRAN LEWIS EBELING • Produced by NICK J. MILETI and PAUL MASON • Directed by A.K. ALLEN

R RESTRICTED
UNDER 17 REQUIRES ACCOMPANYING
PARENT OR ADULT GUARDIAN

From ∕N∖ New Line Cinema   © New Line Cinema MCMLXXXVI

BUDCO
REGENCY
TWIN
16TH & CHESTNUT STREETS
567-2310

STARTS
TODAY!

REGENCY DAILY AT 12:30, 2:30, 4:30,
6:30, 8:30, 10:30
$2.50 'TIL 12:30, FRIDAY ONLY
SENIOR CITIZENS $2.50

ALSO STARTS TODAY AT THESE SELECTED AREA THEATRES

- **AMC BUCKS COLONIAL 2**
  The Market Place—Street Rd.
  at Bustleton Pike

- **BUDCO ANDORRA 6**
  Ridge & Henry Avenues

- **BUDCO CITY LINE TWIN**
  77th & City Line Ave.

- **BUDCO COLLEGE**
  Swarthmore

- **BUDCO GATEWAY 3**
  Devon Exit on Rt. 202, S. of Expy.

- **BUDCO ORLEANS 8**
  Cottman & Bustleton, N.E. Phila.

- **BUDCO QUAKERTOWN 6**
  County Sq. Shpg. Center, Rt. 309.
  Trumbauersville Rd.

- **BUDCO 309 CINEMA 4**
  N. End of 309 Expy. at Rt. 63,
  Montgomeryville

- **ERIC I-95 TWIN**
  Intersection I-95 & Rt. 1

  NEW JERSEY

- **AMC DEPTFORD 8**
  On Clements Bridge Rd.
  across from the mall

- **AMC MARLTON 8**
  800 North Route 73, Marlton

- **BUDCO PRINCE 3**
  Rt. 1, Princeton

- **ERIC TWIN WILLINGBORO**
  Rt. 130 N., S. of Levitt Pkwy., Willingboro

- **ERIC TWIN ROUTE 38**
  Adj. to Cherry Hill Mall, Cherry Hill

  DELAWARE

- **ERIC 5 TRI-STATE MALL**
  Naamans Rd., Claymont

Advertisement for *The Ladies Club, Philadelphia Inquirer*, April 11, 1986

more complex history of sexual trauma. Angie (Patricia Estrin) is a skeptic and has the most measured approaches, demonstrating that the feminist movement was diverse in thought and opinion on how to carry out actions. Nancy (Jennifer Lee) is the most passive and quiet member, meant to be a kind of "hippie pacifist" type.

It is implied that though they are different, with varied reactions to the traumatic event they experienced, they are stronger together. Furthermore, the emphasis on characterization reinforces that the women are stronger as a unit *because* of their individuality; each woman's personality and pathos add to the power of the squad. A nondiegetic example of this is the poster for the film, which features photos of each woman separated by clear white lines and labeled with their name.

"Authority and Government"

Solanas's stance on authority in this section is quite concise: "There's no reason why a society consisting of rational beings capable of empathizing with each other, complete and having no natural reason to compete, should have a government, laws or leaders." She considers the fact that we do have these systems in place as evidence of men's failure to create a society unable to deal with human fallibility without the aid of oppressive authority. Her stance is antipolice, antigovernment, and antireligion.

Rape-revenge films generally share this stance: typically, police are depicted as corrupt, clueless, bumbling, sexist pigs. Girl-gang rape-revenge films are no different, and authority is painted with a scathing brush. In *Act of Vengeance*, there are multiple scenes that show the police as insensitive and incompetent. When Linda is first raped, she immediately reports the assault to the police. They brush her off and humiliate her by asking her intimate questions about the assault in a nonprivate area. One officer suggests that Linda deserved the assault by asking what she was wearing. Linda responds with justified fury. In another scene, the victims of the "Jingle Bells Rapist" are gathered in one room to pick out the assailant in a lineup. After the women fail to agree on which man it could be, a detective tells them he only brought them in there to make exactly that point and show them how difficult their job is. He all but says it is an impossible task and that the women should let it go. They respond angrily, and the interaction is their impetus for forming a "rape squad."

The Ladies Club has similar plot beats. It is clear that Janet Greek's film was inspired by *Act of Vengeance*; the former is an updated, 1980s take on the 1970s exploitation genre. The main character, Joan, is a female police officer who is beaten and raped in her home by a gang of hoodlums. That her fellow officers do not take the attack seriously is a searing indictment of the police as an institution and of capitalist-driven, mainstream feminism. By choosing to make the heroine of the story a police officer who is mistreated by her colleagues in the aftermath of the assault, Greek critiques the project of capitalist feminism that seeks to position women as "equal" to men, no matter the cost. The moments of friction between Joan and her male peers is in line with the antiauthoritarian SCUM ideology that eschews "equality" with patriarchs in favor of revolution. However, there is also a stark contrast between Joan and Constance (a police officer and a doctor) and the working-class domestic workers in the group they organize with. For example, Joan is only able to form the club because as a cop, she can access the records of sex offenders, manipulating the system against itself. Constance has even more privilege: she's educated, white, and wealthy and appears to live in an entire house by herself.

"Prejudice (Racial, Ethnic, Religious, Etc.)"

Solanas's stance on prejudice as a tool of male dominance is written in two succinct sentences: "The male needs scapegoats onto whom he can project his failings and inadequacies and upon whom he can vent his frustration at not being female. And the vicarious discriminations have the practical advantage of substantially increasing the pussy pool available to the men on top." With these two short lines, Solanas condemns all bigotry as a tool of the patriarch to oppress marginalized people. In the world of SCUM, men will do anything to stay in power and use/abuse women, including prejudice of all forms. Prejudice is explicitly linked to male domination and sexual violence. Solanas implies that oppressing marginalized women creates the condition for men to essentially have their pick of any woman they choose to sexually force themselves on.

The link that Solanas makes between prejudice, specifically racism, and sexual violence is demonstrated in the girl-gang rape-revenge film. The rape Karen experiences in *Act of Vengeance* is a notable example. While she is working at home, the rapist breaks in and assaults her in a racialized manner that differs from white Linda's rape at the beginning of the film. The rapist calls Karen "girl" several times and says she has a "nice black bottom." The racist aggression is "subtle" (as much as such a thing can be) and easy to miss for white viewers. But it is an intentional line of dialogue that calls attention to the repulsive nature of the rapist character, as if to say, "Not only is this man a woman hater, he's also a racist, and he will use that fact in his methods of degradation."

The Ladies Club (1986)

VHS cover for *Violated*, aka *The Ladies Club* (1986)

The link between racism and rape culture is more present in *The Black Alley Cats*. As I discussed previously in the chapter, *The Black Alley Cats* is by no means a bastion of antiracist sentiment. It is clearly a cash grab of a film, using the taboos of rape, interracial sex, and lesbianism as shock factors to arouse the audience. That said, it is worth examining in a historical framework how the radical feminist idea that rape and race are linked invades the consciousness of "lowbrow" films like *The Black Alley Cats*. The punch is not as poignant or intentional as in a more fully fleshed-out film like *Act of Vengeance*, but the fact that the ideas show up at all in this more intentionally erotic film is indicative of the relevancy of SCUM within the zeitgeist.

The Black Alley Cats centers around a gang made up of mostly Black women (there are two white women in the gang). It is rare for films of this era outside the Blaxploitation genre to feature more than one Black actress, and even rarer for those actresses to be as dark-skinned as they are in *The Black Alley Cats*. At the beginning of the film, a group of young women (who are actually meant to be teenagers attending a girls' boarding school) are raped by a group of men. They decide to form a gang following this incident to take revenge on the men who raped them, as well as on white society at large by robbing parties of rich white guests. Throughout the film, the Black characters are preyed on and objectified by both white women and men, who they ultimately take revenge on. We are shown various incidents of microaggressions that are meant to be viewed as such. For example, Marsha (Charlene Miles) and Pamela (Sunshine Woods), in an effort to cover their tracks, lie to their white teacher, Miss Woods (Betty Mitchell), that they were out taking Vivian (Sandy Dempsey) and Melissa (Johnnie Rodes), their white friends, to "meet [their] people." Miss Woods responds, "Such fine spirit down there," at which point Marsha sneers and snickers, rolling her eyes.

But the aggression in the film is not limited to the micro. After all, it does open with a gang rape. In a plot move uncharacteristic of rape-revenge films, which are usually focused on graphic, extreme depictions of sexual violence, Pamela is drugged and "date-raped" by a white couple whom she babysits for. They take photos of her naked body that they then use to blackmail her into attending a party at their home. This time, the nefarious couple has a different plan, forcing Pamela to don a skimpy maid outfit and wait on their white guests, encouraging them to inspect her body in a manner reminiscent of slavers plying their "wares" at the auction block. *The Black Alley Cats* explicitly links sexual violence to racism. That one of the rapists is a white woman illustrates what Solanas calls "male-females," women who sell out to the white supremacist patriarchy. Furthermore, the diversity of the gang and their varying races and socioeconomic backgrounds supports Solanas's following sections on competition and friendship, in which she proposes that SCUM-minded women will function on an even playing field in harmony with one another. In fact, the core ethos of the girl-gang film is that of the power of women loving each other and banding together, which is a major theme in the *SCUM Manifesto*.

"Hatred, Violence, and Death"

The final sections of the *SCUM Manifesto* are where Solanas lays out her ultimate goal:

> SCUM will kill all men who are not in the Men's Auxiliary of SCUM. Men in the Men's Auxiliary are those men who are working diligently to eliminate themselves, men who, regardless of their motives, do good, men who are playing ball with SCUM. A few examples of the men in the Men's Auxiliary are: men who kill men ... who tell them a woman's primary goal in life should be to squash the male sex (to aid men in this endeavor SCUM will conduct Turd Sessions, at which every male present will give a speech beginning with the sentence: "I am a turd, a lowly abject turd," then proceed to list all the ways in which he is.

For Valerie Solanas, the solution to the end of male violence is to organize on a mass scale and murder men so that women can take over and eliminate the monetary system and all forms of government. In fact, she says that death "excites [the man] sexually and, already dead inside, he wants to die," and that the hatred men display is evidence of the hate they feel "at the bottom, of his own worthless self."

SCUM's vision of men is the kind that occupies the world of the rape-revenge film: violent, hateful, and sexually excited by death and destruction. These are not nuanced, complex portrayals of men and manhood; they are one-dimensional in exactly the way *SCUM* presents them: to make a point. In the world of these films, men are intentionally reduced to flattened figures of inept, rageful rapists or cowardly enablers to emphasize the all-consuming system the women of the films are up against. They can find no respite, even in their male partners, who dismiss or mock them.

Indeed, discarded and ignored, the women of rape-revenge films are given little choice but to murder and destroy their rapists (as in *Act of Vengeance* and *The Ladies Club*), or at least humiliate them (again in *Act of Vengeance*, and most notably in *The Black Alley Cats*). The narrative arc emphasizes that women undergo multiple humiliations associated with rape, the rape itself being the first, and the subsequent denial and interrogation they undergo from men at large afterward positioned as its own kind of violation. It has been written many times in various texts that the graphic nature of the rape scene in the rape-revenge movie serves to justify the coming revenge act. I would argue that the absolute repulsive hatefulness of the men in these films serves a similar function of justification and catharsis for the characters and viewers. By the time the murder comes, we simply cannot wait for it to happen.

Annie Rose Malamet

"LOOK WHERE YOU'RE GOING, CUNT"

Political Violence in Feminist Cinema of the Late Second Wave

Into the 1980s, feminism's second wave made an indelible mark on the evolution of the developed world. The movement's successes were remarkable—rights to abortion and birth control, access to childcare, opportunities for women to attain job positions usually reserved for men, and on and on— but these victories were a far cry from winning the war. Forty or so years down the track and feminism's fight is yet to reach its finale, with some of its landmark wins, such as the abortion rights offered by *Roe v. Wade*, even being overturned in the US in 2022. What happened in the '80s was the incorporation of feminism's achievements into mainstream society under the guise of a generalized liberal feminism. In fact, the "feminist" label started to lose its association with certain milestones and its momentum, because feminism's gains were no longer considered those of the movement itself; they'd been incorporated and embraced into society. Everyone claimed ownership over what was once considered radical or an affront to the patriarchy. Yet feminists were still angry. And rightly so. Equality was not measured on the outcomes of isolated agendas; it was a cultural shift that needed to permeate every aspect of society. New forms of feminism would start to emerge to meet this end: intersectional feminism, which recognized that inequality for women stemmed from more than just patriarchal forces but from class, race, religious and sexual discrimination as well, among other factors; and difference feminism, which sought to revalue traditionally devalued feminine qualities such as subjectivity, caring, and empathy (as defined by Stanford University's Gendered Innovations project). In the perpetuation of

A Question of Silence (1982)

the feminist fight, the adoption of cinema as an artistic weapon cannot be underplayed, especially at a time when women filmmakers were still few and far between. The fact that women were taking control of film cameras and writing their own on-screen narratives was a feminist call to arms itself, and a revealing insight into the feminist cause as it entered the late second wave.

Here, I consider three powerful examples of feminist cinema of that time—Marleen Gorris's *De stilte rond Christine M* (*A Question of Silence*, 1982), Lizzie Borden's *Born in Flames* (1983), and María Luisa Bemberg's *Camila* (1984)—that teetered on a politically radical precipice because they refused to accept that feminism had achieved its aims. I cast them in the light of radical violence and how, as a cinematic expression of feminism by women filmmakers, the content of these films advocated for an advancement of the feminist cause, one that reached beyond the definition of the second wave to achieve dramatic change at a nuanced, cultural level.

In a 1996 interview with *Cineaste*, Dutch filmmaker Marleen Gorris talked about feminism becoming "the last 'F-word' in American culture" and of the media "having a field day with anything feminist, denigrating it left, right, and center." Feminism's plight in the Netherlands was similar to that in the US, with milestones such as the passing of the legalized abortion bill in 1981, although this bill didn't come into effect until 1984 as the Termination of Pregnancy Act. Gorris's debut film, *A Question of Silence* (1982), is one that polarized opinion and generated an onslaught of outrage at the time of its release. It hinges on an act of violence so brutal it rivals that of any horror movie, but it is also a very political act—in its provocation, in its observations of patriarchal oppression, in its hyperrealized depiction of how such oppression can irreconcilably hurt people, and in how it coerces its audience into exonerating the perpetrators of the brutality as heroes.

Some might argue that such coercion verges on manipulation, which possibly accounts for the film's continuing controversy with critics and audiences—that and the absence of sympathetic male characters (in his *Boston Globe* review of the film, Jay Carr accused the film of positioning all its male characters as straw dogs). However, by expressing its radical message—the subjuga-

Dutch poster for *A Question of Silence* (1982)

tion of women in society and its endemic effect—in a cinematic safe space where there can be positive provocation, *A Question of Silence* achieves something that violence and extremism in real life fails to do: it prompts people to think without causing any real harm. Possibly, the biggest achievement of Marleen Gorris, though, is to construct a rich, dense feminist manifesto through a traditional narrative structure. She does so with layered metaphoric language and symbolism. Literally every line, every gesture, every frame of this film could be analyzed and positioned according to the deeper meaning of its feminist intent.

The brutal act at the fulcrum of this film is the murder of a male shopkeeper. This shopkeeper, who remains nameless, runs a ladies' clothing boutique and runs into three women who were previously strangers to each other but magically—even magnetically—come together in a perfect storm to kick him, stab him with crude weapons such as coat hangers and shopping carts, and mutilate him in a way that goes beyond what could be excused as self-defense. The inciting moment is when one of the women, Christine (Edda Barends), is accused of shoplifting by the man. Rather than accept her crime with shame or regret, she provokes him further by putting more items in her bag. The other women come to her aid (although in a notably somnambulistic manner, almost robotic in their lack of emotion) to form a murdering triumvirate—a spontaneous moment where they rise triumphantly from their oppression to kick and stomp the patriarchy, as represented by this shopkeeper, until he is a mess of lifeless flesh. Yet it's not as gruesome as that description may suggest. It is violent, but it is not the blood and guts (or lack thereof) that we see on the screen that is shocking. It's the verbal relaying of these details by the male coroner to the female psychiatrist, Janine (Cox Habbema), who is assigned to determine the mental state of the women. It is this third-party observation from a man that viscerally paints the picture of violence for us as the audience. Otherwise, what we see on-screen is unfetishized.

The film starts after the murder has already taken place, when the women are being arrested at their respective homes and workplaces. It's only in flashback that the incident gets pieced together as an incremental puzzle with a lack of alibis for all parties involved. As mentioned, it's a notably bloodless incident. As soon as the male shopkeeper falls to the ground, the camera remains on the women, mainly focusing on their unflinching, stony faces from below (from the point of view of the victim) as they systematically beat him. Despite the savage crime being committed, they go about their business as if it's a mundane, routine activity. Seemingly, the shopkeeper has done nothing to warrant this attack, apart from his air of superiority in catching Christine stealing red-handed. Or has he? At the courtroom climax of the film, the prosecutor rhetorically asks the jury to turn the gender tables and consider if it had been a woman shopkeeper murdered by three men. This prompts one of the defendants to burst into uncontrollable laughter that then spreads across the courtroom (to other women witnesses of the crime that stand in solidarity with the defendants through their silence) and forces proceedings to be adjourned. Why the laughter? Because violence against women is rife in society and frequently goes unpunished. It is truly laughable.

A Question of Silence follows the genre hallmarks of a neo-noir detective story. As the protagonist, psychiatrist Janine serves as our private dick lumped with getting to the bottom of the case. On the surface, she seems respected in her professional and private life and appears happily married. She takes on the strange case with an open mind as to whether the three women are insane—or not. However, as she gets to know each individual woman better, their insight opens her eyes to the circumstances of her gender and, as every good detective story goes, she has unintended revelations about herself—about how she too has been caught up in the destructive powers of the patriarchy without consciously realizing it.

For Janine, everything comes into question: her meaning in life, her relationship with her husband, her career, and her professional viability. It

"One of the more delicious and absorbing dramas to be found on the screen. A thriller that becomes a deeply human, poignant drama."
SAN FRANCISCO CHRONICLE

★ ★ ★

"A shocker all right, a terse provocative movie..."
NEW YORK DAILY NEWS

Three women on trial for their lives.
What they didn't say could kill them!

A
Question
of Silence

Written and Directed by
MARLEEN GORRIS

Distributed by **QFi** QUARTET/FILMS INCORPORATED

US poster for *A Question of Silence* (1982)

raises the possibility she is just a stooge for a system endemically positioned to oppress her because she is a woman. Arguably, this questioning begins when the secretary, Andrea (Henriëtte Tol), challenges Janine over her psychiatric report, trivializing its relevance. It further cements the comment of the coroner, "I presume you're usually assigned to women," a comment that effectively undermines Janine's authority as a real psychiatrist. By the time Janine stands up in court to controversially proclaim the women sane, she has become one of them. When she leaves the court—judged in the eyes of the men—it makes sense that another man walking past would derogatorily reprimand her: "Look where you're going, cunt." This unidentified man's statement is loaded, ominous. Has she sounded the death knell on her own professional and personal life? We will never know, because this statement occurs at the finale of the film.

Defendant Andrea is circumspect and practical, a corporate woman with strong leadership potential whose talent is constantly undermined, even exploited, by the men at her workplace. She displays calm fortitude at the prospect of her trial and reacts to the murder by engaging in emotionless, fully clothed sex with a man who mistakes her for a sex worker. She rides her john with the same kind of mechanical dominance she displays when doing away with the shopkeeper. Ann (Nelly Frijda), another one of the killers, reveals a lifetime of unfulfillment to Janine. This includes her marriage, her relationship with her unappreciative daughter, and her demeaning job as a waitress. This culminates in Ann living a rather lonely, insular life where her only pleasure comes from cooking fancy French dinners for one with a bottle of red wine.

In contrast, housewife and kleptomaniac Christine (Edda Barends) remains guarded in silence, which functions as the metaphoric heart of this film. The Dutch title, *De stilte rond Christine M*, refers to the silence surrounding Christine's character, although this is somewhat misleading, because the film treats each of the three women—and the protagonist, Janine—with equal importance. Arguably, the silence of the title refers to the treatment of women in general, who are continually ignored or denied a voice. Christine's decision not to talk is a form of empowered surrender, rather than the catatonia everyone initially suspects. She reflects the sentiments of the other women through her vow of silence because she is wise to the futility of explaining herself within a patriarchal legal system, where judgment on her has already been passed. The audience witnesses the soullessness of her daily existence and loveless relationship with her spouse through flashback sequences. The only time Christine speaks is to provide information about the care of her children to be relayed to her husband; her own defense is a moot point. The film's title refers to a singular question, but the rest of the film also raises many difficult issues through its use of silence, implying that if we're ever going to come up with answers, the questions need to be asked in the first place.

Writing for *Vox* in 2018, Constance Grady observes, "The second wave cared about racism too, but it could be clumsy in working with people of color. As the women's movement developed, it was rooted in the anti-capitalist and anti-racist civil rights movements, but black women increasingly found themselves alienated from the central platforms of the mainstream women's movement." Whereas *A Question of Silence* uses political violence to position the feminist cause within a predominantly white and heterosexual context, Lizzie Borden's *Born in Flames* acknowledges that feminism comes in many colors, sexual guises, and viewpoints and includes incongruent, opinionated voices. She throws feminism into the heated racial and sexual melting pot of a near-future New York, taking a faux documentary science-fiction approach that is presented as a series of largely improvised vignettes from its nonprofessional cast. These scenes are woven together via the narrative thread of factions of women trying to find a unified platform for revolution—to achieve a more egalitarian society, as had been promised to them.

The rub here is these women are already the product of revolution—a successful, peaceful socialist democratic revolution, as the film takes pains to point out—that is now celebrating its ten-year anniversary. But it is failing to reach its zenith for everyone, particularly women, and women are splintered in their agenda for how this inequality should be addressed. Furthermore, they are marginalized by their race (many of the women represented in this film are Black) and their sexuality (lesbianism being an acute threat to the patriarchy). The film focuses on minority groups with limited representation in society, even within the feminist movement itself. In *Born in Flames*, they're not just identified and offered a meaningful role within the cause, but they're also provided with a soapbox to put forward agendas that would otherwise be lost.

Adopting the nomenclature of the infamous axe murderer, a version of her own birth name, Borden found inspiration in the experimentation and naivety of the French New Wave. Filmed haphazardly across a four(ish)-year period on a meager budget of $40,000, she created a film that can be disconcerting due to its unconventionality, combining a patchwork of sequences that remarkably culminate in a three-act structure but otherwise seem to be an eclectic assemblage of both informal and formal debates on feminist

Feminist revolutionaries storming a television network *in Born in Flames* (1983)

issues—including private discussions and media broadcasts, with radio and television playing a huge role. The women of this film jostle for a public platform while under surveillance from gormless men in suits who represent the establishment. Gil Scott-Heron may have claimed the revolution would not be televised, but *Born in Flames* begs to differ. In an interview in *BOMB* at the time of the film's release, Lizzie Borden explains her presentation of the Social-Democratic War of Liberation as wanting

> to show the opportunism of a movement that looks progressive but is just a ploy to enable the society to recover a bit before women are forced back into ordinary, "pre-revolutionary" roles. And there's always the excuse, like "we can't give you the total equality now because of the state of the economy." This is similar to what happens during war—when women are needed they are elevated to the same economic position as men and then when they are not needed they are pushed back again.

Her radical approach to making *Born in Flames* was intrinsically political, shining the spotlight on women ignored by white, middle-class feminism. She says:

> There was no script to begin with and in many ways the characters evolved out of my working with each woman individually. Each woman played both herself and represented a certain aspect of feminism within the fiction of the film. I had to work very much in pieces for two

Honey, the voice of Radio Phoenix in *Born in Flames* (1983)

reasons: first, I jumped in with no money and I had to shoot often just once a month. Second, since I wasn't going to be working with actors I wanted to work very closely with people and how they themselves speak, particularly the Black women.

This includes Jean Satterfield, a real-life basketball player and body-builder cast in the central role of Adelaide Norris. Norris is founder of the militant Women's Army, which resembles a terrorist organization and consequently attracts the attention of the FBI, although its only real act of terrorism is to mobilize vigilantes on bicycles with whistles to intercept assaults on women on the street. However, as Norris's profile rises, she forms threatening international alliances, specifically with the women of the Sahrawi in Spanish Sahara, part of an armed insurrectionary movement that was known for its gender equality, including the active participation of women. Norris eventually travels to North Africa to meet with women leaders and, on her return, is taken into police custody and mysteriously dies, which leads her followers to suspect she has been assassinated. Borden also cast Flo Kennedy, a prominent civil rights activist and lawyer who plays Adelaide Norris's mentor, Zella Wylie. A third is Honey, appearing under her own name, a self-proclaimed evangelist. As the voice of Phoenix Radio (the station that burns to the ground, only to rise from the ashes), Honey is something of a narrator for the film, adapting the political speeches of Malcolm X into her own rhyming, feminist verse. She shares the radio airwaves with her fellow radicals at Radio Regazza, namely Isabel, played by singer-songwriter Adele Bertei. Famously, Oscar-winning film director Kathryn Bigelow makes an early career appearance as one of the white, middle-class newspaper editors whose feminist views tend toward the academic rather than the realities of life on the street.

Born in Flames uses its fragmented presentation as a metaphor. The film posits the feminist cause as rife with variation, of many different voices who are not necessarily in agreement with each other, of segmentation reflected in the staccato snippets of some of its sequences. Given it willfully avoids depicting feminists as unified, many critics have questioned whether the film is a foe to the feminist cause, rather than a friend. On the other hand, we could view Borden's depiction of the feminist agenda as not as easily categorized as some would like to think and, consequently, conveying that women cannot be pigeonholed under one pillar of thought either.

Music plays a huge role in *Born in Flames*, and it would arguably be a very different film without its soundtrack. The driving, anthemic title track by Red Krayola, with its tremulous vocals and frenetic bass line, returns as almost a leitmotif at various points, usually when there is a montage of women's work, such as one sequence that focuses on women doing quotidian tasks with their hands, including rolling a condom on a penis. The film also comes littered with other music tied to the civil rights movement, from the Staple Singers to Stevie Wonder, from funk to punk, further emphasizing how race is reflected heavily in this discourse. The soundtrack contributes to the color and vibrancy of an aesthetic that perfectly taps into the vein of New York City street life at a particularly volatile point in its real-life history.

Stylistically, this is a product of its guerrilla filmmaking—and guerrilla feminism—with Borden turning the limitations of budget and resources into the film's creative rationale. While certainly elevated through music, its grainy, sometimes dark and grimy imagery knit together beautifully thanks to Borden's prowess as both an editor and visual artist. The narrative could have unraveled at any point, but, impressively, she weaves fragmented scenes into a comprehensive story of intrigue, espionage, conspiracy, and political activism. *Born in Flames* eschews on-screen violence, although there is the constant, simmering threat that something could, and will, happen. These women are ready to mobilize, and the unremitting surveillance of their conversations and activities shows the danger they represent to the status quo. Adelaide Norris's death is "reported" after the fact; as a result, the women bear arms to take over a television station and, finally, they blow up the transmitter on top of the World Trade Center, unintentionally prophesying a far more violent act to come. In *Born in Flames*, even with its socialist utopian setting, the plight of women of all colors, creeds, and sexualities is still a work in progress that teeters on, and sometimes tips over, the edge of political violence. But, as acknowledged by Bikini Kill singer Kathleen Hanna during an event held by the Cinemaniacs Film Collective in Melbourne, Australia, in March 2023, Borden's film puts

UK poster for *Born in Flames* (1983)

forward "a blueprint" for the feminist cause—a way forward and a strident argument for the ongoing "good fight," that feminism needs to be a pervasive, persistent movement, otherwise old habits can die hard and women will find themselves right back at the starting block.

Compared to the other two films discussed here—the first displaying a more conventional detective story, the second a low-budget punk aesthetic—Argentinian writer-director María Luisa Bemberg's sweeping epic *Camila* (1984) is a tragic love story in the most Shakespearean sense of the term, where moments of tender romance are intercut with bloody gore and political violence. In this way, it is more explicitly violent than either *A Question of Silence* or *Born in Flames*. Based on historical fact—the scandalous, mid-nineteenth-century romance between a Catholic priest, Ladislao Gutiérrez (Imanol Arias), and a young, upper-class woman, Camila O'Gorman (Susú Pecoraro)—*Camila* uses its bodice-ripping love story as something of a ruse, a counterpoint to political tyranny in Argentina and the limitations placed on women under patriarchal oppression. Importantly, the political backdrop of the 1800s provides a mirror to contemporary Argentina that, at the time of making *Camila*, was still recovering from the Dirty War waged by the military junta that deposed Isabel Perón—third wife of military dictator Juan Perón—in 1976, which involved a bloody campaign against leftists and political dissidents, both real and perceived. The iron-fisted rule of this dictatorship was only loosened three days following Argentina's disastrous Falkland Islands invasion in July 1982, with parliamentary democracy restored through presidential elections in 1983. Producing a film like *Camila*—a story of liberty, of fighting against an extreme right-wing establishment and its punitive dominance—would not have been possible just a couple of years previous.

María Luisa Bemberg, who also went on to direct films like *Miss Mary* (1986) and *De eso no se habla* (*I Don't Want to Talk About It*, 1993), was not a young woman at the time

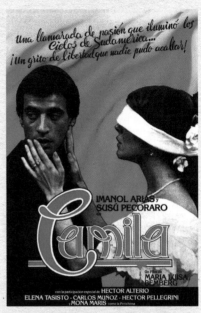

Spanish poster for *Camila* (1984)

of making *Camila*. Born in 1922, she had positioned herself as a feminist long before second-wave feminism or the military junta had taken root. She was one of the founders of the Feminist Union in Argentina in the mid-twentieth century. In many ways, we can assume *Camila* offered a therapeutic expression of her anxieties, as well as those of other left-leaning intellectuals who had lived for many years under the threat of assassination or incarceration in one of the junta detention camps. While based on actual events, the details of Camila O'Gorman's union with Ladislao Gutiérrez and their shocking execution by firing squad is sketchy, with the facts blurred over time as the story became myth. Accordingly, Bemberg took creative license in presenting the character of Camila, positioning her as a somewhat hopeless romantic. A member of the Buenos Aires privileged elite, Camila has the gift of literacy, which results in her burying her head in books and coming up with the kind of fanciful notions that result in an educated woman being deemed dangerous. As her father says to her, "Reality is not a French novel."

The character of Camila's father, Adolfo O'Gorman (Héctor Alterio), acts as the collective embodiment of masculinity. He is crippled by pride and enraged by the shame he still carries after his mother, and later daughter, tarnish the family name with their illicit liaisons. Adolfo's domestic dictatorship reflects the behavior of Federalist governor Juan Manuel de

They paid the ultimate price for their illicit passion.

UK poster for *Camila* (1984)

Rosas (1829–32, 1835–52), who was known for his macho *gaucho* image—the Argentinian version of a Wild West cowboy—and a reign of terror that included mass killings and gruesome fear tactics, such as parading the heads of his enemies on spikes. I could argue that Adolfo figuratively serves his own daughter's head on a spike to the governor, as he is the one who ostensibly hands her over to the authorities.

Describing single women as "chaos" and "a natural disorder," Adolfo pressures Camila to marry, although not to the beau of her choice. Camila has already fallen head over heels for handsome young priest Ladislao. And the priest, despite his vows of chastity, finds it impossible not to love her back. An older priest warns him that "women can be the instrument of the devil," but at no point does Bemberg's depiction of their relationship suggest Camila is the Svengali and Ladislao the victim (or vice versa); both come together as equals, although somewhat naive in their expectations, experiencing their own individual crises in how to handle their situation. In many ways, Camila is the stronger of the pair, resolved in her feelings and comfortable in her faith that they're doing nothing wrong. Ladislao constantly wrestles with guilt and sadness, eventually taking ownership of his choices rather than blaming Camila. He flagellates himself, both literally and figuratively, but never extends this punishment to her.

History has painted de Rosas as using Camila and Ladislao to send a warning to dissenters, especially upper-class women who might have been tempted to rail against the patriarchy; however, Camila's elevation into a legend meant that using her for political maneuvering worked against de Rosas, and he eventually lost power. Some reports say she was eight months pregnant at the time of her death—which made the execution illegal—although Bemberg said this fact could not be confirmed. Nevertheless, she chose to use Camila's pregnancy and the offering of holy water from a priest for Camila to drink to baptize the unborn baby, to give further gravitas to the final moments of the film: Ladislao and Camila, blindfolded, sitting before the firing squad, whispering reassurances to each other: "Right next to you, Camila."

When Bemberg talked about *Camila* to *Cinéaste* in 1985, she didn't refer to equality but to differences between men and women. Rather than anger, she talks about another fiery emotion, passion, and how this is a distinctly feminine quality that women should harness rather than suppress. She talks about these qualities in the context of women being politically active and politically effective: "Most women waste their youth as love junkies, in constant need of that 'fix' of adoration and passion. That I understand. What I want to explore now is how to use that need in the interest of women themselves. There's nothing wrong with passion; it just should not be allowed to consume our lives, or it should be channeled into political struggles.... If we are romantics, we should realize it as a positive force, not a negative one."

Films such as *A Question of Silence*, *Born in Flames*, and *Camila* cannot be expected to speak for all second-wave feminists; however, they are a creative demonstration of feminism's mutation into a complex machine, one where a few victories against patriarchal oppression were not enough to silence activists and send them back to the kitchen. Feminism was at an important yet uncomfortable juncture in the early 1980s, redefining and reorganizing itself for the next phase in its evolution.

Emma Westwood

OUTTAKE: *MAEVE* (1981), PAT MURPHY, NORTHERN IRELAND

There has been no shortage of big-screen films made about the Troubles, the name for the roughly thirty-year conflict over Northern Ireland's status within the United Kingdom, in which over 3,500 people died, the majority civilians, in bombings, assassinations, riots, and tit-for-tat violence between republicans, loyalists, and occupying British military forces. From the early '90s onward, British and American directors produced a series of dramas and thrillers about the struggle. Far rarer were Irish-helmed screen depictions of the Northern Ireland conflict. One notable exception is Pat Murphy's 1981 film *Maeve*.

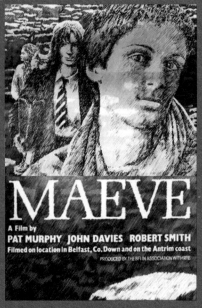

Maeve (1981)

The title character, played by Mary Jackson in her only big-screen role, is a young woman who has escaped Belfast for London and returns home to visit her Catholic family: her once-gregarious traveling-salesman father (Mark Mulholland), still traumatized from being imprisoned by the British on false charges and scared for what the future holds; her mother (Trudy Kelly), exhausted and secretly angry at Maeve for leaving; and her younger sister, Roisin (Brid Brennan). Roisin is spirited and independent, but Maeve is worried she is starting to accept the brutality of the Troubles and the deeply ingrained misogyny of Irish society as her natural lot in life. Maeve also encounters her former lover, Liam (John Keegan), who is profoundly conflicted over the republican cause that his father staunchly supports and struggles to understand why Maeve left.

The narrative is structured along conversations, arguments, or stories shared between the characters, and it shifts backward and forward in time

Maeve Sweeney (Mary Jackson, second from left) and her sister Roisin (Brid Brennan, left) being stopped by British soldiers in *Maeve* (1981)

without any warning. This fractured, nonlinear approach can be confusing, but it mirrors the often disjointed way memory functions. Murphy uses this structure to explore a range of issues: generational differences and the question of what people owe the past, family tensions, her identity as a strong feminist, and how her gender and political outlook relates to the physical and mental violence inflicted on the population by the struggle between loyalists and republicans.

By the early '80s, a sense of weariness about the seemingly intractable conflict was creeping into public discourse in Northern Ireland, and there was growing opposition to paramilitary violence on both sides of the political divide. The year *Maeve* was released was the culmination of five years of protest by republican paramilitary prisoners against changes introduced by the British that sought to strip them of their Special Category Status as political prisoners. This had escalated into hunger strikes that would result in the deaths of ten Irish republican prisoners, including the most famous of them, Bobby Sands. This larger political picture, while not directly referenced, is the backdrop to *Maeve*. The film was shot on the streets of Belfast, largely using natural light, imbuing it with a depressingly vivid sense of verisimilitude—a landscape of gutted buildings, broken windows, graffiti-smeared walls, and unofficial checkpoints manned by sullen, suspicious paramilitaries. The British military presence is everywhere, and the film shows British forces mixing their security functions with routine sexual harassment. The most obvious instance is when Roisin is stopped by British soldiers coming home late at night from her job in a pub. In addition to roughly searching her bag and questioning her about her movements, they insinuate that any woman out so late must be a prostitute and, hence, sexually available.

Pat Murphy on the set of *Maeve* (1981)

Republicans come off little better. Liam's father is inured to the violence he is part of and its impacts on those around him, and contemptuous of anyone who does not wholeheartedly embrace his cause. "I know his trouble," he says to a table of drinkers about his son, who is present. "He's one of those revolutionaries who don't want to get shot." *Maeve* also captures the unpredictable and arbitrary nature of murky civil conflicts like the Troubles: the bomb threats and tension of not knowing who is knocking on the door late at night and what their intentions might be. In one alarming scene, Maeve, her sister, and her friends walk home slightly drunk from a night out and are accidentally caught in a gun battle between unseen assailants.

Maeve may have grown up in Belfast, but she is a complete outsider, because she refuses to accept the lot assigned to women in the conflict, to be wives and daughters who stoically accept that their menfolk will be killed and locked up in the name of a struggle she believes will not do anything for women. In a lengthy argument with Liam, she asserts that much more fundamental social change is required. "Men's relationship to women is just like England's relationship to Ireland," she tells him. "You're in possession of us. You occupy us like an army."

Maeve is one of the earliest examples of a new Irish national cinema that started to emerge in the late 1970s. Murphy was the only female director in this movement, and *Maeve* has been labeled as the country's first feminist film. No doubt speaking to the lack of resources and opportunities available to Irish filmmakers in this early period, as well as the gender inequalities governing how they were allocated, Murphy has only a handful of feature films to her credit. Her next film, *Anne Devlin* (1984), starred Brid Brennan as the housekeeper of Robert Emmett, who led a botched republican uprising against the British in 1803. Devlin, a republican activist in her own right who helped organize the uprising, was left behind to face imprisonment and torture after Emmett fled. Underlining the international connections made by second-wave feminist filmmakers, Murphy had a small role as a newspaper editor in Lizzie Borden's *Born in Flames* (1983), a film examined in the previous chapter. Murphy's early films deserve to be much better known as uniquely feminist takes on Ireland's history and the cost of its violence on women.

Andrew Nette

OUTTAKE: *ON GUARD* (1984), SUSAN LAMBERT, AUSTRALIA

On Guard opens with a documentary film crew attempting to interview staff about the unspecified scientific research they are undertaking in a nondescript building, as the workers leave for the day. The staff are nervous and not prepared to talk on the record, and the crew is moved on by security. The narrative quickly switches gear to something approximating a heist thriller. Female voices talk through the mechanics of an illegal operation they are about to undertake, as the viewer is shown a series of photographs and marked-up floor plans of the inside of the same nondescript building.

Susan Lambert's 1984 film involves four feminist women—Diana (Jan Cornall), Georgia (the wonderfully named Mystery Carnage), Amelia (Liddy Clark), and Adrienne (Kerry Dwyer)—who plan to break into the offices of a mysterious multinational biotech company called U.T.E.R.O. The aim is to reroute the power to set up an electromagnetic force field that will destroy years of sensitive IVF-related research stored on the facility's computer disks. At the same time, the four are collaborating on a documentary to send to the media that will explain and justify the reasons for their sabotage. The promotional artwork for the film's release included the subheading "A Girls' Own Adventure." Lambert told the March–April 1984 issue of Australian magazine *Cinema Papers* that the project originated out of frustrations she had over the lack of strong, capable women on the Australian screen: "We wanted to make a heist movie and have the girls get away with it. That's where we started." What she ended up delivering is an explicitly queer feminist thriller that explores issues around political violence and the then-emerging debate over IVF technology and its relationship to women's reproductive self-determination, with a sophistication and complexity that belies its brief fifty-one-minute running time.

Cowritten by Lambert and Sarah Gibson, the production is strongly grounded in their feminist politics. The cast, a mix of professional and amateur actors, is almost completely female. It was produced by Digby Duncan, whose main credit until that time was directing the 1980 documentary *Witches, Faggots, Dykes and Poofters*, about the community backlash to the police's attempted suppression of Sydney's first gay and lesbian Mardi Gras in 1978. The crew were female, and the atmospheric synth soundtrack—which complements the at times eerie, New Wave color palette of vivid blues and reds—was provided by Sydney feminist post-punk band Stray Dags, fronted by Carnage.

Director Susan Lambert (right) with Mystery Carnage on the set of her 1984 film *On Guard* (*Cinema Papers*, March–April 1984)

Lambert told *Cinema Papers* that she and Gibson wanted to focus specifically on "women as activists." The film shows the four women preparing for and carrying out their sabotage, at considerable risk to themselves, while juggling work, family life, and relationships. Georgie is a nurse who was sacked from the hospital where she was employed for asking questions about U.T.E.R.O.'s involvement in the institution's governance. Diana, a documentary filmmaker and one-half of a lesbian couple with Georgina, has two children from a previous relationship. Tensions arise between Georgina and Diana over the latter's reluctance to take a more direct role in the sabotage plan and identify more openly as a lesbian. The pressure ramps up further in the days leading up to the raid, when Amelia loses a diary in which she has been recording the details of the sabotage plan and unknown assailants ransack the flat of a woman they have been interviewing for the documentary about her experience with U.T.E.R.O. The early 1980s saw IVF technology come to wider prominence as both a medical procedure and a subject of considerable media debate. The documentary film the women are making provides a mechanism to interrogate the wider issues involved, including secrecy, reproductive rights, and control, as well as the government subsidies given to private health research while public hospitals experience funding shortfalls. It also allows Lambert to link the U.T.E.R.O. raid to similar acts of sabotage by radical feminists internationally.

On its release and more recently, critics have noted parallels between *On Guard* and Lizzie Borden's *Born in Flames* (1983). While Borden paints on a much larger canvas, both films have the same feeling of militant feminist agitprop politics that assert a right to protest, violently if necessary, and both merge didacticism with solid genre tropes. On a local level, *On Guard* also exudes a very real sense of the direct-action politics that were part of the mass antinuclear movement in the early 1980s. This movement saw numerous actions, large and small, including women-only actions, against companies involved in uranium mining and disruptions to and the occupying of American military installations on Australian soil and visiting American nuclear-armed ships in Australian ports. "One of the interesting things about the heist in *Guard* is that it is quite domestic in flavour," notes Lambert's interviewer in *Cinema Papers*.

VHS release cover of *On Guard* (1984)

"The mechanics of the crime are so simply explained that the film almost works as a blueprint for a new kind of terrorism." After a limited theatrical release and some exposure in overseas film festivals, *On Guard* largely disappeared and has never had a DVD release.

Andrew Nette

ABOUT THE CONTRIBUTORS

Scott Adlerberg is the author of five novels, including *Graveyard Love* (2016), *Jack Waters* (2018), and *The Screaming Child* (2023). His short fiction has appeared in various anthologies, and he contributes pieces to such places as *CrimeReads*, *Mystery Tribune*, and *Literary Hub*. Each summer, he hosts the Word for Word Reel Talks film commentary series in Manhattan. He lives in Brooklyn.

Uday Bhatia is a film critic with *Mint Lounge* in Delhi. He is the author of *Bullets over Bombay: Satya and the Hindi Film Gangster* (2021).

Lee Broughton is a writer, critic, film programmer, and lecturer in film and media. He is the author of *The Euro-Western: Reframing Gender, Race and the "Other" in Film* (2016) and the editor of *Critical Perspectives on the Western: From "A Fistful of Dollars" to "Django Unchained"* (2016) and *Reframing Cult Westerns: From "The Magnificent Seven" to "The Hateful Eight"* (2020). His research interests include the western, horror films, and cult movies more generally. Lee has contributed chapters and articles to numerous edited collections and academic journals and has worked on the extra features for a number of Blu-ray releases.

Samm Deighan is a film historian, editor, and author of *The Legacy of World War II in European Arthouse Cinema* (2021) and a monograph on Fritz Lang's *M* (2019). She's a special-features producer for Vinegar Syndrome and cohosts the *Twitch of the Death Nerve* podcast.

Harlem native **Michael A. Gonzales** is a cultural critic, short story scribe, and essayist who has written for *CrimeReads*, *Longreads*, the *Paris Review*, and the *Village Voice*. His fiction has appeared in *Under the Thumb: Stories of Police Oppression*, edited by S.A. Cosby (2021); *Get Up Offa That Thing: Crime Fiction Inspired by the Songs of James Brown*, edited by Gary Phillips (2023); *The Book of Extraordinary Femme Fatale Stories*, edited by Maxim Jakubowski (2022); *Killens Review of Arts & Letters*; and *Ellery Queen Mystery Magazine*. He currently lives in Baltimore.

Matthew Kowalski specializes in the history of modern Central and Eastern Europe but teaches broadly in European and global history at Temple University, Delaware County Community College, and the Community College of Philadelphia. His research interests are mainly focused on the intersection between cultural and political-diplomatic history and especially on the role of mass culture (sport-food-film-music) in the Socialist Bloc during the Cold War. He has contributed to a variety of projects, including coauthoring a global history textbook and a forthcoming piece on Soviet and East German "football (soccer) diplomacy" in the Global South.

Kimberly Lindbergs is a writer, researcher, and artist based in California. Her areas of interest include '60s and '70s pop culture and the occult. For almost a decade, Kimberly was a regular contributor to Turner Classic Movies. She has also penned essays for DVD and Blu-ray releases, and her work has appeared in numerous publications, including *Cineaste*, *Publishers Weekly*, *Fandor*, the *Cultural Gutter*, and *Paracinema*. As a volunteer, she has worked closely with local history organizations and participated in the Bernie Sanders 2020 presidential campaign. You can find her online at www.kimberlylindbergs.com.

Annie Rose Malamet is an internationally recognized lesbian vampire expert, freelance film writer, and perverted aesthete. She is the creator of the popular podcast *Girls, Guts, & Giallo*, where she examines controversial and subversive cinema through the lens of queer leather and sex work history and sensibilities. Annie has lectured and presented work at festivals and colleges in both the United States and Europe. She has appeared as a cultural expert in the Shudder documentary *Queer for Fear* (2022) and on the PBS show *Historian's Take*. Her essays and reviews have been in various publications over the last decade.

Andrew Nette is a Melbourne-based writer of fiction and nonfiction. He is the coeditor of three books on the history of postwar pulp and popular fiction, all published by PM Press, the most recent of which, *Dangerous Visions and New Worlds: Radical Science Fiction, 1950 to 1985* was published in late 2021. He is the author of *Rollerball*, a monograph on Norman Jewison's 1975 dystopian classic of the same name. His writing on film, books, and culture has also appeared in a variety of print and online publications. You can find him at his website, www.pulpcurry.com, and on Twitter/X at @Pulpcurry.

Charles Perks is a high school graduate and minimum wage employee who has helped countless coworkers get raises and gain a modicum of class consciousness over the years but has often been fired from various jobs for agitating in favor of syndicalism and forming unions. He currently cohosts the *Twitch of the Death Nerve* podcast and is writing a humorous book of Maoist limericks: "There once was a Marxist from Nantucket."

Robert Skvarla is a freelance writer from Philadelphia who explores conspiracy communities and new religious movements. His writing has appeared in *Creem*, *Diabolique*, and *Atlas Obscura*, and he blogs about the American weird at *Mondo Americana*. You can follow him on Twitter/X at @RobertSkvarla.

Christos Tsiolkas is a Melbourne-based writer. He is the author of seven novels, and he is also a playwright, scriptwriter, and essayist. His short stories were published in the collection *Merciless Gods* (2014). Many of his novels and stories have been adapted for the stage and screen. Christos has been writing on cinema and screen culture for over three decades. He is currently a film reviewer for the *Saturday Paper*. His most recent novel is *7½* (2021).

Emma Westwood is a film writer and commentator from Melbourne, Australia. She has authored three books on cinema—*Monster Movies* (2008), *The Fly* (2018), and *Seconds* (2021)—and edited *Bride of Frankenstein* (2023). You can hear her on a variety of radio shows and podcasts, as well as providing Blu-ray audio commentaries for the likes of Kino Lorber, Umbrella Entertainment, Eureka, Arrow, Indicator, and Second Sight.

Mike White is a highly acclaimed film critic, author, and podcast host of *The Projection Booth*. He began his career as a founder and editor for the groundbreaking film zine *Cashiers du Cinemart*, before devoting his time to writing books, including *Impossibly Funky: A Cashiers du Cinemart Collection* (2010) and *Cinema Detours* (2011). White's podcast, *The Projection Booth*, has become a must-listen for cinephiles worldwide, where he provides in-depth analysis and discussions on a vast range of cinematic genres, from obscure cult favorites to timeless classics. His meticulous research, eloquent delivery, and deep appreciation for cinema have earned him widespread recognition among film enthusiasts and aspiring filmmakers alike.

INDEX

Page numbers in *italic* refer to illustrations. "Passim" (literally "scattered") indicates intermittent discussion of a topic over a cluster of pages.

ABOUT PM PRESS

PM Press is an independent, radical publisher of critically necessary books for our tumultuous times. Our aim is to deliver bold political ideas and vital stories to all walks of life and arm the dreamers to demand the impossible. Founded in 2007 by a small group of people with decades of publishing, media, and organizing experience, we have sold millions of copies of our books, most often one at a time, face to face. We're old enough to know what we're doing and young enough to know what's at stake. Join us to create a better world.

PM Press
PO Box 23912
Oakland, CA 94623
www.pmpress.org

PM Press in Europe
europe@pmpress.org
www.pmpress.org.uk

FRIENDS OF PM PRESS

These are indisputably momentous times—the financial system is melting down globally and the Empire is stumbling. Now more than ever there is a vital need for radical ideas.

In the many years since its founding—and on a mere shoestring—PM Press has risen to the formidable challenge of publishing and distributing knowledge and entertainment for the struggles ahead. With hundreds of releases to date, we have published an impressive and stimulating array of literature, art, music, politics, and culture. Using every available medium, we've succeeded in connecting those hungry for ideas and information to those putting them into practice.

Friends of PM allows you to directly help impact, amplify, and revitalize the discourse and actions of radical writers, filmmakers, and artists. It provides us with a stable foundation from which we can build upon our early successes and provides a much-needed subsidy for the materials that can't necessarily pay their own way. You can help make that happen—and receive every new title automatically delivered to your door once a month—by joining as a Friend of PM Press. And, we'll throw in a free T-shirt when you sign up.

Here are your options:

- **$30 a month** Get all books and pamphlets plus a 50% discount on all webstore purchases

- **$40 a month** Get all PM Press releases (including CDs and DVDs) plus a 50% discount on all webstore purchases

- **$100 a month** Superstar—Everything plus PM merchandise, free downloads, and a 50% discount on all webstore purchases

For those who can't afford $30 or more a month, we have **Sustainer Rates** at $15, $10, and $5. Sustainers get a free PM Press T-shirt and a 50% discount on all purchases from our website.

Your Visa or Mastercard will be billed once a month, until you tell us to stop. Or until our efforts succeed in bringing the revolution around. Or the financial meltdown of Capital makes plastic redundant. Whichever comes first.

Girl Gangs, Biker Boys, and Real Cool Cats: Pulp Fiction and Youth Culture, 1950 to 1980

Edited by Iain McIntyre and Andrew Nette with a Foreword by Peter Doyle

ISBN: 978-1-62963-438-8
$29.95   336 pages

Girl Gangs, Biker Boys, and Real Cool Cats is the first comprehensive account of how the rise of postwar youth culture was depicted in mass-market pulp fiction. As the young created new styles in music, fashion, and culture, pulp fiction shadowed their every move, hyping and exploiting their behavior, dress, and language for mass consumption and cheap thrills. From the juvenile delinquent gangs of the early 1950s through the beats and hippies, on to bikers, skinheads, and punks, pulp fiction left no trend untouched. With their lurid covers and wild, action-packed plots, these books reveal as much about society's deepest desires and fears as they do about the subcultures themselves.

Girl Gangs features approximately 400 full-color covers, many of them never reprinted before. With 70 in-depth author interviews, illustrated biographies, and previously unpublished articles from more than 20 popular culture critics and scholars from the US, UK, and Australia, the book goes behind the scenes to look at the authors and publishers, how they worked, where they drew their inspiration, and—often overlooked—the actual words they wrote. Books by well-known authors such as Harlan Ellison and Lawrence Block are discussed alongside neglected obscurities and former bestsellers ripe for rediscovery. It is a must read for anyone interested in pulp fiction, lost literary history, retro and subcultural style, and the history of postwar youth culture.

Contributors include Nicolas Tredell, Alwyn W. Turner, Mike Stax, Clinton Walker, Bill Osgerby, David Rife, J.F. Norris, Stewart Home, James Cockington, Joe Blevins, Brian Coffey, James Doig, David James Foster, Matthew Asprey Gear, Molly Grattan, Brian Greene, John Harrison, David Kiersh, Austin Matthews, and Robert Baker.

"*Girl Gangs, Biker Boys, and Real Cool Cats is populated by the bad boys and girls of mid-twentieth-century pulp fiction. Rumblers and rebels, beats and bikers, hepcats and hippies—pretty much everybody your mother used to warn you about. Nette and McIntyre have curated a riotous party that you won't want to leave, even though you might get your wallet stolen or your teeth kicked in at any given moment.*"
—Duane Swierczynski, two-time Edgar nominee, author of *Canary* and *Revolver*

Sticking It to the Man: Revolution and Counterculture in Pulp and Popular Fiction, 1950 to 1980

Edited by Andrew Nette and Iain McIntyre

ISBN: 978-1-62963-524-8
$34.95   336 pages

From Civil Rights and Black Power to the New Left and Gay Liberation, the 1960s and 1970s saw a host of movements shake the status quo. The impact of feminism, anticolonial struggles, wildcat industrial strikes, and antiwar agitation was felt globally. With social strictures and political structures challenged at every level, pulp and popular fiction could hardly remain unaffected. While an influx of New Wave nonconformists transformed science fiction, feminist, gay, and black authors broke into areas of crime, porn, and other paperback genres previously dominated by conservative, straight, white males. For their part, pulp hacks struck back with bizarre takes on the revolutionary times, creating vigilante-driven fiction that echoed the Nixonian backlash and the coming conservatism of Thatcherism and Reaganism.

Sticking It to the Man tracks the changing politics and culture of the period and how it was reflected in pulp and popular fiction in the US, UK, and Australia from the 1950s onward. Featuring more than 300 full-color covers, the book includes in-depth author interviews, illustrated biographies, articles, and reviews from more than 30 popular culture critics and scholars. Works by science-fiction icons such as J.G. Ballard, Ursula Le Guin, Michael Moorcock, and Octavia Butler, street-level hustlers turned bestselling black writers Iceberg Slim and Donald Goines, crime heavyweights Chester Himes and Brian Garfield, and a myriad of lesser-known novelists ripe for rediscovery, are explored, celebrated, and analyzed.

Contributors include Gary Phillips, Woody Haut, Emory Holmes, David Whish-Wilson, Susie Thomas, Bill Osgerby, Kinohi Nishikawa, Devin McKinney, Scott Aldeberg, Andrew Nette, Victor J. Banis, Cameron Ashley, Mike Dalke, Danae Bosler, Rjurik Davidson, Rob Latham, Michael Gonzales, Iain McIntyre, Donna Glee Williams, Nicolas Tredell, Brian Coffey, James Doig, Molly Grattan, Brian Green, Eric Beaumont, Bill Mohr, J. Kingston Smith, Steve Aldous, David Foster, Joe Weixlmann, and Cheryl Morgan.

Dangerous Visions and New Worlds: Radical Science Fiction, 1950 to 1985

Edited by Andrew Nette & Iain McIntyre

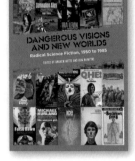

ISBN: 978-1-62963-8836 (paperback)
   978-1-62963-932-1 (hardcover)
$29.95/$59.95   224 pages

Much has been written about the "long Sixties," the era of the late 1950s through the early 1970s. It was a period of major social change, most graphically illustrated by the emergence of liberatory and resistance movements focused on inequalities of class, race, gender, sexuality, and beyond, whose challenge represented a major shock to the political and social status quo. With its focus on speculation, alternate worlds, and the future, science fiction became an ideal vessel for this upsurge of radical protest.

Dangerous Visions and New Worlds: Radical Science Fiction, 1950 to 1985 details, celebrates, and evaluates how science fiction novels and authors depicted, interacted with, and were inspired by these cultural and political movements in America and Great Britain. It starts with progressive authors who rose to prominence in the conservative 1950s, challenging the so-called Golden Age of science fiction and its linear narratives of technological breakthroughs and space-conquering male heroes. The book then moves through the 1960s, when writers, including those in what has been termed the New Wave, shattered existing writing conventions and incorporated contemporary themes such as modern mass media culture, corporate control, growing state surveillance, the Vietnam War, and rising currents of counterculture, ecological awareness, feminism, sexual liberation, and Black Power. The 1970s, when the genre reflected the end of various dreams of the long Sixties and the faltering of the postwar boom, is also explored along with the first half of the 1980s, which gave rise to new subgenres, such as cyberpunk.

Dangerous Visions and New Worlds contains over twenty chapters written by contemporary authors and critics, and hundreds of full-color cover images, including thirteen thematically organized cover selections. New perspectives on key novels and authors, such as Octavia Butler, Ursula K. Le Guin, Philip K. Dick, Harlan Ellison, John Wyndham, Samuel Delany, J.G. Ballard, John Brunner, Judith Merril, Barry Malzberg, Joanna Russ, and many others are presented alongside excavations of topics, works, and writers who have been largely forgotten or undeservedly ignored.

The Red Army Faction, A Documentary History—Volume 1: Projectiles for the People

Edited by J. Smith and André Moncourt with Forewords by Russell "Maroon" Shoats and Bill Dunne

ISBN: 978-1-60486-029-0
$34.95   736 pages

The first in a two-volume series, this is by far the most in-depth political history of the Red Army Faction ever made available in English.

Projectiles for the People starts its story in the days following World War II, showing how American imperialism worked hand in glove with the old pro-Nazi ruling class, shaping West Germany into an authoritarian anti-communist bulwark and launching pad for its aggression against Third World nations. The volume also recounts the opposition that emerged from intellectuals, communists, independent leftists, and then—explosively—the radical student movement and countercultural revolt of the 1960s.

The Red Army Faction, A Documentary History—Volume 2: Dancing with Imperialism

Edited J. Smith and André Moncourt with an Introduction by Ward Churchill

ISBN: 978-1-60486-030-6
$26.95   480 pages

The long-awaited *Volume 2* of the first-ever English-language study of the Red Army Faction—West Germany's most notorious urban guerillas—covers the period immediately following the organization's near-total decimation in 1977. This work includes the details of the guerilla's operations, and its communiqués and texts, from 1978 up until the 1984 offensive.

This was a period of regrouping and reorientation for the RAF, with its previous focus on freeing its prisoners replaced by an anti-NATO orientation. This was in response to the emergence of a new radical youth movement in the Federal Republic, the Autonomen, and an attempt to renew its ties to the radical left. The possibilities and perils of an armed underground organization relating to the broader movement are examined, and the RAF's approach is contrasted to the more fluid and flexible practice of the Revolutionary Cells.

The Angry Brigade: A History of Britain's First Urban Guerilla Group

Gordon Carr with Prefaces by John Barker and Stuart Christie

ISBN: 978-1-60486-049-8

$24.95   280 pages

"You can't reform profit capitalism and inhumanity. Just kick it till it breaks." —*Angry Brigade, communiqué*

Between 1970 and 1972, the Angry Brigade used guns and bombs in a series of symbolic attacks against property. A series of communiqués accompanied the actions, explaining the choice of targets and the Angry Brigade philosophy: autonomous organization and attacks on property alongside other forms of militant working class action. This book covers the roots of the Angry Brigade in the revolutionary ferment of the 1960s, and follows their campaign and the police investigation to its culmination in the "Stoke Newington 8" conspiracy trial at the Old Bailey—the longest criminal trial in British legal history. Written after extensive research—among both the libertarian opposition and the police—it remains the essential study of Britain's first urban guerilla group. This expanded edition contains a comprehensive chronology of the "Angry Decade," extra illustrations and a police view of the Angry Brigade. Introductions by Stuart Christie and John Barker (two of the "Stoke Newington 8" defendants) discuss the Angry Brigade in the political and social context of its times—and its longer-term significance.

The Angry Brigade: The Spectacular Rise and Fall of Britain's First Urban Guerilla Group

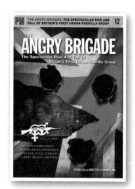

$19.95   DVD (NTSC) 60 minutes

This documentary, produced by Gordon Carr for the BBC (and first shown in January 1973, shortly after the trial), covers the roots of the Angry Brigade.

Extra: The Persons Unknown (1980, 22 minutes) The so-called "Persons Unknown" case in which members of the Anarchist Black Cross were tried (and later acquitted) at the Old Bailey on charges of "conspiring with persons unknown, at places unknown, to cause explosions and to overthrow society." Featuring interviews and footage of Stuart Christie, Nicholas Walter, Crass, and many other UK anarchist activists and propagandists of the time.

Lonely Hearts Killer

Tomoyuki Hoshino

ISBN: 978-1-60486-084-9
$15.95   232 pages

What happens when a popular and young emperor suddenly dies, and the only person available to succeed him is his sister? How can people in an island country survive as climate change and martial law are eroding more and more opportunities for local sustainability and mutual aid? And what can be done to challenge the rise of a new authoritarian political leadership at a time when the general public is obsessed with fears related to personal and national "security"? These and other provocative questions provide the backdrop for this powerhouse novel about young adults embroiled in what appear to be more private matters—friendships, sex, a love suicide, and struggles to cope with grief and work.

PM Press is proud to bring you this first English translation of a full-length novel by the award-winning author Tomoyuki Hoshino.

We, the Children of Cats

Tomoyuki Hoshino
Translated by Brian Bergstrom

ISBN: 978-1-60486-591-2
$20.00   288 pages

A man and woman find their genders and sexualities brought radically into question when their bodies sprout new parts, seemingly out of thin air. . . . A man travels from Japan to Latin America in search of revolutionary purpose and finds much more than he bargains for. . . . A journalist investigates a poisoning at an elementary school and gets lost in an underworld of buried crimes, secret societies, and haunted forests. . . . Two young killers, exiled from Japan, find a new beginning as resistance fighters in Peru. . . .

These are but a few of the stories told in *We, the Children of Cats*, a new collection of provocative early works by Tomoyuki Hoshino, winner of the 2011 Kenzaburo Oe Award in Literature and author of the powerhouse novel *Lonely Hearts Killer* (PM Press, 2009). Drawing on sources as diverse as Borges, Nabokov, Garcia-Marquez, Kenji Nakagami, and traditional Japanese folklore, Hoshino creates a challenging, slyly subversive literary world all his own.

Look for Me in the Whirlwind: From the Panther 21 to 21st-Century Revolutions

Sekou Odinga, Dhoruba Bin Wahad,
Jamal Joseph
Edited by Matt Meyer & déqui kioni-sadiki
with a Foreword by Imam Jamil Al-Amin,
and an Afterword by Mumia Abu-Jamal

ISBN: 978-1-62963-389-3
$26.95   648 pages

Amid music festivals and moon landings, the tumultuous year of 1969 included an infamous case in the annals of criminal justice and Black liberation: the New York City Black Panther 21. Though some among the group had hardly even met one another, the 21 were rounded up by the FBI and New York Police Department in an attempt to disrupt and destroy the organization that was attracting young people around the world. Involving charges of conspiracy to commit violent acts, the Panther 21 trial—the longest and most expensive in New York history—revealed the illegal government activities which led to exile, imprisonment on false charges, and assassination of Black liberation leaders. Solidarity for the 21 also extended well beyond "movement" circles and included mainstream publication of their collective autobiography, *Look for Me in the Whirlwind*, which is reprinted here for the first time.

Look for Me in the Whirlwind: From the Panther 21 to 21st-Century Revolutions contains the entire original manuscript, and includes new commentary from surviving members of the 21: Sekou Odinga, Dhoruba Bin Wahad, Jamal Joseph, and Shaba Om. Still-imprisoned Sundiata Acoli, Imam Jamil Al-Amin, and Mumia Abu-Jamal contribute new essays. Never or rarely seen poetry and prose from Afeni Shakur, Kuwasi Balagoon, Ali Bey Hassan, and Michael "Cetewayo" Tabor is included. Early Panther leader and jazz master Bilal Sunni-Ali adds a historical essay and lyrics from his composition "Look for Me in the Whirlwind," and coeditors kioni-sadiki, Meyer, and Panther rank-and-file member Cyril "Bullwhip" Innis Jr. help bring the story up to date.

At a moment when the Movement for Black Lives recites the affirmation that "it is our duty to win," penned by Black Liberation Army (BLA) militant Assata Shakur, those who made up the BLA and worked alongside of Assata are largely unknown. This book—with archival photos from David Fenton, Stephen Shames, and the private collections of the authors— provides essential parts of a hidden and missing-in-action history. Going well beyond the familiar and mythologized nostalgic Panther narrative, *From the Panther 21 to 21st-Century Revolutions* explains how and why the Panther legacy is still relevant and vital today.

On the Ground: An Illustrated Anecdotal History of the Sixties Underground Press in the U.S.

Edited by Sean Stewart
with an Introduction by Paul Buhle

ISBN: 978-1-60486-455
$24.95   208 pages

In four short years (1965–1969), the underground press grew from five small newspapers in as many cities in the U.S. to over 500 newspapers—with millions of readers—all over the world. Completely circumventing (and subverting) establishment media by utilizing their own news service and freely sharing content amongst each other, the underground press, at its height, became the unifying institution for the counterculture of the 1960s.

Frustrated with the lack of any mainstream media criticism of the Vietnam War, empowered by the victories of the Civil Rights era, emboldened by the anti-colonial movements in the third world and with heads full of acid, a generation set out to change the world. The underground press was there documenting, participating in, and providing the resources that would guarantee the growth of this emergent youth culture. Combining bold visuals and innovative layouts, and eschewing any pretense toward objectivity, the newspapers were wildly diverse and wonderfully vibrant.

Neither meant to be an official nor comprehensive history, *On the Ground* focuses on the anecdotal detail that brings the history alive. Comprised of stories told by the people involved with the production and distribution of the newspapers—John Sinclair, Art Kunkin, Paul Krassner, Emory Douglas, John Wilcock, Bill Ayers, Spain Rodriguez, Trina Robbins, Al Goldstein, Harvey Wasserman, and more—and featuring over 50 full-color scans taken from a broad range of newspapers, the book provides a true window into the spirit of the times, giving the reader a feeling for the energy on the ground.

"*On the Ground* serves as a valuable contribution to countercultural history."
— Paul Krassner, author of *Confessions of a Raving, Unconfined Nut: Misadventures in the Counterculture*

"One should not underestimate the significant value of this book. It gives you real insights into the underground press and its vast diversity of publications, which translated into a taste of real people's power."
— Emory Douglas, former Black Panther Party graphic artist and Minister of Culture

Asia's Unknown Uprisings
Volume 1
South Korean Social Movements in the 20th Century

George Katsiaficas

ISBN: 978-1-60486-457-1
$28.95   480 pages

Using social movements as a prism to illuminate the oft-hidden history of 20th-century Korea, this book provides detailed analysis of major uprisings that have patterned that country's politics and society. From the 1894 Tonghak Uprising through the March 1, 1919, independence movement and anti-Japanese resistance, a direct line is traced to the popular opposition to U.S. division of Korea after World War Two. The overthrow of Syngman Rhee in 1960, resistance to Park Chung-hee, the 1980 Gwangju Uprising, as well as student, labor, and feminist movements are all recounted with attention to their economic and political contexts. South Korean opposition to neoliberalism is portrayed in detail, as is an analysis of neoliberalism's rise and effects. With a central focus on the Gwangju Uprising (that ultimately proved decisive in South Korea's democratization), the author uses Korean experiences as a baseboard to extrapolate into the possibilities of global social movements in the 21st century.

Asia's Unknown Uprisings
Volume 2
People Power in the Philippines, Burma, Tibet, China, Taiwan, Bangladesh, Nepal, Thailand, and Indonesia, 1947–2009

George Katsiaficas

ISBN: 978-1-60486-488-5
$26.95   448 pages

Ten years in the making, this book provides a unique perspective on uprisings in nine places in East Asia in the 1980s and 1990s. While the 2011 Arab Spring is well known, the wave of uprisings that swept East Asia in the 1980s became hardly visible. This book begins with an overview of late 20th-century history—the context within which Asian uprisings arose. Through a critique of Samuel Huntington's notion of a "Third Wave" of democratization, the author relates Asian uprisings to predecessors in 1968 and shows their subsequent influence on the wave of uprisings that swept Eastern Europe at the end of the 1980s. By empirically reconstructing the specific history of each Asian uprising, significant insight into major constituencies of change and the trajectories of these societies becomes visible.

The Global Imagination of 1968: Revolution and Counterrevolution

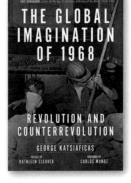

George Katsiaficas with a Preface by Kathleen Cleaver and a Foreword by Carlos Muñoz

ISBN: 978-1-62963-439-5
$24.95   360 pages

This book brings to life social movements of the 1960s, a period of world-historical struggles. With discussions of more than fifty countries, Katsiaficas articulates an understanding that is neither bounded by national and continental divides nor focused on "Great Men and Women." Millions of people went into the streets, and their aspirations were remarkably similar. From the Prague revolt against Soviet communism to the French May uprising, the Vietnam Tet offensive, African anticolonial insurgencies, the civil rights movement, and campus eruptions in Latin America, Yugoslavia, the United States, and beyond, this book portrays the movements of the 1960s as intuitively tied together.

Student movements challenged authorities in almost every country, giving the insurgency a global character, and contemporary feminist, Latino, and gay liberation movements all came to life. A focus on the French general strike of May 1968 and the U.S. movement's high point in 1970—from the May campus strike to the revolt in the military, workers' wildcat strikes, the national women's strike, the Chicano Moratorium, and the Black Panther Party's Revolutionary Peoples' Constitutional Convention in September—reveals the revolutionary aspirations of the insurgencies in the core of the world system. Despite the apparent failure of the movements of 1968, their profound influence on politics, culture, and social movements continues to be felt today. As globally synchronized uprisings occur with increasing frequency in the twenty-first century, the lessons of 1968 provide useful insights for future struggles.

"A well-informed survey of the global 'New Left' of 1968."
—Eric Hobsbawm, author of *The Age of Extremes: A History of the World, 1914–1991*

"George Katsiaficas's work presents an understanding how we of the New Left used our education as a practice of freedoms: confronting the racist, warmongering status quo with the objective of creative participatory democracy. As we continue to work toward cooperational humanism here at home and the world over, this insightful analysis provides a useful backdrop for social activism and the struggle for future democratic human rights."
—Bobby Seale, former chairman and cofounder of the Black Panther Party

A History of Pan-African Revolt

C.L.R. James with an Introduction
by Robin D.G. Kelley

ISBN: 978-1-60486-095-5
$16.95   160 pages

Originally published in England in 1938 (the same year
as his magnum opus *The Black Jacobins*) and expanded
in 1969, this work remains the classic account of
global black resistance. Robin D.G. Kelley's substantial
introduction contextualizes the work in the history and
ferment of the times, and explores its ongoing relevance today.

"*A History of Pan-African Revolt* is one of those rare books that continues to strike
a chord of urgency, even half a century after it was first published. Time and
time again, its lessons have proven to be valuable and relevant for understanding
liberation movements in Africa and the diaspora. Each generation who has had the
opportunity to read this small book finds new insights, new lessons, new visions for
their own age . . . . No piece of literature can substitute for a crystal ball, and only
religious fundamentalists believe that a book can provide comprehensive answers
to all questions. But if nothing else, *A History of Pan-African Revolt* leaves us with
two incontrovertible facts. First, as long as black people are denied freedom,
humanity and a decent standard of living, they will continue to revolt. Second,
unless these revolts involve the ordinary masses and take place on their own terms,
they have no hope of succeeding." —Robin D.G. Kelley, from the Introduction

"I wish my readers to understand the history of Pan-African Revolt. They fought,
they suffered—they are still fighting. Once we understand that, we can tackle our
problems with the necessary mental equilibrium." —C.L.R. James

"*Kudos for reissuing C.L.R. James's pioneering work on black resistance. Many brilliant
embryonic ideas articulated in* A History of Pan-African Revolt *twenty years later
became the way to study black social movements. Robin Kelley's introduction superbly
situates James and his thought in the world of Pan-African and Marxist intellectuals.*"
—Sundiata Cha-Jua, Penn State University

"*A mine of ideas advancing far ahead of its time.*"
—Walter Rodney

"*When one looks back over the last twenty years to those men who were most far-
sighted, who first began to tease out the muddle of ideology in our times, who were
at the same time Marxists with a hard theoretical basis, and close students of society,
humanists with a tremendous response to and understanding of human culture,
Comrade James is one of the first one thinks of.*"
—E.P. Thompson